MARCIA DAVENPORT was born in 1903 in New York City. After attending Wellesley College and the University of Grenoble in France, she joined the editorial staff of *The New Yorker*. Marcia Davenport has contributed articles to *The Saturday Evening Post*, *McCalls*, *Reader's Digest*, *The New Yorker*, and *Fortune*, and has written several novels. *Mozart* was Marcia Davenport's first book and the first American biography of the great eighteenth century composer. In the truest sense, *Mozart* was a labor of love, during which the author "retraced every journey he made, saw every dwelling then extant in which he had ever lived, every theatre where his works were first performed, every library and museum where his manuscripts were then to be seen." *Mozart* is a biography of such commanding stature that it has remained unassailable since its publication in 1932.

Other Avon Books by
Marcia Davenport

THE VALLEY OF DECISION

MOZART

MARCIA DAVENPORT

AVON BOOKS NEW YORK

AVON BOOKS
A division of
The Hearst Corporation
105 Madison Avenue
New York, New York 10016

First Avon Books Printing: September 1979

AVON TRADEMARK REG. U.S. PAT. OFF. AND IN OTHER COUNTRIES, MARCA
REGISTRADA, HECHO EN U.S.A.

Printed in the U.S.A.

OPM   20   19   18   17   16   15   14   13

The Bicentenary Edition of this book
is dedicated to my lifelong friend

ARTURO TOSCANINI

A NOTE FOR 1979

At the two hundredth anniversary of Mozart's birth, I wrote a new foreword, which follows this note, for the bicentenary edition of this biography. That introduction brought matters about Mozart up to 1956, but the ensuing twenty-three years have outrun it. Mozart gives ever more impressive proof that there really is immortality. First in his music; then in the fascination that he holds for people of all persuasions and ages. The phenomenon is that more of Mozart's music is being performed, recorded, and listened to at this time than ever before; perhaps, though statistical proof is impossible, more of Mozart than of any other composer. The explanation must be the simple one of universal response to beauty; of the delight of possessing music with the peculiar personal emotion that people feel for Mozart.

When I was first working on this book there was relatively little of Mozart's music to be heard in American concert halls and opera houses, and comparatively little elsewhere except in Austria and Germany. Only in those countries could I hear as much of the music as I needed. American orchestras, far fewer in number than now, still leant to nineteenth-century taste in symphonies. Their concerto repertoire almost ignored Mozart's astonishing assortment of twenty-five concertos for seven different solo instruments besides the twenty-nine piano concertos which he composed for himself, or occasionally for a pupil, to play. Chamber-music was absolute caviar to the general public. As for the operas—until 1929 and 1939, *Don Giovanni* and *Figaro* had been absent from the Metropolitan since early in the century, and *Die Zauberflöte* was seldom heard before 1941. Today, two of these three appear every season in New York, as at all other international houses, while in this country and abroad, smaller and regional opera entities are eagerly presenting hitherto rarities like *La finta giardiniera*, *Il rè pastore*, *Idomeneo*, and *La Clemenza di Tito*. For the last there is a current vogue. Personally, I wonder why. I may feel too keenly Mozart's situation in the autumn of 1791. To a libretto of a pompous type that he had long outgrown, Mozart composed *Tito* in dire, hurried necessity, distracting him from graver and greater considerations—*Die Zauberflöte*, the Requiem, and his own imminent death, about which he had premonitions, only three months later.

It is a long time since a pilgrimage to Central Europe was necessary in order to hear Mozart in abundance. Who could have predicted that almost all of Mozart's six hundred and twenty-six works would now exist on records? Or that every summer in New York there is a whole month of daily Mostly Mozart concerts, which draws audiences so appreciative, motley, and contemporary as to make Mozart a sign of these times as well as of all time? Mozart lives with us in all our variegations of humanity. I think we love him, among our other reasons, for his versatility, unmatched by any other composer in all music. We can hear Mozart in every form of composition, and we know that the enormous body of his work assures us of surprises and of new experiences seasoned by the instant recognition that touches every Mozartean everywhere.

M.D.

FOREWORD
TO THE BICENTENARY EDITION

THE LOVE of Mozart and his music, inseparable entities, has always been a dedication of initiates. When late nineteenth-century romanticism thundered loud, the lay votaries of Mozart were a quiet minority, although Wagner, Brahms, Berlioz, Verdi, and Strauss acknowledged their debt to him in words as well as in their music. Haydn and Beethoven had been the first to say that from Mozart they had the most to learn. Their successors have repeated this ever since. To us whose love and necessity keep music alive, Mozart has more to say in depth and breadth at this time than ever before. At the two hundredth anniversary of his birth the small company of initiates has grown to numbers who from every evidence prove that Mozart, with Beethoven and Bach, is one of the composers to whom more people prefer to listen than to all others.

I reflect upon this with undiminished regard after a lifetime of saturation in Mozart's music. I cannot remember when it was that this music first gripped my infant heart. But it must have been when my mother, Alma Gluck, sang arias of Mozart with nobility of style, perfection of technique, and beauty of voice unequalled since. To this day my ear echoes her wondrous classic sostenuto in *L'amerò, sarò costante;* her dazzling bravura in *Un moto di gioia,* the lovely alternative final aria for Susanna which Mozart composed three years after *Le Nozze di Figaro* and which, alas, is never sung in performance. But the deepest Mozartean impression was graven by listening to my mother and Marcella Sembrich, then elderly and retired,

Foreword

singing the Letter Duet. I was standing, a small child, spellbound near the piano. There was nobody else in the room. Sembrich's voice was not beautiful, but she was a good musician. She was seated at the piano accompanying and singing the Contessa's part while my mother stood, one hand on her shoulder, singing Susanna's. The elder voice was reedy, the younger fresh and glowing. Something in the contrast and the blending was moving beyond a child's comprehension. I did not know the sense or the context of what they were singing, but I realize now that they personified a world not only of Mozart's creating, but one which created him.

My childish reactions were naturally component with my adoration of my mother. With rare exceptions I loved whatever she sang because she sang it. But the music of Mozart stands apart in retrospect from this childlike readiness of acceptance. It had magic of its own, beauty separate from my mother's beauty of voice and face, tenderness different from but matched only by hers, identification with Mozart's name at a time when I was too young to know other composers' names or music of themselves. All my life since, while my musical taste and capacity have widened, I have found in Mozart's music the quintessence of all that I feel most keenly in mind and in emotion. Most of us do find in the music we love best the transmutation of its creator's expression into terms intensely personal to us—and quite as fraught with paradox as the mysterious human heart.

The classic perfection of Mozart's music, the seraphic, godlike ease in which it seems to have been conceived, are highly formalized veils which hide from all but the wholly sensitive the tragedy, universal measure of human fate,

Foreword

which most of the great and many of the lesser works express. It is a mistakenly romantic notion to read into music personal statements of tragic experience which may be synchronous in the composer's life with the creation of the music in question. Mozart composed music of radiant vivacity, sparkle, and wit at times when he was crushed by neglect, debt, and the awful discouragement of living his whole life insufficiently compensated and recognized. But he also composed such haunting evocations of mystic tragedy as the C minor Piano Concerto, K.491, at the same time that he was working, full of confidence and optimism, on *Le Nozze di Figaro*, the most glorious comic opera ever written. The juxtaposition of such extremes of musical mood is found repeatedly throughout his life. This can but mean that his genius transcended all the concerns and burdens, the passing pleasures too, of a pitifully harried existence, to soar into that realm which can only be called divine, where man assumes the robe of immortality.

Such thoughts stir ever-recurrent wonder about the vessel which housed this most perfect and spontaneous of all musical genius, the unimposing small-statured man who died a starveling at the age of thirty-five. When I wrote this book I did not evoke an imaginary Mozart; there has always been a real one. He exists for anyone to know, in his voluminous letters and in his still more voluminous works. After that, as I noted in my introduction to the original edition, it is necessary to have read the definitive biographies and it is helpful to know the letters and memoirs of contemporaries. Then come the few slight gaps in documented history which dogmatic biographers have avoided for lack of material of which to make foot-notes, and which romanticizers once gilded and sugared into the preposterous

Foreword

eighteenth-century confection that many thought Mozart's life to have been. I tried to chart an honest course between the two.

I have also known Mozart as truly as it is possible to know a man long dead; have metaphorically, as Dr. Johnson said the biographer must, "eat and drunk and lived in social intercourse with him." As Mozart's music had enchanted me always, so Mozart's life occupied me for years, during which I retraced every journey he made, saw every dwelling then extant in which he had ever lived, every theatre where his works were first performed, every library and museum where his manuscripts were then to be seen. I combined this knowledge with conscientious study of his known life and set down in a continuous record what I believe to have happened. This in some instances is an unconventional procedure but I did not follow it unauthorized. I was helped by several of the foremost scholars of the subject, who read and criticized and endorsed my presentation, and who were also generous with their own material.

The conspicuous instance of my conscientious reconstruction was the meeting in Prague in 1787 of Mozart, Lorenzo DaPonte, and Casanova, when *Don Giovanni* was being written there. In 1926, two sheets of manuscript were found among some Casanova relics at Schloss Hirschberg, near Dux in Bohemia, where he died. These papers were pronounced by qualified authorities to be genuine, and they bear in Casanova's handwriting some fragments of verse that are clearly part of a scene from DaPonte's libretto for *Don Giovanni*. How this came about was the concern, like so many other instances of historical reconstruction, of several scholars of international repute, among whom the

Foreword

following gave me their generous help: Dr. Paul Nettl, then Professor of Musicology in the German University at Prague, now at Indiana University, who first published the contents of the Schloss Hirschberg papers and who is as well known for his Casanova studies as for his musical research; the late Dr. Vlastimil Blazek, then Archivist of the State Conservatory of Music at Prague, whose knowledge of Mozart in Prague was authoritative; and the late Dr. Arthur Livingston, then Professor of Romance Languages at Columbia University, editor of the definitive English translation of DaPonte's memoirs. These scholars agreed that the incident responsible for the Casanova papers must have been essentially what I presented.

I make no apology for my abandonment of formal documentary technique. This book uses original documents in direct quotation, quoted so directly that they are integral with the text. Foot-notes would have thrown each of them back into the source-material from which I extracted them for the purpose of letting the characters speak for themselves. Readers for pleasure are not troubled by this, and readers for duty know, like all Mozart students, whence each quotation comes. Furthermore, the bibliography covers all sources from which quotations have been made. Throughout the book, double quotation-marks have been used to designate this original source-material. All imaginary conversation, written by me, is placed in single quotation-marks. There is no imaginary description. Streets, houses, rooms, furniture, clothes, and all other objects are described only as I have seen them, or as they are represented in original documents, paintings, and prints of the period.

In the years between the original publication of this book

Foreword

and the present writing, two major contributions to definitive literature on Mozart have appeared. The first is the revised Köchel *Chronological and Thematic Index of the Works of Mozart,* edited by Alfred Einstein and published by Breitkopf & Härtel at Leipzig in 1937. The previous 1905 revision of the Köchel Index had become obsolete in relation to a large part of Mozart's work. The late Dr. Einstein undertook the most exhaustive study of all the manuscripts and the circumstances of their composition that had ever been made. It was grimly fortunate that he was able to complete his great labor before the outbreak of the Second World War. Two-thirds of all Mozart's manuscripts and a vast part of those of the other composers had long been in the Prussian State Library at Berlin. Before the holocaust the music manuscripts were removed for safekeeping to four scattered hiding-places, and after the fall of Berlin it was found that at least one of these had become part of Poland. Mystery still surrounds the whereabouts in Communist hands of the dispersed and missing manuscripts, which include half of *Figaro,* all of *Die Zauberflöte, Tito,* the Requiem, and many of Mozart's major instrumental works. The manuscripts of Bach's St. Matthew Passion and Beethoven's Ninth Symphony are among the other incalculable treasures which have had the same fate.

Dr. Einstein's researches resulted in correction of the chronological sequence and of many other factors pertaining to all but the best-known of Mozart's works. In renumbering the more than six hundred and twenty-six compositions Dr. Einstein retained the old Köchel numbers in heavy type, and placed the revised numbers beside them in light-faced type, which eliminates any possibility of con-

Foreword

fusion. Few changes were made in the numbers of the major works, which were catalogued by Mozart himself, especially after 1784. The Köchel numbers in my text are those of the 1905 edition of the Index.

The method of numbering the symphonies, concerti, quartets, and other instrumental music from Number One upwards, which often appears on programmes and gramophone records, is presumably the result of such numbering in the collected works of Mozart published by Breitkopf & Härtel late in the nineteenth century. It is neither so accurate nor so informative as the Köchel Index listing.

The second major work on Mozart is *The Letters of Mozart and His Family*, Chronologically Arranged, Translated, and Edited, with an Introduction, Notes, and Indices by Emily Anderson, published in 1938 by Macmillan at London. This extraordinary piece of scholarship is the result of many years of trained and painstaking research. It is the only complete, wholly unexpurgated edition of these letters in any language, since its German predecessors, the Schiedermair edition and less complete ones, were expurgated and drastically cut. The Mozart family were copious, indefatigable letter-writers, expressing themselves with such startling freedom, frankness, and coarseness of humor that every previous editor of their correspondence felt called upon to bowdlerize it. Miss Anderson has given us in English exactly what Mozart and his family wrote, and in doing so, has presented a more perfect likeness of Mozart than any biographer has ever drawn.

All but one or two of the letters of Mozart himself had been published, though with excisions, in one or other of the previously existing collections. Miss Anderson has pub-

Foreword

lished them complete, noting that some letters Mozart is known to have written have never been found and may still come to light. In some instances she has included passages never before reproduced from the original letters. The great bulk of her work, enormously enlightening in its formative influence upon Mozart's character and life, is the mass of Leopold Mozart's letters, many of which had never previously been published. And with the exception of a few familiar phrases, none of the letters of Anna Maria, Mozart's mother, had ever been translated into English until Miss Anderson published them. These, together with letters of Mozart's sister and his wife, complete a picture of unparalleled intimacy, vividness, and immediacy.

The letters in my text are quoted from the editions previously available; most from the Bozman translation edited by Hans Mersmann, some from Pauline Townsend's translation of the Jahn biography, and the rest I translated from the Schiedermair edition of the Mozart family letters. All inconsistencies or mistakes in spelling and grammar that appear within quoted material are as nearly true to their originals as translation permitted. To correct them would have dimmed their vivid quality and would have suggested a more formal education than Mozart and his lively contemporaries possessed.

Miss Anderson considers that two letters attributed to Mozart are spurious. Both are quoted in my text, without better proof of their authenticity than any other student has been able to supply up to now. The first is the letter, quoted on Page 283, said to have been written to a certain Baron von P., who was supposed to have inquired of Mozart what his methods of composition were. Granted that Mozart's so-called reply is spurious, the facts of which it

Foreword

is compounded are none the less true, for the writer of the letter made a compendium of notes about Mozart's habits of composing, all of which were remarked time and again by himself, his wife, and his close associates.

The second letter is quoted on Page 366, and was ostensibly written in September, 1791, to Lorenzo DaPonte after he had left Vienna. Miss Anderson considers this letter also spurious, but the late W. J. Turner does not agree with her. He quotes it on Pp. 368–69 of his *Mozart*, stating that until there should be actual proof to the contrary, he prefers to follow the tradition which has ascribed it to Mozart. I not only agree with Turner's view, but as in the case of the spurious letter to Baron von P., I find the content of the "DaPonte" letter reflective of the true circumstances—in the latter case, of Mozart's state of mind in September, 1791. This was less than three months before he died. He was at an extremely low ebb of health and mood, obsessed with thoughts of death inseparable from his work on the Requiem. I cannot agree with Miss Anderson's opinion that the letter is doubtful because it indicates extreme depression at a time, she says, "when Mozart, though in poor health, was feeling unusually stimulated and exhilarated."

There is no proof that Mozart was enjoying any sense of wellbeing in the autumn of 1791, except his pleasure in *Die Zauberflöte*. His output was more prolific at that time than for eighteen months past. But this was consequent upon the sporadic manner in which commissions came to him, and its result was the "race with death"—his own oft-repeated words—which spurred the frenetic work of his last months. It does not imply a spontaneous resurgence of his creative forces. If the letter in question was written by Mozart from Vienna, this must have been after his return

Foreword

from Prague, where he had had a sad and exhausting three weeks over the composition and presentation of *La Clemenza di Tito,* which was a failure. He returned to Vienna particularly depressed by the contrast between that experience in Prague and his earlier triumphs there. It was the likeliest of moments for him to think nostalgically of DaPonte, and to write to him.

Its present remoteness makes the point unrealistic, but this is nevertheless the place to note that in writing of Prague, I used in this book the old German nomenclature of streets and landmarks. Subsequent intimacy with Prague in the years of its freedom fixed me in the habit of referring to its streets and buildings by their Czech names. But the German usage here is consistent with that of the eighteenth century, long before the Czech national revival, when Prague was a provincial capital of the Habsburg Empire, and German the language in public and written use.

For their helpful advice on this book I am still indebted, as I was originally, to a group of scholars, musicologists, and librarians, few of whom are now alive. They include the late Dr. Johannes Wolf, until 1934 head of the Musical Section of the Prussian State Library, who gave me unlimited access to the treasures in his charge. The late Carl Engel of New York, former head of the Music Division of the Library of Congress, gave me valuable opinion, as have the present head, Dr. Harold Spivacke and his associates. The late Dr. Livingston and Dr. Blazek, already mentioned, were most helpful. I was and am indebted to the Mozartgemeinde of Salzburg, and particularly to its retired General Secretary, Alfred Heidl, for indispensable help. Herr Heidl was generous with time, thought, and his own material on Constanze Mozart, which he placed at my dis-

Foreword

posal. He read and corrected my manuscript and made many valuable suggestions. Other librarians and curators in Munich, Leipzig, Mannheim, Prague, Vienna, and Paris without exception put their knowledge and their documents into my hands.

This book has not been rewritten, but has been carefully correlated with documentation made available since it was first published. Some of my work could stand rewriting, and I should like to have done that if it had been practicable. I might in that case have tempered some evidences of the youthful fervor with which I flung myself into a labor of love; but then I would be writing a different book. Today I would not write the imaginary conversation already mentioned, though that little which is in the text is thoughtfully and conscientiously distilled from careful study of and saturation in the source-material. Still, that is not considered serious biographical practice, and this is a serious biography.

It is a sobering thought, and one to make a writer humble, that the heritage of genius such as Mozart's can outlast seeming permanencies of our civilization which we have seen destroyed in this "terrible twentieth century." When I was studying to prepare this biography, I was able to see and work and live in a world which has largely disappeared. Most of my work was done in Vienna, in Salzburg, in Prague, in Leipzig, and in the Prussian State Library at Berlin. All but the first two now lie beyond the so-called curtain which has fallen to cut us off from many sources of our common culture. And the spiritual and intellectual toll of man's brutality is far more tragic than war's destruction of treasured places. The gleaming steel vaults of the great library in Berlin, so vividly described by Dr. Einstein in his preface to the revised Köchel, where the saintly Dr.

Foreword

Wolf left me, a total stranger, alone to work among the opened cabinets, were buried beneath the rubble of the grand building. But the dispersal of the manuscripts is a greater grief to those who were privileged to work with them and their dedicated curator.

We have lost music's hallowed "publishing quarter" and we do not even know what else in the once-lovely city of Leipzig, where I used to wander through the linden-shaded streets and sit for hours beneath the austere vaults of the Thomaskirche, listening to the great organ and the proud choir for whom Bach composed, a quiet artisan at his daily stint. We can no longer gaze on the magical Gothic spires soaring from the green hills and grey mists of Prague, nor visit the tranquil garden of the Bertramka, where Mozart composed *Don Giovanni* and I have spent weeks of time, happily at work. Who knows when we shall see again the golden baroque houses, the brooding arcaded squares, the little jewel that is Stavovské Divadlo, the theatre where *Don Giovanni* had its glorious premiere? Vienna we have; but sadly changed. Much of its oldest quarter, the Innere Stadt, where Mozart and his silly Constanze leaped from house to house ahead of their creditors, was crushed by the fury of man. Unscathed Salzburg, at which Mozart scoffed in his gamiest idiom, may become again the place of delighted pilgrimage we used to know, but ten years' military occupation has not enhanced its traditions or its charm.

We of my generation, that of the two world wars, are the last to suffer these pangs when we return, if we can reach them, to the places where we first met and loved the tangible symbols of our heritage. Younger people are more fortunate, as is right; they can appreciate what remains

Foreword

without mourning what is lost. But all of us, living on what terms we can with the knowledge that total barbarism or annihilation can yet overwhelm us, might despair altogether except that immortal beings like Mozart live in their art to tell us that man himself, through the creations of his mind and spirit, is the only permanence.

I am grateful for the opportunity to present this book anew, and grateful too that in nearly twenty-five years it has not been out of print. That has nothing to do with the authorship or with the work itself: only with the subject. It means, I think, that my original intention has been well understood. I wanted to write for the lay reader a book about one of the world's best-loved immortals which, I said, was neither a romance nor a text-book. I tried then to tell the truth, and to truth there can be no emendation except further enlightenment.

Marcia Davenport

Limonta, Como, 1955

ILLUSTRATIONS

PART 1

"... a gentle trace
Of light diviner than the common sun
Sheds on the common earth, and all the place

Was filled with magic sounds woven into one
Oblivious melody . . ."
—SHELLEY, "The Triumph of Life."

I

1756–1762

ON a bitter winter Sunday, January 27, 1756, he was born at Salzburg. Throughout the long day Anna Maria groaned in torture, tended by pious, clumsy neighbors and a distraught husband. Toward evening the groans swelled to shrieks, and at eight o'clock a frail child was precariously delivered. Next morning the bundle of wool was carried through the snow to the baroque cathedral on the Domplatz. Sharp blades of wind cut down between the close overhanging mountains and flung white robes around the scowling saints at the church doors. Inside, dwarfed among the square, soaring columns, a few worshippers knelt hugging their coarse green cloaks and shivering at contact with the chill marble floor. Deep in prayer, they blew on their purple fingers, moved their trussed feet, and took no notice of this town commonplace, this christening party at the left-hand rear corner of the nave, where the high iron font was open and filled with icy holy-water. In a moment the ceremony was over, town-chaplain Leopold Lamprecht bestowing on the feeble child the names Johannes Chrysostomus Wolfgangus Theophilus. The Theophilus became Gottlieb by German translation, and was converted into the Italian Amadeus after a journey to Italy. Hence the signature, Wolfgang Amade Mozart

Mozart

The boy's father later added Sigismundus as a confir-
mation-name, but it was never used. Whether the choice
was prompted by courtesy to Archbishop Sigismund, the
family patron, or by optimism, record does not say. Sigismund was ruling prince of the archiepiscopal See of Salzburg; a noble adventitiously turned churchman. Among
the destinies he held in his greedy, lace-rimmed hands was
that of Leopold Mozart, Wolfgang's father, a capable violinist and composer. Leopold had come fortune-seeking
to Salzburg, forsaking his native Augsburg where his people were simple, honest bookbinders—something he set
out at once to forget. They had produced him in 1719;
beyond that he acknowledged them as little as he could.
In 1747, established after ten years in Salzburg, as court
composer and assistant conductor to the orchestra, with a
fixed though inadequate income, he married Anna Maria
Bertlin, daughter of a lay official at the court. He had
courted her long and faithfully, and won her with the
complacent observation, "Good things take their time."
She was mild and cheerful and blessed with the humorous
bump indigenous to true Salzburgers, and quite devoid of
any talents. She gave her son Wolfgang his gay disposition, his love of fun, and the humanizing simplicity that
enabled him to carry gracefully the burden of genius. She
was a good Catholic wife, trusted Leopold absolutely,
never questioned his plans, submitted to his rigid opinions, and devoted herself to housekeeping and to the birth
of one child every year for seven years. She lost all but
Marianne (Nannerl), born July 30, 1751, and Wolfgang
(Wolferl), the youngest. One wonders how he survived
his first trip to church. Leopold and Anna Maria were
called the handsomest couple in Salzburg, and their chil-

Mozart

dren promised to inherit their good looks. But Wolfgang lost his early beauty in consequence of his prodigious childhood, and turned out to be an insignificant-looking man.

They lived in the house in the Getreidegasse which is now the Mozart Museum—a five-story tenement (using the word in its better sense) of cream-colored plaster, built like all European town dwellings around a centre court. It is a short walk from the court chapel where Leopold went to work every day. An old street arch leads into the Löchelplatz, on which the building faces, and in the centre of which there was the usual well, the water-supply for the neighborhood, where the housewives gathered for cleanliness' sake and gossip. The house belonged to Lorenz Hagenauer, a good bourgeois merchant who lived in it and was on the friendliest terms with his fourth-floor tenants. Visitors entered the dim downstairs hall, climbed three flights of dark, but well-kept stairs, knocked on a heavy door, and found Mama, in a stuff gown, spotless white cap, fichu, and ruffled apron, smiling in the anteroom. *Grüss-Gotts* were exchanged, with hand-kissing or a hearty salute on both cheeks. Mama then led the way into the square low-ceiled drawing-room, with three casements on the Löchelplatz. Each window had a show of flowering plants and here was Herr Canari in his cage, chirping cordially to friendly advances. Pushing forward a chair, bustling about the tidy room, calling to Theresa to hurry with the coffee, Mama put her head through a door and called, 'Nannerl, Wolferl, *kommt her.*' Marianne appeared, leading Wolfgang by his chubby hand. At eight, she was a quiet little girl with a slender body and a serious expression. She had the broad Mozart forehead, the large, steady blue-gray eyes, the fine blond hair.

Mozart

Her brother was a round pudding of a boy of four, with the same brow and eyes as his sister's, set in an unusually wide head. He bounded up to his mother, climbed into her lap, kissed her, stroked her cheeks, climbed down, climbed into the guest's lap, repeated his demonstrations, climbed down, and trotted back to Nannerl. Noisily and comfortably, above all, unaffectedly, they went about their play, singing and chasing each other round the room, greeting intimate family friends who dropped in for coffee, *Kuchen*, and music. One visitor brought trios, another a new quartet, for they all composed and all played. Papa came in from his day's work as assistant director of the orchestra, accompanied by his most intimate friend, Andreas Schachtner, the court trumpeter, at whose appearance the children shouted for joy.

The home was as comfortable as it was happy. The furniture was good walnut; each room had its big tile and porcelain stove; the drawing-room held the black-keyed clavier. The bedroom was in the middle, with the children's trundle-beds under their parents' big one. To the rear was Papa's study and the writing-table where he recorded Wolferl's first compositions. Wolferl wrote notes before words. Outside, down the bare stone hall, was the warm kitchen where Theresa was roasting the capon for her darling's dinner—it was always his favorite dish—and where the dog jealously watched every morsel she touched. Theresa, Herr Canari, the dog and the capons all shared tender messages in Wolfgang's letters when he was away from home.

In the drawing-room, the baby had his lessons at the clavier. Leopold had begun to teach Nannerl when she was seven, and Wolferl, barely three, would not stay

Mozart

away. He would sit on the floor playing with blocks or a kitchen spoon, and at certain sounds suddenly drop his toys, rise, and move almost unconsciously to the clavier. He would stand, spellbound, ignored by his father and sister; and after Nannerl's lesson would reach up and tentatively, delicately touch the keys. His midget fingers found a third; ah! He gurgled, cooed, and touched the next two keys in order; another third! Ecstatic delight. Then the fingers moved on, but missed the lower note, struck two together, a discord. The baby stopped, gasped, began to bawl with disappointment. Next day he could remedy the mistake; a little later, try to pick out what he had heard Nannerl playing. When he was four, Leopold started, half in fun, to teach him too.

After a year of learning, the baby cared for nothing but music. He sat at the clavier for any length of time, willingly, eagerly. He had soft, sandy hair which straggled over his ridiculous coat-collar, a miniature of that worn by Leopold, standing by. One paternal hand was lifted to beat time, the other was clenched in his big patchpocket. Papa had cold, prominent eyes; a mouth whose curled upper lip and heavy lower lip suggested passion at once disciplined by the hard jaw. The chin was dominant, deeply moulded, jutting out under a firm transverse line below the mouth. It was strongly cleft, a mark that appeared as a dimple in the baby, for Wolferl had inherited this broad face but not the rigid character that stamped ungentle lines on it. Leopold wore his wig and his formal clothes with hauteur—his artisan birth had no bearing on his present court tenure. To Wolfgang his tone and his manner were tender, but his assertive self-importance was plainly to be seen. Gently removing the chubby right hand

Mozart

from the keyboard, he said, 'Each hand must first play perfectly alone. Then together. So—*einz*——'

The tiny back was soldierly, the round eyes, later to protrude with ill-health and strain, were eagerly fixed on the exercise-page written out in Papa's copper-plate hand. The visitor marvelled that the soft, stubby fingers, not strong enough to butter their own bread, could be so precise, so firm, such complete masters of the shallow keys. Watching the child's abnormal concentration, his willing slavery, and seeing the mixture of reverence and conscience in the father, it is plain that this is not so much a lesson as a checking-up on what wonder God has wrought since yesterday; for Leopold is already convinced that this genius is the mark of divine favor, so to be received and guided. With each day's manifestation the father first gave thanks, then went on to develop. Wolferl never heard a precept more than once. Each moment of his learning time was priceless, equal to weeks in an ordinary life; he seemed to know everything before it was told him, and such was his musical instinct that he probably did know.

The lesson over, Wolfgang having learned in half an hour to play a minuet perfectly and in precise time, Leopold told him to jump down, run away and play. No sudden joy, no leap for freedom answered this. The child would stay and tease for duets, ask for his sister to play them with him. Leopold said, 'Nannerl is finished for the day, and you, too!—off with you!' But first there must be an embrace, for there was no stinting of demonstrative love between this pair. Then Wolferl would seize his father's cane, straddle it, and turn in a twinkling into the baby he was, prancing through the rooms on his hobbyhorse, and singing, in perfect time, you may be sure. He

Mozart

had no interest in games for which no musical accompaniment could be devised. When Papa's friends came in, they had to join Wolferl's play. Whoever did not carry toys in the procession from one room to another must sing or play a march on the fiddle. And every night at bedtime there was an infantile ceremony. Standing on a chair beside Papa, Wolferl sang to a tune of his own invention the meaningless words, *"Oragna figata fà, marina gamina fà,"* then kissed the end of Leopold's nose, promised to keep him in a glass case when he grew old, and so went to sleep.

A monk named Bullinger was one of the family intimates, and Schachtner the trumpeter was the adored of both children. Schachtner went home with Leopold after the afternoon service, one Thursday, and they went upstairs to find four-year-old Wolferl busy with music-paper, pen, and ink—a great deal of ink. He had dug his quill into the very bottom of the sticky ink-well, and then wiped away the drops shed on his opus by smearing them with the palm of his hand. Leopold instantly showed his extraordinary instinct for the child's psychology. He did not scold him for spilling ink and making a mess of his clothes, nor tease him for pretending to be grown-up and a composer. Gravely he asked him what he was doing. Without looking up, Wolferl answered:

"Writing a concerto for the clavier and"—smearing away another blot—"it will soon be done."

"Let me see it."

"Oh, no, Papa, it is not finished. You cannot tell yet what it is like."

But Leopold won the gentle argument and picked up the paper.

He and Schachtner exchanged the expected smiles.

Mozart

Then he began to study the "apparent nonsense," to note its construction and theme. His eyes widened, filled with tears. Silently he handed the paper to Schachtner and called his attention to the details. At last he observed, with an incredulous sigh, "The child has not only written a concerto, but one so difficult that nobody can possibly play it."

Here Wolferl, waiting patiently to get back his manuscript, chirped, "*Aber ja, Papa,* you are right! It is so hard, that is why it is a concerto. One must practice it until it is perfect, but see"— He trotted to the clavier, spread his fat fingers, but could only indicate what he meant. He had made it hard purposely; playing concertos and working miracles were the same thing!

The next year, after the family had returned from Vienna, Schachtner took a court violinist named Wentzl to the Mozarts' one afternoon. Wentzl had composed six trios which he wanted to play over with Papa and Schachtner, Leopold being an able violinist and the author of a text-book on violin-study. Wolferl, hanging around, was on the *qui vive* as soon as the fiddles and scores were taken out. He had a tiny violin of his own, but had never had a lesson. Clutching his toy, he nosed into the group and began begging to play second fiddle.

Leopold reproved him.

'How can you play second fiddle when you have never had a lesson?'

Trying to control his trembling lip, Wolferl said, "*Aber Papa,* one need not have learnt in order to play second fiddle."

Ignoring this wisdom from the mouth of his babe, Leopold answered sharply, "Wolferl, we are ready to begin,

Mozart

and you are delaying us. You are a nuisance. Go away at once."

Now the tears fell; hugging his little fiddle, the baby crept away, crying bitterly.

This was more than the tender Schachtner could bear.

'Oh, see here, Leopold,' he protested, 'let the *Bübchen* play along with me'—winking at Papa—'you won't be able to hear him,' he added.

Leopold, still ruffled, finally gave in.

'But Wolferl,' he said, shaking his finger, 'you are not to play loud enough for anyone to hear, verstehst *Du?* or you will be sent away at once.'

Someone wiped the baby's nose and set a chair for him. The first trio began. Schachtner played with one eye on Wolferl. In a very few minutes, it was obvious that the old trumpeter was quite superfluous. The five-year-old was carrying the whole second fiddle perfectly. Schachtner quietly laid down his fiddle and stole a glance at Leopold, sawing away with the tears running down his cheeks. Little was said until all six trios had been played. Then Leopold could not restrain the guests any longer. They swooped on the baby with exclamations and kisses, which so excited him that he insisted on trying first violin, and carried it off, far from perfectly, but never breaking down altogether.

Here was the child's genius, the inborn flame glowing at white heat. But marvellous as the feat may have been, the truth is that many violinists have shown similar genius as children; many a little Russian boy could play second fiddle at sight at the age of five. Mozart is differentiated from other prodigies less by his perfection in performing than by his native urge to compose. Here is the true, the rare seed of greatness. He had the requisite talent for superb performance on the violin or clavier, but that alone would have made him just one more immortal interpreter of music. But he hardly functioned at all, musically, before he identified himself with creation. When he left his play to sidle up to Nannerl's lesson, he was drawn not so much by the pleasing sounds as by the compulsion to answer an urge that filled his child's soul, and that paced the growth of that soul until it dominated his world.

The notable part played by Leopold was his recognition of the child as a creative musician more than as a performing prodigy. Whether or not one blames him for dragging the helpless infant around Europe to be the pet of sensation-loving courts, he was certainly profoundly right in his emphasis on the creative. We dare not think what would have been lost had not Leopold had his pedantic conscience, and had he not been able to temper this with his great love. Wolfgang would surely have been a flash-in-the-pan, a brief blaze destined to be extinguished by his own weaknesses, of which he had many. He could have been cheap, would have been impermanent. As it happened, God was for once intelligent as well as kind. He planted in Wolfgang Mozart what is probably the purest, sheerest genius ever born in man, and then placed it in the care of Leopold. The resultant flowering was no accident.

Leopold had a most difficult course to navigate, and he did it consummately. Too much pressure, too rigid application of his pedagogic ideas would have dampened the boy's flame, as well as caused him to revolt from discipline. Too much tenderness, too much yielding to his own natural instinct merely to praise and marvel would have pro-

Mozart

duced a slipshod musician, if one at all; would never have developed the incomparable polish that distinguishes the merest phrase of Mozart. Leopold could, while training the child to write manuscripts in the beautiful, orderly pattern that became a life habit, so balance the young sense of values that the mechanics never obtruded over the supremely important flow of ideas. In the same way, Wolfgang was not allowed to be carried away by the excitement of success in concert. He was kept constantly aware of music, not of himself as a performer of it. He was treated as an adult (which he was) in musical judgment. So he could, at twelve, form reliable opinions of contemporary composition, untinged by juvenile prejudices—caprice, jealousy, or personal conceit. Like all serious workers, he knew the true worth of his own productions; and while modesty is not just the word to apply to his mental attitude, only true modesty allows a man to realize how good his own work is. This judicial faculty he possessed at a very early period. He could have been obnoxious with it, but he never was.

Nobody knows whether it ever occurred to Leopold Mozart to question the wisdom of exploiting his two children publicly. After all, he was only an indigent musician. And musicians, of whatever condition, were not expected to have taste and judgment in the eighteenth century. They were servants of courts, in station little above menials, in practice never above turning their talents into bread. Fame was their first requisite, for they depended utterly on their reputations to obtain situations. If Wolfgang was ever to reach the highest position in the service of some royalty, he could not begin too soon to acquire fame. As for Nannerl, she would of course never be a

Mozart

conductor or composer, but the severest and most jealous critics admitted that she was an extraordinarily fine cla-vier-player. It could only add to the boy's glamour to present her along with him. Marvellously as she played at ten, he played quite as well at six; no harm, but a great deal of profit might derive from any comparisons the world chose to make. It must be remembered that children, as such, were not thought of then in the complicated psychological terms of to-day. Everybody had a great many children, usually one a year, few of whom (for which thanks were surreptitiously given) survived. If those who lived were undistinguished they were just more townspeople, and if they had any talents parents rushed to exploit them because they appeared so remarkable while children were small, and the golden days would be num-bered. Leopold would not have admitted this his moving idea; he claimed to be concerned with the future.

Mozart, however, was dowered with real genius enough to have overpowered the physique of an ordinary child. The mystery is that he, with a delicate body, survived at all the fantastic handicaps of twelve years of hard travel-ling, hard living, and public performances. Still more as-tonishing is the steady stream of music that flowed dur-ing those years from his child's brain—for he did have the brain and soul of a child and kept them in spite of the abnormal demands made of them.

At the same time, he did not escape the sophistication that would naturally overtake a boy living among mu-sicians whose free-and-easy lives and baldness of speech were not much different then from now. Salzburgers were noted for bawdy language, coarse jokes, and suggestive buffoonery, to which Wolfgang was exactly suited by

Mozart

temperament. In spite of every serious, every sorrowful aspect of his life, he always loved a good laugh—and started one at every opportunity. As soon as he began writing letters he peppered them with sly references to unmentionable things that cause innocent readers of "that dear, dainty little Mozart" to gasp in incredulous horror. The thirteen-year-old boy who observes of a *grotesco* at the Mantua opera that ". . . . he leaps well, but does not write as I do, that is, as the sows piss . . . ." is not quite the mincing minuetist he has sometimes been pictured.

His public life began in September, 1761, when he was five. He played the part of a chorister in a Latin comedy given to mark the close of the year at the Salzburg Gymnasium. The music for the piece was written by Eberlin, the court organist, and Wolferl was one of a hundred and fifty children engaged to play in it. Leopold looked down on the whole performance, but was always ready to encourage anything that brought Wolferl into public notice. This was the year when Leopold wrote down Wolferl's first composition in the music-book from which he learned his minuets. The melodies, of course, are simple and are plainly the ideas of a child; yet their treatment is perfection, and instantly identifiable as Mozart's. There could be no better proof of his innate musical purity and soundness; many trained harmonists would do no better than the baby who merely played what he heard inside his head.

Until just before his sixth birthday, then, Wolferl led a happy and not too burdened life. His disposition was angelic, the last thing to expect of a child genius. He was sweet, docile, obedient, affectionate to the last degree.

Mozart

No tempers or tantrums, never a yowl of rage nor a foot stamped on the floor. He learned his lessons, whatever they were, easily and quickly. His mind was usurped by music until he discovered the rudiments of arithmetic. Suddenly the house erupted with figures scribbled on every bit of space—walls, floors, tables and chairs. This passion for mathematics is plainly in close alliance with his great contrapuntal facility. Music, however, was his only real interest. All his playfulness, expressed in trivial jokes and pranks, was forgotten the moment he touched a clavier or harpsichord. Leopold wrote to him reminiscently, in later years, "Your countenance, even, was so grave that many intelligent persons, seeing your talent so early developed and your face always serious and thoughtful, were concerned for the length of your life." This horrible prophecy might not have been so smugly quoted by Leopold had he realized that his own misguided ambition was to be the chief cause of his son's hardships and pitiably premature death.

Of course he did not realize, and carefully he made his plans. Munich, the Bavarian capital, seat of the Elector's court, was his first goal; whatever sensation the children made there would quickly travel back to Salzburg. This was what Leopold wanted in order to increase his importance with Archbishop Sigismund. Mama received her orders. She brushed up the children's warmest clothes for travelling and their very best for concerts; polished their buckles and buttons, knitted new warm stockings and mittens, packed band-boxes. On the 12th of January the big travelling coach pounded across the dirty, snowy cobbles of the Löchelplatz, and stopped at Getreidegasse, 225. Mama bustled downstairs loaded with rugs and blankets, following the excited children. Leopold, in tricorne and greatcoat, stood aside while she bundled them into their places, along with packages of food and flasks of nourishing drinks. She wrapped up their throats, admonishing Nannerl to take good care of Wolferl, see that he eats nothing *schrecklich*, keep him out of draughts, don't let him get his feet wet, give him his rhubarb *wenn er es braucht*, and be a good girl yourself. She gave each child a big, brisk hug and a kiss on both cheeks, backed out of the coach, and embraced Papa in farewell. He sprang in, the door was slammed, the step was folded, the postillion's whip cracked like a shotgun. Mama retreated into the doorway to escape the flying slush, waving her apron at the two little faces pressed against the back pane as the coach turned and lurched away. If there were no tears in her eyes, she was not the mother we know her to be. The carriage lumbered its way through the little town, skirted the frozen Salzach, and moved off between the steeply-cut mountains. A new and never-to-be-forgotten rhythm is implanted in the youngest passenger—the pitching beat of heavy wheels, the broken thumping of sixteen big hoofs.

The brief, candent life has begun.

II

1762–1763

LEOPOLD was not only a good father and a good teacher; he was a first-rate publicity man as well. Busily, he set about circulating news of his wonder children as soon as they arrived in Munich. They were soon invited to play at several of the best houses, and shortly, before the Elector Maximilian Joseph III at his palace. They made a fine impression, were extravagantly admired, and handsomely received everywhere. The remuneration for such performances was whatever the noble patron chose to give; ducats, when the luck held. There were times, however, to which a huge collection of rings, snuff-boxes, and other bibelots is witness, when the full precariousness of this custom was borne in on Leopold. But the first trip was financially profitable, for Papa started home in three weeks with bigger plans in his eye. They stayed quietly at Salzburg for the next nine months, practicing, studying, preparing to acquit themselves faultlessly of any musical challenge. Wolfgang also worked at his violin and composed minuets and small pieces which Leopold, with scrupulous care, wrote down in Nannerl's copy-book. This book later found its way into the hands of a family at Graz, who sold it to the Princess Pauline of Russia, who returned it to its original home just a hundred years after the children had used it.

In September, when he knew the important people would be returning to town from country-seats and watering-places, Leopold ordered the coach to take the whole

Mozart

family to Vienna. This time Mama packed her own best silks and real lace fichus along with the children's finery. Funds were conveniently raised by borrowing from Hagenauer, the obliging landlord, and the Mozarts started for Linz, the first stop on the way. They had to take everything with them—the clavier, two fiddles, cases of music, bulky boxes of clothes, all strapped to the roof of the coach. They travelled *noblement*—that is, in a private vehicle hired by Papa instead of in a post-chaise or diligence. This extravagance was due partly to bad roads and the importance of protecting the children's health, and partly to what Leopold called the honor and reputation of their court. What he really meant was that he considered himself and his family superior to the wandering performers who got around Europe as best they could and made their bids for patronage in bald rather than in genteel ways. Leopold was courting royalty, and was shrewd enough to know that nothing succeeds like success —or, *faute de mieux*, the appearance of it.

Wolfgang captivated the fat bishop of Passau, who, with many kisses and blessings, made them remain for five days, against Leopold's better judgment. Poor Papa's reasoning was confirmed by the bishop's reward of one ducat for almost a week of constant performing, but the children finally gave a concert at the next stopping-place, Linz, under the patronage of Count Schlick, the provincial governor, which somewhat minimized the expense of being in high favor with the church. Two local nobles, Count Herberstein and young Palffy, heard them play and carried the news of the coming sensation to the capital, ahead of the children's arrival. This delighted Leopold, who wrote Hagenauer long accounts of everything

Mozart

that happened, probably as a partial way of discharging his many obligations. But the patronizing tone of the letters leaves little doubt that Papa thought he was doing poor provincial Hagenauer a great favor by giving him glimpses of the smart world. And where could Leopold better strut his pride than in letters sure to be read aloud to the whole admiring community at home?

They travelled from Linz to Vienna by boat on the Danube. Even at the custom-house Wolferl contrived to beguile savage breasts and so charmed the revenue-officers with a minuet on his fiddle that they passed the baggage without the usual irritating delay. (Six years later, he signed a letter to Nannerl, *"Wolfgang de Mozart, Edler von Hochenthal, Freund des Zahlhausens."*) Herberstein and Palffy had done nobly by the family cause, and aristocratic Vienna was keen in anticipation of the prodigies. In no time they were the talk of the town, countesses and princesses vying with each other to present the newest sensation. All this was gratifying, but Leopold's eye was fixed in one direction—Schönbrunn—and shortly, to his overwhelming joy, the command came, unsolicited. The children were perfectly calm about it, but Mama's flustered preparations, her scrubbing and brushing and curling and polishing were a sight to see. The private treasurer came in one of the Imperial carriages to fetch them from their lodgings, the White Ox in the old Fleischmarkt. Their entrance into the royal presence was as awesome to Leopold as it was a matter of course to Wolfgang, who saw Maria Theresa as a kind, motherly woman, and so climbed into her lap, took her round the neck, and kissed her heartily.

The Empress was just the person to appreciate this

Mozart

spontaneity. She bore sixteen children altogether, and though, of necessity and tradition, she played the ones who lived in the game of politics, she loved them far more than royal mothers were apt to love in those involuntarily fecund days. She was too real a woman and too much a German not to be charmed by an attractive, talented child. She was also a good musician. The Emperor Charles VI, her father, had had her taught to play the clavier and to sing, and she herself had engaged the composer, Wagenseil, to live at court and teach her children. Her son, Joseph, who was later to have the honor of being Mozart's appreciative patron while allowing him to starve, was a credit to Wagenseil, but his younger brother, Leopold, was barren ground for music. Their father, the Emperor Francis I, enjoyed Wolferl more than anyone in the royal family, but he took more pleasure in trifling fun with the boy than in any appreciation of his music. His idea of a marvel was to make Wolferl play with one finger or with the keys hidden by a cloth. Fortunately the child was not long acquiring contempt for such inartistic nonsense. He soon learned to trust his own instinct not to play for people who could not appreciate what he was doing. As a man he usually lost his temper, and refused to play, if his audience did not listen respectfully.

For the first appearance at court, Francis and Maria Theresa had chosen a quiet day when the children could play without any interruptions. Within the private salon the royal family was ranged about in comfortable, unaffected attitudes of interest, the younger children with their fingers in their mouths, round-eyed with wonder at the two little mountaineers. Rigid forms of address and behavior were left aside—Wolferl's introduction to royalty was such that no king or emperor ever confused him. The children stayed three hours and covered themselves with glory. During the next four weeks they appeared repeatedly in the imperial salons, playing clavier duets, solos, and violin and clavier sonatas. Wolferl also improvised, and accompanied the royal children. They became the court pets, and the rage of society. On her name-day, the Empress sent her treasurer to the Mozarts' lodging with two state costumes; Wolferl's had been made for the archduke Maximilian, and Nannerl's for one of the little archduchesses. "Would you like to know how Wolferl's dress looks? It is of a lily-color, of the finest cloth, with a waistcoat of the same, the coat with double broad gold borders. Nannerl's . . . is of white brocaded taffeta, with all sorts of ornaments. . . ." These are, of course, the clothes in which Leopold had the two familiar portraits of the children painted during this visit.

Wolferl was entirely unimpressed by the external grandeur of the little Habsburgs, and played with them as if they were villagers from home. He was particularly fond of seven-year-old Marie Antoinette. One day he slipped and fell on the polished floor, while walking between her and one of her sisters. She picked him up and comforted him while the sister walked on.

"You are good," Wolferl said, "and when I grow up I will marry you."

The Empress asked him why.

"Because I am grateful," he answered. "She was kind to me, but her sister paid no attention."

If Marie Antoinette had chosen to remember, fourteen years later, a grateful little boy at Schönbrunn, she might have eased for Mozart some of the bitterest grief a youth

Mozart

ever endured. But she was busy milking cows at the Trianon.

He was invariably earnest about music, and absolutely truthful in criticism, exclaiming in his piping voice, *Pfui, Off-key!* or *Bravo!* when he stood in the anteroom listening to Joseph play violin duets with his teacher. He soon tired of showing off like a pet monkey to amuse the court, and one day demanded that the Emperor, who was sitting beside him at the clavier, be replaced by Wagenseil. When the composer came, Wolferl said, "I am going to play one of your concertos, Herr Wagenseil, and will you kindly turn over for me?" Sometimes it is hard not to believe that Leopold coached him in these artless demonstrations, but such utter simplicity of behavior would never have occurred to Papa as the way to win royalty.

Generous gifts of money were bestowed from the royal treasury, and Leopold delightedly watched society follow suit. Until late every night the children's time was filled with engagements at fashionable houses. "To-day we are at the French Ambassador's, and to-morrow we go to Count Harrach's. We are everywhere fetched and sent home in the carriages of the nobility. . . . On one occasion we were at a place from half-past two until near four o'clock; then Count Hardegg sent his carriage for us, which took us at full gallop to the house of a lady"— (obviously Hardegg's mistress)—"where we stayed till half-past five; afterward we were with Count Kaunitz till near nine." Such an unnatural regime could not long continue without harm. On the 21st of October, after a concert at Schönbrunn, Wolferl fell sick, broke out in high fever and a red rash. Leopold wrote home to order masses to local saints, but scarlet fever was stronger than the prayers of Salzburg, and for four weeks the family was isolated, with no profit accruing except the polite inquiries of the nobility who sent their lackeys with messages, but not with money.

When Wolferl, pale and a little shaky, reappeared, most of his patrons showed plain aversion to his company, fear of infectious diseases being quite naturally a mania; and the remaining performances were acknowledged with shoe-buckles, verses, and gracious smiles from the Empress. So Leopold accepted an invitation to appear at Pressburg in Hungary, barely accessible through a wilderness. That his insanity in taking the children on such a wild ride in the dead of winter went unpunished by fate is miraculous. They reached Salzburg again in January, 1763, after struggling with roads of indescribable condition, and in some places with no roads at all. They had been away four months, much longer than Leopold's leave of absence, and Sigismund's reaction was anything but tolerant. This warfare between Leopold and his patron endured for the remainder of Wolfgang's childhood. In justice to the Archbishop it must be admitted that Leopold did as little as possible to earn his salary, and that he never hesitated when faced with choosing between his duty to his post and his determination to ride to wealth and fame on the tail of Wolfgang's comet.

As the Mozarts threaded its formidable roads, Europe was a jumble of small courts, sporadic wars, shifting frontiers, public and private intrigues, and rivalries of every sort from those of princes for thrones to those of women for princes. Only a few countries, notably England, France, and Russia, pretended to united governments. Germany and Italy were made up of hundreds of

Mozart

disharmonious little principalities, each with its own ruler
and court, all subject to the titular authority of the Holy
Roman Emperor, at this time Francis I of Lorraine, duke
of Tuscany, who was elected only because he was Maria
Theresa's consort. The office of emperor was theoreti-
cally elective, but it came to be accepted (at the point of
the sword) that the archdukes of Austria, likewise kings
of Hungary and Bohemia, should hold the title, though
the formality of an election was subscribed to, and the
emperor always crowned, according to tradition, at Frank-
fort-am-Main.

Bavaria, of which Salzburg was then a part, was ruled
by an elector, Prussia and Saxony by kings, the Palatinate
—Germany along the Rhine—by an elector; Parma, like
other Italian courts, enjoyed an archduke, Naples-and-
Sicily a king, Venice the doge, and the rest of southern
and central Europe similar petty powers. Holland, Flan-
ders, Luxembourg, Lorraine, and endless other duchies
belonged to Austria; the greedy Habsburgs had married
into almost every ruling family, from the greatest to the
least. Maria Theresa married daughters to the king of
France, the king of Naples, the archduke of Parma, and
the duke of Saxe-Teschen; and sons to the daughters of
Spain and the duchy of Modena. Like every other large
family party, this one could not continue indefinitely without strife. So there were wars, not only between directly
opposed powers like Prussia and Austria, Sweden and
Russia, but between those allied by marriage and in supposed allegiance to the Empire.

Until Napoleon, however, these wars were mostly of
the *opera-buffa* type. There was fighting, certainly, but a
battle was a day's affair fought by professional soldiers on

Mozart

some open field where neighboring towns were not in danger of bombardment, and where ample food for the armies could be had without causing adjacent cities to starve. Travellers had their troubles, but not those to be expected as the result of wars. Rather were accidents to coaches and horses, dirt, highway-robbers, cold and hunger, and above all, the execrable village inn to be dreaded, "where by or against one's will one was forced to sleep as the only alternative to spending the night under the stars. There one met every horror or danger. There, without remorse, the host made the most of the traveller's necessity. There flourished fleas, bugs, and rats, clouds of flies, dirt unbounded, the traces of bygone foods with their attendant odors, dirty linen, and the smells of drains, if such things chanced to exist." This was what Leopold chose as the setting for his children's tender years; this, and the false adulation of courts, the evanescent acclaim of superficial people. The Mozarts did travel, like everyone else at that time, wherever they pleased. Their troubles were not the devastation of war or interference by the military. They had sufficient, if unlovely food and drink, and fresh, if not admirable post-horses.

War, far from being a national catastrophe, was part of a king's ordinary business; the rest was intrigue, love and license, and gloriously, patronage of the arts. Painting, sculpture, poetry, drama, and music flowered under the benevolence of kings and princes. For all their condemnation of these magnificent little courts, modern proletarians cannot point to anything so deliciously democratic as the friendly intercourse of the great aristocrats with the artists who surrounded them by invitation. Of course there was a black side to this picture, that the artist who had

Mozart

neither the luck, the charm, nor the influence to be recognized by a royal patron was in danger of starving to death. While Haydn lived a happy, sheltered life at Prince Esterhazy's court, Mozart died thirty years too soon, the victim of the vicious side of patronage. There is much to be said for modern democracy, in which the writer or composer can take his works to a publisher, stand an even chance of being well and fairly paid, and perhaps become a popular idol overnight; but it often seems that great plays and great music were written in the days when royalty commanded them, and that they were offered to cultivated audiences who were more concerned with the graces of life than with the profits of trade. Be that as it may, eighteenth-century Europe swarmed with small courts whose rulers, partly in genuine devotion to beauty, and partly in rivalry with their contemporaries, were magnificent patrons of all the arts. Music flourished as never before. An introduction to a prince was almost as good as a command to play for him. Casting his eye over this golden field, Leopold could not but believe that Europe was his oyster, and Wolfgang's genius the sword with which to open it.

So Papa sat in Salzburg for six months after the triumphal tour to Vienna, grudgingly fulfilling his duties at court, busily laying plans for the next journey. No potential patron was mentioned that Leopold did not somehow obtain a letter to him, to store away with his other talismans. Between Salzburg and Paris, his ultimate goal, lay any number of courts. . . . He announced his plans to the family in May. Obediently, Mama began her preparations, with a heart aching at the thought of another long absence from home, how very long she could not

Mozart

then tell; at leaving her kind, homely friends, and Theresa, and the pets. She loved the squares and arches and quays of Salzburg; its churches; the *Peterskeller*, dark, saintly retreat of plain familiar food and cool white wine, where the family supped sometimes, bowing their heads and crossing themselves when a gentle father made his rounds of benediction. She loved the houses of her boisterous friends, where a game of quoits and a sally of broad jokes was ample entertainment for her simple soul. And, above all, she loved the clean, sunny home that no lodging in the world could equal, no matter what its proximity to a palace. Nevertheless, the packing went forward on a larger scale than ever before. Wolferl was seven, and Nannerl eleven, when they left home the third time, on the 9th of June, 1763. Leopold had laid out a route to Paris that included all the important courts along the way. He planned to visit country-seats, as the nobility would be away from their capitals during the warm weather.

Hardly a day away from home, the coach broke down —without injuring anyone, for a wonder—at Wasserberg. Wolferl played the organ there, for the first time, while they waited for the repairs to be made. Munich next, where they played again for the Elector, who kept them waiting for their money; then Augsburg, where they stayed two weeks visiting the Mozart relatives and where Wolferl played with his four-year-old cousin, Maria Anna Thekla Mozart, whom they called *"Das Bäsle."* He was to know her much better one day. Leopold deplored this waste of time. They received their first rebuff at Ludwigsburg, where their introductions to the Duke of Württemburg did not gain them an audience at his summer palace. Leopold ascribed this to the influence of Jomeili, the Duke's Italian *Kapellmeister*, but laid himself open to the charge of pettishness, for Jomelli was a fine musician, and far too important to belittle himself with jealousy of a child. Wolfgang had real enough battles with jealousy later; the truth of the Jomelli episode is merely that the world was not so impressed with Leopold and his children as he liked to think.

Schwetzingen was the next stop, the summer court of the Elector Palatine Karl Theodore, who maintained one of the best orchestras in Europe at his permanent capital, Mannheim. The orchestra played at the summer residence and its profound influence on the sensitive child, who had never heard such music, can hardly be overestimated. One of the players was the flautist Wendling, who became a lifelong friend of Wolfgang's. Leopold was full of pompous praise for the band; "it is incontestably the best in Germany, composed entirely of young men of good character, neither drinkers nor dicers, nor yet clownish persons; their conduct is as praiseworthy as their talent." This is a slap at Salzburg and its folk-ways. He adds, "My children have set all Schwetzingen in commotion." This was probably true. From there they went to Heidelberg, where Wolferl again showed amazing precocity at the organ. Whenever they had time to kill in a town, they did it by visiting the best organ, as modern travellers drop into a movie while waiting for a train. At Mainz they had to give public concerts because the Elector was ill, and from there they went to Frankfort. One concert had been planned, but a press notice, a good sample of Papa's talents as promoter, gives further details:

"The universal admiration excited in the minds of the

Mozart

audience by the astounding genius of the two children of Herr L. Mozart, *Kapellmeister* at the court of Salzburg, has necessitated the threefold repetition of the concert which was announced to take place on one occasion only.

"In consequence, therefore, of this universal admiration, and in deference to the desires of many distinguished connoisseurs, the next and positively the last concert will take place this evening, Tuesday, August 30, in the Scharfischen Saal, on the Liebfrauenberge.

"The little girl, who is in her twelfth year, will play the most difficult compositions of the greatest masters; the boy, who is not yet seven, will perform on the clavecin or harpsichord; he will also play a concerto for the violin, and will accompany symphonies on the clavier, the manual or keyboard being covered with a cloth, with as much facility as if he could see the keys; he will instantly name all notes played at a distance, whether singly or in chords, on the clavier, or any other instrument, glass, bell, or clock. He will finally, both on the harpsichord and the organ, improvise as long as may be desired and in any key, thus proving that he is as thoroughly acquainted with the one instrument as with the other, great as is the difference between them.

"Each person pays half-a-thaler. Tickets may be had at the Golden Lion."

In one of these audiences sat a beautiful, dark-haired, sentimental boy of fourteen, very much the father to the man that was to be. Johann Wolfgang Goethe already knew French, Italian, Latin, and Greek, but listened, open-mouthed, to the *kleiner Hexenmeister* in powdered wig and sword. Nor did the memory of the poor little monkey doing his musical tricks in grown-up clothes sway Goethe in maturity from coupling Mozart with Raphael, and placing the two at the head of all achievement, for their "ease and blitheness in art."

Mozart

The rest of the long Paris journey through Coblenz, Bonn, Cologne (where they thought the cathedral dingy), Aix, and Brussels, yielded enough trinkets to start a shop, but not enough money to pay hotel bills and post-horses —a purpose to which, Leopold remarked sourly, he could not put the Princess Amalie's kisses. No mention is made in his letters of the wonderful Rhine country, but the beauties of nature were redundant to the Mozarts; only the elevation of their estate mattered to them. The travelling was so slow!—Papa's temper made the long days, cooped up in the smelly, lurching coach, a trial for them all. The children jabbered and fidgetted, Mama had headaches, Papa wrestled with the snarls of finance and the caprices of aristocratic pockets. Nannerl's English hat, toilet bottles "worth four ducats," and Flemish lace; Wolferl's swords, watches, and snuff-boxes were source at once of pride and despair. Leopold would rather have had money, but would not bring himself to turn them into cash; so boxes "full of Peruvian treasure" were shipped back to Salzburg at great expense, and Papa continued to scheme and solicit, more mercenary at every turn.

III

1763–1766

THE streets of Paris were too deep in filth to permit much walking at any time. In November, with cold rains and no purifying sunlight, they were impossible. Anyone whose clothes were worth keeping clean had either to ride in a carriage which bounded over the rough cobbles spattering slime and slops on hoipolloi, or be carried in a sedan-chair. Leopold hired three of these—fantastic ostentation—to take the children about, leaving letters at important doors and waiting while he pulled, or tried to pull wires. For all the kind offices of Count von Eyck, the Bavarian Ambassador, and for all the letters from influential German nobles, the Mozarts might have left Paris unnoticed. But Leopold had a letter addressed by a merchant's wife of Frankfort to one Friedrich Melchior Grimm, which proved to be the key to the charmed circle.

This gentleman, famous later as a baron of the Empire, an ambassador, an encyclopædist, Diderot's intimate, the lover of Madame d'Épinay and probably of Catherine the Great, and the writer of the enormous *Correspondence Littéraire* with half the crowned heads of Europe, was at that time merely a German fortune-seeker voluntarily exiled in Paris. The longer he stayed there, the more his native Teuton virtues gave way to acquired French faults. When the Mozarts first addressed themselves to him, he was secretary to the Duc d'Orléans, which gave him the entree to every great *hôtel*. He was brilliant in conversation and recognized as the first among musical connoisseurs in Paris. It was all to his advantage to further the Mozart cause and be recognized as their sponsor. He soon opened all the desirable doors to the children; also managed their public concerts, and engineered the presentation at Versailles, which took place shortly before Christmas.

The domestic arrangements of the court nonplussed the Mozarts; Louis XV in one suite; his wife, poor Maria Leczinska of Poland, in another, with her kind and homely daughters; the Dauphin in another; on the ground floor, in unparalleled magnificence, Pompadour. Ladies of every rank and condition came and went, charging the none too delicate atmosphere with futile perfumes. Dandies with lice in their wigs pursued them into the dank *entresols*, where they loved, slept, and did their various *devoirs*. Blasts of frigid air swept the vastness of marble and mirror. The wine was not unknown to freeze on the tables. The fashion for fur, naturally the result of such chill surroundings, had become a rage; "the ladies wear their clothes trimmed with fur summer as well as winter; they wear fur round their necks, fur in their hair instead of flowers, and on their arms instead of bands. . . . The most laughable thing is to see a sword-band ornamented with a fur border. That must be a capital method to prevent the sword from freezing."

Priceless tapestries hung on the damp marble walls, and lap-dogs befouled the corners. Stately staircases were backed by dirty flights and stinking passages used by wenches on their way to the king's bed—*bouchées* procured by Pompadour between orgies at the Parc aux Cerfs.

Mozart

There was a vast amount of outward form, but no privacy of any kind; what was not completely obvious was witnessed by spying eyes at keyholes. The Mozarts saw it all, dumbfounded by the contrast with Schönbrunn, for with all the surface etiquette of the stiff Vienna court and the Emperor's unofficial peccadilloes, Francis and Maria Theresa led a simple, intimate family life which Wolferl and Nannerl had shared.

They played for Pompadour in "her apartments toward the gardens, like a paradise," on a harpsichord of gilt, beautifully ornamented and painted. On the walls were her portrait and the King's, both life-size. When she set Wolferl on a gilt table, thinking to amuse herself with the little mannikin, he bent forward to kiss her. She pushed him away coldly, whereupon he piped, "Who is this that does not want to kiss me? The Empress kissed me." Who indeed!—a lady with unpleasant diseases, hardly the ideal recipient for the innocent kisses of a well-washed little boy. Leopold thought her figure imposing and described her as large and plump, with a fair complexion and eyes somewhat resembling those of the Empress. He must have been dazzled by her grandeur, for she died the next year and was sick at this time; pale, with a bad skin, and subject to fits of coughing and spitting.

In other apartments, they played for the Queen and the Princesses, who departed from all precedent—anything resembling normal behavior being taboo at Versailles—by kissing and playing with Wolferl and Nannerl in their own rooms and even in the draughty corridors. On Christmas day, they heard matins and three masses at the court chapel, which elicited opinions from Leopold that colored certain of Wolfgang's later ideas. "I heard music that was

Mozart

both good and bad. Everything performed by single voices, intended to pass as an air, was vapid, cold, and miserable, in a word, French; the choruses, however, were all good; indeed, excellent." This was in the midst of the Parisian war between adherents of the French and Italian schools of music. Needless to say, Leopold found all the good in the Italian and all the bad in the French. There is more than accident in Wolfgang's lifelong contempt for French music and art; the seeds were planted early. French choirs, though, were admitted good even by Papa; and, as usual, he took care that Wolferl should hear them, as he had him hear everything from which there was anything to learn.

The most prominent composers in Paris were Schobert, clavecinist to the Prince de Conti, and Eckard, a pupil of Philip Emmanuel Bach. Nannerl played their compositions "with incredible clearness; indeed, in such a manner that the envious Schobert cannot conceal his jealousy." Here is Leopold at his worst again. He thought he was taking a shot at a jealous Frenchman, but Schobert, the leader of the French school, was a Silesian, as Eckard was a Bavarian, and he was not jealous in the least. Leopold merely borrowed the bias of Grimm, who hated Schobert and was not above scheming to use the Mozart geniuses to discredit him by comparison.

On New Year's day, 1764, the family was privileged to witness the spectacle of Louis dining in state with his wife and children. They were not invited to the table, of course, but during the meal the Swiss Guard cleared a passage for them into the royal dining-hall, which was horribly damp and cold. They had the honor of standing like lackeys beside the chairs while the Bourbons ate their dinner. Wolferl stood close to the Queen, who fed him bits from the table and talked to him in German "which she speaks as well as we do." She had to interpret to the King, who, it may be assumed, did not care much whether he understood the distinguished conversation or not. Leopold stood by Wolferl, which smacks of prompting some of the child's remarks, and Mama and Nannerl on the other side of the King, near the Dauphin and Madame Adelaide.

The net profit of all the Versailles performances appears as an entry of the year 1764 in *Des Comptes des Menus Plaisirs du Roi:*

"Sieur Mozart la somme 1,200 livres pour avoir fait exécuter de la musique par ses enfants en présence de la famille royale."

Other cash received included eighty *louis-d'or*, proceeds of three hundred and twenty tickets sold by Grimm for the first public concert; "he also gave us our wax lights." These concerts were given at a little theatre in the private house of M. Félix, rue et porte St. Honoré; aside from Versailles, the fashionable world still centred in the Faubourg St. Honoré, not far from the Louvre, which had been deserted as a royal residence eighty years before. Pompadour had a magnificent town house in the district. The Mozarts lodged at the Hôtel Beauvais in the rue St. Antoine, on the fringe of the smart circle, and made their appearance at most of the great houses nearby.

At one of these, Wolferl astonished a brilliant gathering by accompanying by ear a lady singing an Italian cavatina. Never having heard the air, he improvised each passage by developing from the previous one. When she had finished he begged the lady to repeat the song, playing a perfect accompaniment of melody and bass; then he played it over ten times, each time with a different set of variations, and would have continued indefinitely if he had not been stopped. And at the Hôtel Beauvais, perched on a chair with his little feet dangling, in a pinafore to protect his clothes from ink, he wrote the first of his works to be printed and published; two sets of piano sonatas with violin accompaniment. These show one distinct and permanent influence of the Paris sojourn; a precision and delicacy which permeated like a perfume every note he ever wrote. Grimm and Leopold put their shrewd heads together and decided to dedicate the first pair of sonatas (K. 6 and 7) to the King's daughter, Victoire; and the second pair (K. 8 and 9) to the Comtesse de Tessé, one of the Dauphine's ladies. So Grimm wrote, addressed to Madame Victoire de France, a long obnoxiously crawling dedication, inscribing the defenseless child, *"Votre très humble, très obéissant, et très petit serviteur."* Victoire had the unexpected good taste to decline this effusion and insist on something simpler. The title-page of the published sonatas read, *"Par J. G. Wolfgang Mozart de Salzbourg, agé de sept ans."* No overlooking anything miraculous with Leopold in charge!

By April they had garnered a big harvest of loot, fame, and admiring patrons; "The people are all crazy about my children." So, with a delightful impression of Paris that the future was to do everything to destroy, they left on the 10th for Calais, en route to London. Leopold made the children keep diaries, preferably in the languages of the countries they visited, knowing well that Wolfgang would some day be glad of all the culture he could acquire. Armed with the usual multifarious letters of introduction,

er sonderer Vogel genannt bason, einer Klapermühlung, ein ... von braun rind, und Herr von den ge... von braun rind. Kensington Hüß, ein ... von den ... Freisäulen, ... Sachen, die in war wachst, ... Seiner, indischen balsam, die welt Engel und Gruels Engel, und ... und die Sachen
greenwick habe ich gesehen, das Invaliten Hous, der Königin ihr Schiff, den Chark in welchen ich eine sehr schöne aussicht gesehen habe, London bridge, St: Chaul kirch, Soudwark, Monument, foundling hospital, enchange, Lincolnsin fiels garten Tempelbar, Sommerset heüß. Zu Canterbury die heüpt kirch, und von Canterbury sind wir 4 meil auf country die country so nt: man at burn plas ge= gangen, diese war eine sehr schöne land güt. das Sort reren.

A double page from Nannerl's diary, which she kept during the three-
write in the language of each country visited. At the left are her
on the way to Holland. Courtesy of the

Dover,

den Port

Calais.

den Port, wie man drÿ Fort und den Schifhort ge=
brucht, wie man das schif in das wasser lasse.

Donkirch.

den Port.

Lille

neuvelle aventure, ein Kloster gewönt
das Exercisium, die Kirworde, den der dÿt stell.

Gent

das Rothhous und Türn welcher drÿ hundert und
26 Stafel hoch ist. ein bernardiner Kloster in welchen
ich die Sacrestÿ soz gitel Zimer, das dispüt Zimer, und
den garden gesehen haben.

Antwerpen.

unser lieben frouir kirch, die Kres S.t Jacob kirch, ein
ein Kloster, rambark carmeliter kirch wo die unser liebe
frau don silber und die capel don wisen marmel

year tour. She carried out as well as she could her father's orders to
observations of London and its vicinity, at the right are her entries
Gesellschaft der Musikfreunde, Vienna.

Mozart

Leopold settled the family in Frith Street, Soho, in the house of a Mr. Williamson, and used his recommendations to such advantage that they were presently invited to play at court, on the 27th.

St. James's was another novelty in their experience of courts. Having been thwarted in his desire to have the "blooming beauty," Lady Sarah Lennox, for his queen, young George III submitted to sage counsel and married Charlotte of Mecklenburg-Strelitz. So the Mozarts found themselves once more in the midst of homely German domesticity, which took even less cognizance of surrounding etiquette than Schönbrunn. King George and Queen Charlotte got on very well, having a common taste—later a mania—for plain living, typified by such mortification to the flesh of the court as boiled beef washed down with barley-water. Their residences were well managed, and like all London dwellings of the better sort, cleaner than the cleanest in France. When Casanova, a few years later, took a furnished house in Pall Mall he was astonished to find that "each storey has two rooms in front and a lavatory behind (in London every floor has this accessory)"! But it does not follow that godliness preceded this most British virtue of cleanliness, for outside the court, society behaved no better than it should, and London was notably gay in its tastes and casual in its morals.

Nobody cared whether or not the King and Queen entertained, for everyone else did, and everyone else was far more amusing—as Horace Walpole has said so vividly. Gambling never saw palmier days than in the London of 1764, and the macaronis who sat all night over the tables at Brooks's, White's, and Almack's with leather cuffs over their ruffles and farmers' hats to shade their eyes,

Mozart

were the husbands of the ladies who got into trouble at the house of the famous adventuress, Madame Cornelys. This dame, the mother of Casanova's little daughter Sophie, ran an immense establishment, Carlisle House, Soho, where she gave public dinners and balls that kept her in momentary terror of the sponging-house, where she often landed. Someone had the fantastic idea of staging a concert by the Mozart children in her palace of iniquity, but nothing came of it.

They did play repeatedly for the King and Queen. George III, whatever American school children have been taught to call him, was at that time kind, gentle, and democratic. He was greatly interested in Wolferl. He put pieces by J. C. Bach, Händel, and Wagenseil on the clavier before him, and sat by while he played them. Wolferl "then accompanied the Queen in an air, and a performer on the *flauto traverso* in a solo. At last he took up the bass part of one of Händel's airs that by chance lay in the way, and upon the mere bass performed a melody so beautiful that it astonished everybody. In a word, what he was on leaving Salzburg is but the shadow of what he is at present; he surpasses all that you can imagine." On going away, they received twenty-four guineas from the Queen; a week later, "we were walking in St. James's Park when the king and queen came driving by, and although we were all differently dressed, they knew us and saluted us; the king, in particular, threw open the carriage window, put out his head, and laughing, greeted us with head and hands—particularly our Master Wolfgang."

Leopold had a benefit concert for himself—and family —for which, to his horror, he had to hire an English or-

Mozart

chestra. He moaned over the expense, but calculated things to the British taste by permitting "Wolfgangerl to play the British patriot and perform an organ concerto upon this occasion. Observe," says the shrewd parent, "that this is the way to gain the love of the English." Even more shrewd was Leopold's selection of June 5— the King's birthday—as the date for the benefit. The publicity conformed with all of Papa's other methods.

By this time Wolferl had acquired a sense of orchestration, and was ready to demonstrate it. When Papa contracted a bad quinzy, the little boy took advantage of the quiet that was prescribed, to sit down, with Nannerl beside him to "remind me that I give the horns plenty to do," and write his first symphony (K. 16). He was then eight. This was followed by three more symphonies, interspersed with numerous violin and piano sonatas. A set of these was dedicated to Queen Charlotte and presented to her on the fourth anniversary of the king's accession. She acknowledged the artless courtesy with fifty guineas. On the 24th of November, Wolferl, himself wide-eyed with excitement as so many others had been in listening to him, was taken to the opening of the Italian Opera Company, where he heard really fine singing for the first time. Giovanni Manzuoli, a celebrated *castrato*, and a great favorite with London audiences, was enchanted by him and gave him some lessons in singing, by which he profited instinctively as if absorbing the knowledge through his skin.

Wolferl also captivated Johann Christian Bach, son of "the great" Bach, Sebastian. Christian had settled in England and held an appointment as music-master to Queen Charlotte. He took the boy on his knees at the clavier, and alternating every few bars, they played a whole sonata at

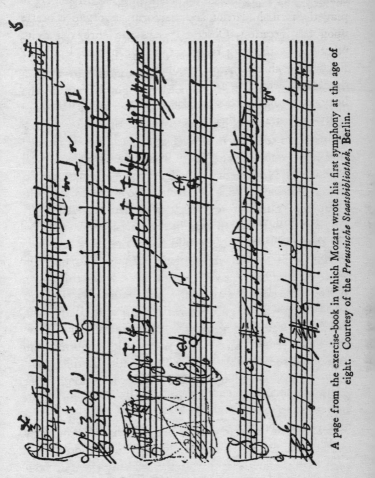

A page from the exercise-book in which Mozart wrote his first symphony at the age of eight. Courtesy of the *Preussische Staatsbibliothek*, Berlin.

Mozart

sight, as if by one pair of hands. Wolfgang was deeply impressed and never forgot his "English" friend.

When Leopold recovered from his quinzy they moved out to the suburb of Chelsea, where they remained while Papa recuperated and Wolferl composed. They returned to town to give several subscription concerts in a mean coffee-house, to which Leopold thought to attract the public by flaring blurbs proclaiming Wolferl a "Wonder of Nature." Leopold had, evidently, neither the sense nor the pride to see that even real genius can be submerged in cheap sensationalism. There was some suspicion of the Wonder of Nature, and one learned gentleman named Daines Barrington took the trouble to write to Leopold Lamprecht, our Salzburg friend who had baptized Wolferl, to verify the birth date in the parish register. Satisfied that no lies were being told about the boy's age, Barrington went to see him at their lodging, and put him through a number of severe musical tests, which, of course, Wolferl tossed off like some new game. Barrington's doubts of his true age were really only dispelled when, "whilst he was playing to me, a favorite cat came in, on which he left his harpsichord, nor could we bring him back for a considerable time." The results of this inquisition were summed up by Barrington in a long paper which he printed in the *Philosophical Transactions of the Royal Society*.

Leopold had appeared to be planning an indefinite stay in England, for they had already been there more than a year, with the unpleasant welcome awaiting them at Salzburg growing more unpleasant, when he decided that England was stupid and unappreciative after all; and godless besides. "What does it signify to talk much of a mat-

Mozart

ter? . . . I am determined not to bring up my children in so dangerous a place as London, where people for the most part have no religion and there are scarcely any but bad examples before the eyes. You would be astonished to see how children are brought up here, to say nothing of religion." Could Leopold be astonished—after Paris, where the streets were thick with maimed beggars, the bastards of aristocrats, abandoned in infancy? Before leaving London, Papa presented an anthem of Wolferl's, *God is our Refuge*, to the British Museum, and received an official letter in acknowledgment:

"Sir: I am ordered by the Standing Committee of the Trustees of the British Museum, to signify to You, that they have received the present of the Musical performances of Your very ingenious son, which You were pleased lately to make Them, and to retourn You their Thanks for the same.

British Museum,
July 19, 1765.

M. Maly
Secretary"

With this, some small profit in money, increased reputation, and decreased health, they set sail, in September, 1765, for the Hague.

There was no real reason for drawing out the long journey any further. Leopold knew perfectly well that his position with the Archbishop was growing more precarious daily, yet he could not quite resign himself to going straight home to servitude and oblivion. So he cast about for some apparently legitimate excuse for protracting the trip. The Dutch Ambassador in London had been urging them to go to the Prince of Orange. Leopold had not taken his invitation seriously, until, on the day they left London, the Ambassador "conjured us again to go to the Hague, as the Princess von Weilburg, sister of the Prince of Orange, had a vehement desire to see this child. I complied the more readily as nothing must be refused a lady in her delicate state." This was sufficient excuse—Leopold taking care that Sigismund should hear about it—for their spending eight months near the delicate princess whose condition must surely have been relieved before they left.

However, there was a serious delay during the stay in Holland, for both the children fell ill. Nannerl first, with an infectious fever so violent that she was given up, lying for days on end in semi-conscious delirium. When she had lucid moments, Papa lectured her on the blessedness of dying and the wickedness of living. And when she was getting better and looking forward to a long and anything but wicked life, Wolferl caught the fever and had his turn in bed. This was his second really serious illness, and both collapses can be ascribed to his excessive mental activity combined with his parents' utter ignorance of the first principles of hygiene. A life so exhausting and exciting would have caused any child to collapse. The age was one when intelligent attention to diet and exercise were unheard of, and the only hope of raising children without constant violent illnesses was the chance of their being let alone in the fresh air to grow up like little animals. When, in the light of modern knowledge, we look back upon the variety of vitamins that were definitely not available, it is quite wonderful that Wolfgang was not actually crippled with rickets, instead of merely growing up with a spindly little body, thin weak arms and legs, and an over-large head. So ignorant was Leopold of the necessity for children to have mental and physical rest, if only to keep their strength, much less gain more, that he began to fret on the long journey back to Salzburg. He was afraid they would not have enough to do at home! "Every moment that I lose is lost forever, and if I formerly knew how valuable time is to youth, I know it more now. You are aware that my children are used to work; should they learn to make excuses . . . my whole building would fall to the ground. Custom is an iron path."

In the late spring they started travelling again. But not home to Salzburg; no indeed, they made for Paris once more. Leopold could not resist the temptation to return there and reap whatever gold and notice might have accrued in their absence. But this stay was very short. They were received with the usual acclaim and enjoyed visiting their former acquaintances, particularly Grimm, who overflowed with cordiality. Grimm was now possessed of a mistress, the charming Madame d'Épinay, whose memoirs fit so well into the contemporary pattern. She was a dear friend of Voltaire, then in his long exile at Geneva, and when Leopold told her that he might take his family back by way of Switzerland, she wrote Voltaire and told him to be ready to welcome the prodigies. But when in September they turned up in Geneva Voltaire was not on hand. He explained to Madame d'Épinay that "your little *Mazar*"—(sic)—"has chosen, I think, a poor enough time to bring harmony into the temple of Discord. You know that I live two leagues from Geneva: I never go out: I was very ill when this phenomenon burst upon the black horizon of Geneva. Now he has gone without, greatly to my regret, my having seen him." Wolfgang did not know what he missed; and when told, twelve years later, cared little enough, as we shall see.

Mozart

Leopold was very nervous about arriving home, perhaps to find that he had been replaced in the Archbishop's service. All during the long trip across Germany he fussed about it, and about his financial condition, which was no better than when he started. He had spent, for him, a fortune, keeping up appearances with fine clothes, the best hotels, smart servants and the actual cost of giving concerts—hiring halls, printing advertising, and sometimes, as in England, engaging orchestras. But the awful day could not be put off forever, and in December they finally crossed the mountains and rolled into Salzburg, three and a half years after they had left it. Mama was the only member of the family who was glad to be at home.

The children were so used to being nomads that home meant mainly the cat and dog and canary, whom they were overjoyed to see. But Leopold, torn between the necessity for keeping a permanent position and the desire to fling his children's fame in his employer's face, put on a sober gray coat and went to the *Residenz* to report. There he found that he had not been dismissed but that his salary had long ago been stopped and that he would not receive any further pay except for time actually spent serving Sigismund in Salzburg. He went back to the Getreidegasse and started to plan for the next phase of Wolfgang's career.

IV

1769–1771

Naples, 19th May, 1770

"C. S. M., [Cara Sorella Mia]

"Please write to me soon and every post-day. I thank you for having sent me the arithmetic books and beg you, if you ever wish for me to have a headache, to send me a few more of these examples. Haydn's 12th minuet which you sent me pleases me very much; you have set the bass to it incomparably and without the smallest mistake. Pray make such essays more often. . . .

"Pray let me know how Herr Canari does? Does he still sing? Does he still whistle? Do you know what has brought the canary to my mind? There is one in our front room here which makes just such a noise as ours. . . . We put on our new clothes yesterday; we were beautiful as angels! . . . We have seen the king and queen at Mass in the royal chapel at Portici, and we have seen Vesuvius too. Naples is beautiful but as crowded as London and Paris. Comparing the impudence of the townsfolk of London and Naples, I really do not know if Naples does not outdo London; for the populace here, the Lazzaroni, have a chief of their own who gets 25 *ducati d'argento* every month from the king simply to keep the beggars in order."

Wolfgang was not only in Naples, but setting the town, in the height of the season, quite by the ears. He was now fourteen. His early roundness of face was narrowing into the rather sharp lines of maturity, his nose developing the length he joked about later, his eyes growing more prominent and less bright. The hollow under his firm chin was already softening to form the characteristic baggy little

Mozart

fold. He had shot up rather suddenly. "Everything is too small for him; all his limbs have grown bigger and stronger. He has no voice for singing. It is completely gone; he has neither high notes nor low, and not five pure tones. This is very vexing to him, for he cannot sing his own things which he would like to do." But he could play them, and he did. He was the pet of the fashionable circle, and was now appearing almost daily at the house of Sir William Hamilton, the British Ambassador, whose wife (the first Lady Hamilton, not Nelson's mistress) was a notedly fine clavier-player "though she trembled before Wolfgang." The Hamiltons were as kind to him as their compatriots had been in London, an added reason for his always high regard for all English people. The new clothes of which Wolfgang was so proud were an apple-green coat with rose-colored facings and silver buttons, with which he wore handsome silk stockings, satin small-clothes, fine lace ruffles, and a well-fitted white dress wig. The smiling, rosy-faced boy made a charming picture in the ornate Hamilton drawing-room. In the background stood Leopold, in a new coat of maroon-colored watered silk with sky-blue facings. After the daily concert, they usually went out to take the air on the Strada Nuova, joining the formal *passagio* of nobility and visiting grandees. They stopped sometimes at coffee-houses for ices, which Wolfgang had never tasted before. He loved them, and also the wonderful fruits and the chocolate, all new treats for him.

He had left Salzburg with Papa five months before, in December. Leopold had been planning this Italian trip for years, and had finally got away with Sigismund's grudging consent. His salary was stopped from the time he left Salzburg, but he did not care. He set about enjoying Italy to the very limit of his ability, though it was only a few weeks before he was observing, "We shall not, I am convinced, make much money in Italy. My sole satisfaction is that we are regarded with considerable interest and appreciation here, and that the Italians recognize Wolfgang's talent. For the rest, one must be content with admiration and applause in lieu of payment, though I must tell you that we are everywhere received with every imaginable courtesy and are presented to the *haute noblesse* on all occasions." Vital, of course, to Papa's peace of mind. Wolfgang scribbled a postscript to Nannerl, "*Addio*, my children, farewell! I kiss Mama's hand a thousand times and imprint a hundred little kisses or smacks on that wondrous horse-face of thine!"

More than the lure of fame had brought Leopold to Italy. The country was then the centre of the musical world, and nobody could get any recognition as a real musician without some training in one of the great Italian cities. Rome and Bologna were supreme in ecclesiastical music, and Naples was the undisputed capital of opera. Not only did the greatest composers come there on commission to write their operas, but the productions were lavish beyond description. At the San Carlo Theatre, the ballet for Paisiello's *Disfatta di Dario* was mounted with four hundred persons and eighty horses. And, of course, every great singer in the world had either been born a Neapolitan, been trained in Naples, or at least made his reputation there. Aprile, Farinelli, Morelli, Marchesi— these were some of the great names among the men, and there were plenty of women to complement them. Student singers who hoped to shine in the highest musical heavens

Mozart

came from all over Europe to study with Finaroli at the famous *Conservatorio*. Leopold saw to it that Wolfgang should be steeped in every form of Italian music. For this, Papa is to be thanked. Wolfgang's firm Italian grounding enabled him to write opera in that style, and later, to introduce a new era in musical drama by the combination of his Italian equipment with the German *Singspiel*. Thus the importance of the Italian trip in Wolfgang's musical development cannot be overestimated. He heard each musical form in which the country excelled; chiefly opera, but also church music of all sorts, and learned all the possibilities of song. In turn, he astonished and delighted the Italians with his clavier-playing and his already comprehensive grasp of instrumental composition.

When they had settled at home after returning from their three-year tour of Germany, France, England, and Holland, Papa had set Wolfgang seriously to mastering counterpoint. For models he gave him Philip Emmanuel Bach, Händel, Hasse, and Eberlin, the latter a Salzburg composer of rather more than average ability. He could hardly have chosen better preceptors, unless he had had access to the works of the great Bach, which were then lying hidden in the shelves of the Thomasschule in Leipzig. It was not until years later that Wolfgang was introduced to Bach, and the experience was almost overwhelming in its force and in the surprise he received. However, between the ages of eleven and thirteen he put in two years of hard and profitable study.

But at the end of the first year Papa had one of his unconquerable fits of ambition and decided that the time had come for Wolfgang to write his first opera. Accord-

Mozart

ingly the whole family departed for Vienna in the fall of
1767. The celebrations were about to begin for the wedding of Maria Theresa's daughter, Maria Josefa, to the
King of Naples. But the Mozarts had no sooner settled in
lodgings on the Hohe Brücke than a smallpox epidemic
broke loose and raged through the capital. The bride was
one of the first to be carried off, and her ambitious mother
promptly married the bereaved bridegroom to her next
daughter, Maria Carolina. But Wolfgang and Nannerl
had no share in the festivities because they both caught
smallpox and suffered very severely. Wolfgang was unable
to see for several weeks, and finally recovered with im-
paired eyesight, but without pockmarks on his face. When
the children went to court again, Maria Theresa received
them and Mama with great kindness and showed the most
motherly solicitude for them in spite of her own bereave-
ment. She had been a widow for some time now, and her
son Joseph had been crowned emperor. This was his second acquaintanceship with Wolfgang. They were to meet
many times in the future, but though Joseph loved music
he never attached much significance to his life-long famil-
iarity with one of its brightest lights. Joseph had not yet
taken the firm grasp on Viennese art that he presently
would, and there was no court opera. Instead an Italian
impresario named Affligio ran the Vienna opera house,
and engaged in professional intrigues with all the composers who were resident there. Every sort of rivalry was
rife, and when a twelve-year-old boy suddenly appeared
upon the scene, a genius so great that he could dismiss the
most difficult challenges without a flicker of his eyelid, the
whole musical community rose in a body to extinguish
him.

Mozart

Leopold was determined that Wolfgang should have an opera to write. He pulled every available wire and finally arrived at an agreement whereby the child was to compose a score for a libretto entitled *La Finta Semplice* (K. 51). Leopold had the backing of the young emperor, who had practically ordered Affligio to commission the opera. But when it was finished, Affligio launched upon a long series of puzzling delays in staging it. Leopold fumed and fulminated in long letters home to Salzburg wherein he revealed clearly his real and utterly shallow feelings about Wolfgang's talent. "The whole hell of music has bestirred itself to prevent a child's talent from being recognized." He went on to protest at the unjust fate which seemed to exact that "I should perhaps set myself down at Salzburg sighing for better fortune until Wolfgang is grown up, and see myself and my children led by the nose till I am an old man and unable to undertake a journey, and Wolfgang *is of an age and growth that have diminished the wonder at his performances.*" Seeing these words in black and white is sufficient conviction that however good a musician Leopold may have been he was no such paternal idealist as he has sometimes been described. He was a calculating opportunist if one ever lived.

La Finta Semplice was not an inspired piece of work—the boy did not know enough to write a substantial opera. Leopold did not believe this, and while Affligio's tactics were evasive and dishonorable, there was some justice in his unwillingness to go to the expense of staging the piece. But the musical mob of Vienna were frankly and grimly determined to discredit the child and his work by any means, however foul. The upshot of it was that the opera

Mozart

was not given and Leopold sought an audience with Joseph, at which he made violent complaint. All sides of the case were considered, and *La Finta Semplice* found to have enough merit for the emperor to order Affligio to pay Leopold one hundred ducats as compensation. The incident was thus closed. But Doctor Anton Mesmer, the famous physician and hypnotist, had heard of Wolfgang's misfortunes and offered him consolation by commissioning a miniature opera—*Bastien und Bastienne* (K. 50)—which was promptly written and privately produced at Mesmer's house. It was much better, musically and in subject, than the rejected *Finta Semplice*. Naturally, however, Wolfgang did not yet know enough to compose a sound opera. The real significance of that Vienna journey lies in its being a foretaste of so much of Wolfgang's later life—heartbreaking struggle against the intrigues of foreign musicians who enjoyed all the favor and success in the capital where he should have reigned.

Upon their return to Salzburg Wolfgang was given a minor position with Archbishop Sigismund to which was attached the empty title, *Kapellmeister*. This meant almost nothing, except that he would be called on from time to time for the composition of church music, to which, accordingly, "I have been accustomed from my earliest youth." As a member of the episcopal retinue his place on state occasions was somewhere below the house servants and lackeys. Until his departure for Italy with Leopold in December, 1769, his compositions consisted largely of canons and *Missa Breve* for the cathedral, and suites, *divertimenti*, and cassations for string ensembles, intended as incidental music for the Archbishop's banquets. There were also some arias and other vocal pieces,

but all of a juvenile quality which was completely changed
after he had had the opportunity really to study Italian
song. Wolfgang made, of course, phenomenally rapid
strides toward real proficiency in serious composition. His
genius for melody was as innate as his gay disposition,
and his magnificent musical thinking a natural gift. His
marvellous aptitude for characterization in song appeared
later still, after he had created a place of his own in the
musical world.

The Italian tour had been laid out systematically. They
followed the natural route southward from Salzburg to
Milan, then straight down the peninsula, stopping at every
important city for visits of varying length. They stayed
in Milan long enough to make a cordial friend of Count
Firmian, a local noble of importance, who proved his interest in Wolfgang by commissioning an opera for the
Christmas celebrations of the following season. Then to
Mantua and Parma, where Wolfgang heard the world-
famed Italian singing at its best, first at the Mantua
opera and then at the house of the notorious "Bastardella"
in Parma. This was the celebrated Lucrezia Agujari who
sang unbelievably high notes with perfect ease and purity
of voice. "I could not have conceived it possible to sing
to *C in altissimo* if my ears had not convinced me. . . .
She is not handsome nor yet ugly, but has at times a wild
look in her eyes, like people who are subject to convulsions; and she is lame in one foot. Her conduct formerly
was good, consequently she has a good name and reputation." Thus Papa, pompous as ever; but Wolfgang merely
took the pen and appended the notes and passages Bastardella actually sang. They are almost incredible.

Rome was Papa's cherished goal, and he insisted on

reaching it for Holy Week. Wolfgang assured Nannerl that "this town would certainly please you well, the Church of St. Peter's being *regulair* and many other things in Rome being *regulaire*, also! . . . Now I have just been drawing Saint Peter with his keys, Saint Paul with his sword, together with Saint Luke and my sister, etc.; and I have had the honour of kissing Saint Peter's toe in Saint Peter's, but because I have the misfortune to be so little, someone had to lift up the undersigned old rascal, Wolfgang Mozart!"

The Vatican, nothing less, was Papa's aim, and thither they repaired:

"Our handsome dress, the German language, and the freedom with which I desired my servant to tell the Swiss Guard to make way, soon helped us through every difficulty. Some took Wolfgang for a German nobleman, others for a prince, and the servant did not undeceive them. I was taken for his tutor. In this manner we proceeded to the table of the cardinals. There it happened that Wolfgang placed himself between the chairs of two cardinals, one of whom, Cardinal Pallavicini, beckoned to him and said: 'Will you have the goodness to tell me in confidence who you are?' Wolfgang told him. The cardinal replied with the greatest astonishment: 'What, are you that famous boy of whom so much has been written to me?' Upon this Wolfgang rejoined: 'Are you not Cardinal Pallavicini?' The cardinal said, 'Yes, why do you ask?' Wolfgang then observed that 'we had letters to his eminence, and desired to wait upon him.' Upon hearing this the cardinal expressed the greatest pleasure, complimented Wolfgang on his Italian, and added: '*Ick kan auck ein benig deutsch sprekken.*' At our departure Wolfgang kissed his hand, and the cardinal taking his baret from his head made him a very polite compliment.

"You are aware that the celebrated *Miserere* of this

Mozart

place is in such high esteem, that the musicians of the chapel are forbidden, under pain of excommunication, to take any part of it away, to copy it themselves, or through another person. However, *we have it already*. . . . Meantime, we will not entrust this mystery to strange hands; *ut non incurremus mediate vel immediate in censuram ecclesiæ.*"

The mystery not to be entrusted was the result of one of Wolfgang's typical feats. More than anything they desired to possess the Allegri *Miserere* which was sung in the Sistine Chapel during Holy Week. This was considered so sacred that the singers were forbidden to carry any of the parts out of the chapel on pain of excommunication. Wolfgang and Leopold went on Wednesday afternoon, where, instead of gazing at Michaelangelo's ceiling, Wolfgang sat, tense with concentration, and allowed every note to engrave itself on his brain. Then they rushed back to their lodging. Wolfgang seized paper and pen, climbed onto a chair, and wrote down the whole work. Some of the matters he had to retain were the notes of a double choir, the traditional forms of the ancient church style, and the absence of a perceptible rhythm. On Good Friday he put his score in his hat and went back to the chapel, where he sneaked in the few corrections that were necessary. Of course the story got out, and instead of excommunication, Wolfgang was made to bring his score to a large party where Christofori, one of the Sistine singers, confirmed its correctness.

Before leaving Rome, Wolfgang received from the Pope the order of the Golden Spur, with its attendant gold medal and title, *Signor Cavaliere*. Gluck had received the same honor, and clung to *Ritter* all his life, but

Mozart

Wolfgang forgot it almost immediately and only called himself *Cavaliere* when he wanted to tease Nannerl and impress her with his importance. Leopold, needless to say, used the title at every possible chance. A much sounder honor awaited Wolfgang at Bologna, where he was made a Member of the Accademia Philharmonica, after going through the usual rigid admittance test:

"On the 9th of October, at four in the afternoon, he had to appear in the hall of the Academy. There the Princeps *Accademiæ* and the two *Censores* (all one-time kapellmeisters) gave him, in presence of all the members, an *antiphona* from an *antiphonarium*, which he was to set in four parts in an adjoining room, whither he was conducted by the *pedellus*, who locked the door on him. When he had completed this piece of work it was examined by the *Censores* and all the kapellmeisters and composers, who thereupon voted with black and white balls. All the balls being white, he was called in; his entrance was acclaimed by general clapping of hands and congratulations, the *princeps* of the academy having previously informed him, in the name of the Society, of his election. He returned thanks and that closed the proceedings. Meanwhile Herr Prinsechi and I were locked into a room on the other side of the hall of the library of the Academy. Everyone was astounded at the rapidity with which he finished his task, as many have spent as much as three hours over an *antiphona* of three lines. You must know, however, that it is by no means easy, as a number of things are not permissible in this kind of composition, as he had been forewarned. He finished it in a little over half an hour."

Also at Bologna Wolfgang came under one of the most valuable of all the Italian influences, that of Padre Martini, the great theorist, teacher, and composer. He examined Wolfgang thoroughly and "speaks of him with

Mozart

amazement," but he also recognized that there was much room for further development. He gave Wolfgang several lessons and took such real interest in him that Leopold went away considering him a powerful ally in the struggle to get the boy established. But Padre Martini had done all he would ever do. He was a sympathetic correspondent, but never an influential sponsor.

The long series of honors and grave preoccupations had not changed Wolfgang's merry and childlike character a particle. He filled his letters full of nonsense and boyish clowning. He drew pictures in the margins, he made up unpronounceable names for the people he described, he sent tender and longing messages to the dog, the canary, and the servant. He described things in any outrageous terms that occurred to him, and he told Nannerl stories that could only have originated in a small Salzburger's brain. From Naples he wrote:

C. S. M.,
"Vesuvius is smoking furiously to-day. *Potz Blitz und ka nent aini. Haid homa g'fresa beym Herr Doll. Dos is a deutscha Compositor und a brawa Mo.* I shall now begin to write an account of my life. I wake at nine o'clock, sometimes not till ten, and then we go out, and then we dine at an ordinary, and after dinner we write, and then we take a walk, and afterwards we sup. On a meat-day half a chicken, or a morsel of roast, on a fast-day a little fish; and then we go to sleep. *Est-ce que vous avez compris? Redma dafir soisburgarisch, don as is gschaida. Wir sand Gottlob gesund, da Voda und i.* I hope you also are well, and likewise Mama. Naples and Rome are two sleepy cities. *A scheni Schrift! Net wor?* Write to me and don't be so lazy. . . . The King is a rough Neapolitan in manners and always stands on a stool at the opera to appear a little taller than the Queen. The Queen is beau-

tiful and courteous, for she has greeted me six times at least on the Molo (which is a public parade) in the friendliest manner.

"P.S.—I kiss Mama's hand!"

But much more noteworthy are his really significant and intelligent criticisms and analysis of the music he heard everywhere. This was the beginning of Wolfgang's freedom of opinion which earned him innumerable enemies in the ranks of musicians less able than he. He had a lifelong knack of summing up all the virtue or the trash in a piece of music or its composer and dismissing the whole thing in pithy remarks like the "opera here . . . is beautiful, but too discreet and old-fashioned for the theatre. . . . The dances are wretchedly pompous. The theatre is handsome." Or, on another occasion, "the *prima Donna* sings well but not loud . . . she cannot open her mouth, but whimpers everything. *La seconda Donna* has a presence like a grenadier. . . . *Il primo Uomo* sings well, but has an uneven voice. . . . *Il secondo Uomo* is getting old and does not please me. *Prima ballerina* good, and they say she is no scarecrow. . . . The rest are just like all others."

After they had been in Italy nearly a year, Wolfgang was given his first opportunity to show what his study of *bel canto* had done for him. Count Firmian's commission for a Milan opera had not been forgotten, and during most of the late summer and early fall Wolfgang had been writing recitatives and posting them back to the Milan director. On the 18th of October, 1770, he and Papa arrived and settled down to finish the work. The opera was *Mitridate, Re di Ponto* (K. 87). Though it appears juvenile in comparison with Wolfgang's later work, it

Mozart

did not seem so then, in contrast with the pieces being written by local composers. It may properly be called Wolfgang's first opera, certainly the first written with any real grasp of operatic technique, and the first to be given a full stage production. The text was written by Vittorio Amade Cigna-Santi of Turin, and the classic tale it told was so dolorous that it affected Wolfgang's spirits. Also, "my dear Mama, I can write but little, for much recitative writing has made my fingers very painful. I beg Mama to pray that my opera may go well, and that we may then be happily reunited."

The sailing was far from smooth. Wolfgang seemed to have no trouble with his composing, but once again the whole local musical fraternity rose up in an attempt to wreck his work and discredit him. Here he had to contend not only with envy of his ability and fear of his youth, but with jealousy of his nationality. The Italians refused to believe that a German boy could write an Italian opera, no matter what he might write for the Germans. The singers leagued with the other Italian plotters and an attempt was made to subvert the great soprano, Bernasconi, and have her sing some other composer's arias in place of Wolfgang's. She finally refused to do it. Wolfgang and Papa were kept in miserable suspense. But after the stage rehearsals began, with an orchestra of sixty pieces, the intriguers and detractors "are struck dumb. . . they have not a word to say. The copyist is full of glee—a good omen in Italy, since when the music is a success the copyist often makes more money through the distribution and sale of arias than the *Kapellmeister* gets for the composition." The premiere was on the 26th of December. Count Firmian's judgment was vindicated. "You may pic-

Mozart

ture to yourself Maestro Don Amadeo at the clavier in the orchestra"—where the conductor was always placed, accompanying the recitatives himself—"and myself in a box as spectator and listener." The spectator and listener was overjoyed at the real enthusiasm of the audience; spontaneous bursts of handclapping and cries throughout the house of *"Evviva il maestro! Evviva il maestrino!"*

There was a trip home to Salzburg after this, but a quick return to Milan in five months, for Count Firmian had procured from Maria Theresa a command for Wolfgang to compose a stage serenata for the approaching wedding festivities of another of her innumerable progeny, this time the Archduke Ferdinand. This piece was *Ascanio in Alba* (K. 111), which Wolfgang wrote in lodgings so thickly tenanted by musicians that there were violinists above and below him, a singing master on one side, and an oboeist on the other. "It is capital for composing; it gives one new ideas," was his unruffled reaction to the pandemonium. The poet's delay in preparing the libretto allowed Wolfgang the privilege of writing the whole score in twelve days, which he did, though again driven to complain that his fingers ached. Some fine singers were engaged for this production; Caterina Gabrielli, and Wolfgang's old friend, Manzuoli of London, whom he was enchanted to see. And for once the intrigues of the jealous were in abeyance. Hasse, who had dominated the Italian opera for years, was in Milan doing an opera with the great poet Metastasio, and freely declared Wolfgang equal to himself, adding, "This boy will throw us all in the shade." Later he wrote to a Venetian friend:

"Young Mozart is certainly a prodigy for his age and I am really extremely fond of him. The father, so far as

Mozart

I can see, is unceasingly discontented with all that I myself complain of here. He adores his son a little overmuch, and does all he can to spoil him; but I have so good an opinion of the innate goodness of the young man that I hope that, despite the adulation of his father, he will not allow himself to be spoilt but will turn out an honourable man."

V

1771–1777

IT was in the next six years that Salzburg earned its real identity as Wolfgang's home, and acquired his sworn hatred. From 1771 to 1777 the whole family was together in the Getreidegasse, with the exception of a few short trips to Munich and Milan, which Papa took with Wolfgang when operas had been commissioned. Papa was still vice-*Kapellmeister* at court, Wolfgang had a lesser position, and Nannerl, helping Mama to keep house, gave a few lessons on the side. Bimperl was acquired now, the dog they loved better than any of his predecessors. The family shared in the social life of the community, and the routine of the children became somewhat more normal.

The alignment of social rank was rather rigid. The archbishop and a few nobles of importance kept very much aloof. Just below them there was a group of minor nobles and gentlemen, all attached to the court. With these the Mozarts sometimes associated, but their real friends were among an even lower class—good, substantial townspeople, like Lorenz Hagenauer, the landlord, and the Haffner family for whose private celebrations Wolfgang wrote the lovely "Haffner" symphony (K. 385), and the equally beautiful serenade (K. 250), both in D major. Below this Mozartian social level there was the typical lower class of the eighteenth century, poor and uneducated, concerned only with the price of salt and the cost of sausage. The town and its habits were summed up in an observation that

"the country gentlemen hunt and go to church; those next
below them go to church and hunt; the next lower rank
eat, drink, and pray; and the lowest of all pray, drink, and
eat. The two latter classes conduct their love-affairs in public, the two former in private; all alike live in sensual indulgence."

That was of course something of an exaggeration. The
Salzburgers were easy-going and fun-loving, fond of
music, games, and dancing. They were less sensual than
they were ignorant and provincial. For all their having a
court of their own, and for all its magnificence, it was a
petty court, and it suffered by the comparisons of an im-
pressionable mind that had seen the great capitals of Europe. Enjoying the amusements, criticizing the boorishness,
Wolfgang became rather paradoxical. He had a delicate
taste for all the arts, yet he had a distinctly coarse turn of
humor. He could crack jokes and exchange buffooneries
with his wittiest neighbors, yet he was always on the verge
of being revolted by them. He liked to eat and drink and
play their games with them, and yet he could turn round
in a moment and damn them for their grossness. He took
the extraordinary natural beauty of his surroundings so
much for granted that he seemed indifferent to it, yet it
had its effect in his intense love of birds and the outdoors.
He always preferred to work in gardens when he could,
and the serene clarity of his music is not unrelated to this
early Salzburg influence.

The favorite sport of the Mozarts was quoit-throw-
ing, which they had every Sunday afternoon at some
friend's house. Sometimes they played cards, and sometimes there was chamber-music. Except in Lent, there was
constant dancing, and Wolfgang was always being asked

Mozart

to compose for it. There was a carnival-hall attached to the town hall and there frequent masquerades were held at which Wolfgang was conspicuously present. About this time a theatre was built, to which the excellent company from the nearby capital, Munich, came and gave performances. This was the highlight of social life in the town. Wolfgang enjoyed it, but never so whole-heartedly that he could associate with his neighbors without criticizing them. However, he was sixteen; gay, lively, and handsomer than he would ever be again. His color was high, set off by his large gray eyes and fine blond hair which, of course, was hidden under a wig on dress occasions. He had always loved clothes and he had always had good ones, that being part of his necessary equipment. He was graceful, and his early if superficial acquaintance with the great world gave him poise and a creditable command of manners. The time was ripe, and Wolfgang began to hear the rustle of petticoats.

Wolfgang has been too much likened to Cherubino— the ardent, amorous youth in love with love, sighing out his delicate passion in terms of plaintive and exquisite melody. Sometimes it might have been true, for anything that may be said of young love is applicable to some phase of every youth's life. But to picture Wolfgang in terms of idle, amorous pursuit; to try to see him constantly slipping away to masked rendezvous in moonlit gardens is to admit him an eighteenth-century puppet and not a flesh-and-blood boy. He caught and kissed the girls, and what more he may have done will have to take its own shape in the imagination of each person who knows him well. But it is impossible to think of Wolfgang as a lustful youngster in search of mischief without remembering

Mozart

something in his background—Leopold. For all his pomposity, his bombast and his materialism, Leopold was at heart a devoutly careful and loving father. He managed, in spite of his false ambition, to instil in Wolfgang a youthful respect for virtue and temperance that is nothing short of amazing in view of the age in which he lived, and the sophistication in which he had steeped his son. To be sure, Leopold's calculating materialism and cold reasoning went farther in teaching Wolfgang restraint than any amount of preaching might have done. From a very early age, Wolfgang realized that promiscuity was almost certain to result in disease. All around him he saw it happening, and if he had had no personal standard of chastity—which he did have—his common sense would have kept him quite continent as a youth.

That there were, a little later, occasional lapses, is also true. But Leopold's very unexpected wisdom in this quarter was proved when he wrote during Wolfgang's early manhood that "I will not enter on the subject of women, wherein nature herself is our enemy, and he who does not strenuously resist at first will strive in vain to escape from the labyrinth, and will find no release but death. How blindly one is often led on by jokes, flattery, etc., until returning sense awakens one to shame, you may, perhaps, have already experienced. I do not mean to reproach you. I know that you love me not as your father alone, but as your closest and surest friend."

But for a young boy there was always amorous dalliance—something else again. Stolen kisses and sly handclasps; kissing-games in which he was often the ringleader; naughty remarks and nearly naughty actions; these were all clearly in the picture. Some one girl usually occupied

Mozart

him in this way, a sweetheart to whom he would be passionately devoted for a few weeks, after which one or the other would find a new love. He made Nannerl his confidant in these tiny but very absorbing affairs. When he went away with Papa he wrote most of his letters home to Nannerl rather than to Mama, and filled his scrawls with cryptic allusions to his temporary beloveds. "Tell Mlle. von Mölk that I expect the same reward from her as for the last quartets. She knows what that is." Half of his nonsense was fantasy. "My compliments, pray, to Roxelana, and she is bidden to take tea with the Sultan this evening. Give my very kindest regards, I beg, to Miss Mizerl, and tell her she must not doubt my love and that she is ever before my mind's eye in her enchanting negligée; I have seen many pretty girls here but no such beauty as she."

He did not always write foolishness. "My opera" *(Il Re Pastore)*, "thank God, was put on yesterday"—January 13, 1775—"and all went so well that I cannot possibly describe the uproar to Mama. In the first place, the whole theatre was packed so full that many people were forced to turn away. After each aria there was a terrible uproar, with clapping and shouts of *'Viva Maestro!'* . . . The interval between the close of the opera and the beginning of the ballet was filled with clapping and shouts which no sooner died down than they broke out afresh, again and again. . . . My Papa and I afterwards went . . . and kissed the hands of the Elector and Electress and other eminent persons, who were all very gracious. . . . My compliments to all good friends of both sexes. . . . Adieu! A thousand kisses to Bimperl." He had ended a previous letter, "Farewell, my little heart. I kiss you, my little liver, and am as ever, my little stomach, thine unworthy

$$\left.\begin{array}{l} \text{frater} \\ \text{brother} \end{array}\right\} \text{Wolfgang.}$$

"Pray, pray, my dear Sister, something is biting me—scratch me!"

These trips to Milan and Munich to write operas were occasioned by the growing certainty that there was no future for Wolfgang in Salzburg. It was vitally necessary that his talent should be known outside, where there were more promising patrons. Leopold's original employer, old Archbishop Sigismund von Schrattenbach, had died in 1772 when Wolfgang was sixteen, and had been succeeded by the well-known Hieronymus, Graf Colloredo. There had been trouble with Sigismund because of his narrow bigotry and comprehensible unwillingness for Leopold to draw a salary and spend most of his time touring Europe. But trouble with Hieronymus was even more acute. The new Archbishop was hated by the Salzburgers for a number of reasons, and he retaliated by stingy treatment of them, conspicuously of men like the Mozarts. He gave all the desirable positions at his court to foreigners, most of the good musical jobs being held by Italians. Yet Colloredo was an intelligent man. Where Salzburg, under Sigismund, had been church-ridden, dreary, and full of hypocrisy, it was free, gay, and amused under his successor. And Hieronymus was no fool. Though he had no great appreciation of music, he knew perfectly well just what Wolfgang amounted to—contrary to the familiar idea that he was ignorant. But he thought he could keep Wolfgang at his court for nothing, producing anything he was asked for, and receiving no recognition. Hieronymus's reason for this was more a general desire to be contemptuous of Salzburg and its people than to be pointedly unfair to Wolfgang.

Of course Leopold hated him with a deadly loathing, chiefly because he failed to make him head *Kapellmeister* when the position was vacant. Then one year after another went by, in which Wolfgang might have been given some respectable appointment, instead of which he retained his ignominious position at 150 gulden a year, and for it wrote a huge amount of very creditable music—masses, litanies, canons, suites and divertimenti of all sorts, quantities of concerti and numerous symphonies. All this time his work improved in noticeable degree. When anything worth writing came along, it meant a journey. In this way he wrote *Lucio Silla* (K. 135) in Milan; the next year the wonderfully vivid motet, *Exsultate, Jubilate* (K. 165) for the great *castrato* Rauzzini; in Munich, *La Finta Giardiniera* (K. 196), and *Il Re Pastore*. Nothing stands out of this period like the *Alleluia* air from the motet, which is in essence and quality immortal, and almost inconceivable as the work of a boy of seventeen. But with Hieronymus all this profited Wolfgang nothing. When he was twenty-one, he stood, a miraculously gifted and splendidly trained composer and a great piano virtuoso, almost unknown, with no position and no prospects.

It was a problem greater than either Leopold or Wolfgang could cope with. Leopold tried, with letters and secret word-of-mouth emissaries, to angle for a position for Wolfgang. He was in terror of Hieronymus, knowing well that he and Wolfgang would both be dismissed instantly if his efforts became known. He might have spared himself his worry, for nobody responded to his advances.

Mozart

This impossible situation could not continue forever, and there were long conferences in the drawing-room at home, Wolfgang and Leopold staring at each other across the table, Mama and Nannerl sitting by with their sewing and shaking their heads. Wolfgang thought he and Papa should both resign from the court service and that all four should pack up and go on a grand tour of Europe. He thought it would be a triumphal progress like that of their childhood. Leopold was wise enough to know that that could not be so. It was much easier to make a sensation with child prodigies than to acquire a paying public for two able but obscure young pianists.

It became apparent that a permanent appointment as *Kapellmeister* at some important court was the only solution for Wolfgang. He himself would have welcomed such a position much more eagerly if it carried with it any possibility of writing opera. From his earliest feeble efforts to his last great works, Wolfgang adored opera. He never came so near despair about his career as at the times when he longed to have operas to write and was forced to support himself in other ways. But now, Leopold reminded him, it was more important to become well known; the opera opportunities would follow. Wolfgang must not forget that he was a pianist as well as a composer —he must pin some of his hopes to that. Wolfgang had not forgotten. He had spent much of his time during the past year perfecting his clavier technique, and copying his piano music into small, neat notebooks that could easily be packed for travelling. Furthermore, he had written in quick succession six piano sonatas (K. 279 to 284) to have ready to play. These of course have become a part of every piano library, universally familiar.

Mozart

Leopold finally reached the decision that he and Wolfgang would have to undertake another tour. This time every effort should be made to get Wolfgang established at some court, and leave him there. So Papa applied to Hieronymus for leave of absence for himself and Wolfgang. The unpleasant bishop flatly and sourly refused. Leopold was flabbergasted. He had not expected to draw his salary while away travelling—but to be refused leave! Wolfgang, however, asserted himself for the first time in his life. To Leopold's utter consternation, and before anyone could stop him, he handed in his resignation. Hieronymus was taken entirely by surprise. He had thought to be able to bully both the Mozarts; it was a shock to find that the younger one, the apparently light-hearted and light-headed boy, would defy him. He accepted the resignation contemptuously. Leopold had some bad hours of suspense while waiting to learn his own fate, sure that he would be dismissed. But Hieronymus, in the most insulting way, told him he was to stay. Poor Leopold was trapped. While he was, like all other self-important people, a big talker and consequently possessed of no real pride, he would have had to stay even if he had had the spirit of a Castilian. For the family must live— and how, if nobody had any permanent source of income?

Wolfgang thought the whole problem solved. He would simply go on tour alone, making his way to Paris with stops at any likely courts. But here Papa rose from the slough of despond and lifted the hand of authority. Wolfgang would do no such thing. It was unthinkable.

He was no more able to go off alone and make his way in the world than a baby. Leopold shuddered as he looked over the possibilities. Wolfgang missing this opportunity,

Mozart

bungling that introduction, failing to pay his respects here, wasting too much effort there. That was bad. But Wolfgang's own traits would make things worse. He would spend his time in nonsense with any young fools he might run into. He would associate with the wrong people. He would dance, drink, keep late hours, run after girls. . . . Not only girls . . . but women. He might make a fool of himself over some woman. He might—oh God!—he might become entangled . . . marry . . . or even worse . . . scandal . . . disease. . . . Leopold tramped the floor clutching his head between his hands. Wolfgang had gone to his room in a mood as dark as he had ever known. He had protested, pleaded, asserted himself. There was no use. He had stirred up enough trouble with his sudden flare at Hieronymus. Now Papa had whirled round on him, ordered him to be silent. Wolfgang thought it wiser to obey. It was bad enough to have Papa in a state like this. But it would be much worse if the proposed tour should fall through altogether. Nothing was so important as a chance to get out of Salzburg. Let Papa work out anything he wished, anything at all, so long as he might only get away.

Eventually the obvious plan took shape. Wolfgang could not go alone, there was no question of that. The boy had never spent a whole night or day without his father. He could not be cast out on the world like a tramp. So the decision was finally made, indeed really made itself. Mama should go. She would not be of any use in the delicate diplomacy incidental to getting the permanent position. But Papa could supervise every aspect of that by letter. He would write daily, and Wolfgang must send him every detail of each meeting. And Mama—she will

Mozart

keep you company, Wolfgang, she will make you comfortable and happy and it will be just like being at home. (Oh, God, help her to keep him out of trouble. Let her watch him every moment. Do not let him out of her sight!)

Wolfgang did not protest. He had not yet any violent urge to be alone and independent. He was much more eager to leave Salzburg, and better with Mama than not at all. Besides, he adored his mother, and while twinges of consternation occasionally seized him, he did not yet know the strength of every man's ultimate urge to be free. He had not even smelled the cup of independence, much less tasted a drop of the exciting wine. This was nearer to it, at least, than he had ever been. And Mama was only going to stay with him until he had found his place and become established in it. Then she would come home, and he would be launched—a man of the world and an artist. Poor Mama had the hard side of the load. She grieved so over leaving home that she could hardly collect herself and attend to her packing. She had hated the long, futile journey when the children were little, hated all its upsets and changes and discomforts. She hated Protestant Germany through which they would pass, with its heathenish people and the meat they tried to serve her on Fridays. But she was a better wife and mother than anything else, and she followed her duty, if with streaming eyes. She and Nannerl went to Mass and offered prayers for them all, for Wolfgang's success, for Papa's and Nannerl's consolation. Meanwhile Leopold was scurrying round raising money and preparing an outfit worthy of a young artist starting out on what should be a triumphal tour. He must have a fine, well-swung travelling coach, neat luggage, handsome clothes, the best clavier that could be made. Leopold made heavy financial sacrifices, and though Wolfgang was kept acutely aware of them, he never had occasion to doubt Papa's devotion.

They left on the 23rd of September, 1777. Mama was dissolved in tears and buried herself against the cushions in the corner as the coach swung into motion. But Wolfgang, after the pang of parting, sat up at once and looked out of the window at the receding peaks and the spires of Salzburg. He was sorry to have left Papa behind, "exceedingly faint and depressed," and Nannerl, weeping "so passionately that I was obliged to do everything in my power to console her." But he was eager and glad to be on his way.

VI

1777–1778

AFTER a short stay in Munich, where Wolfgang made an unsuccessful attempt to "lay myself and my services most humbly at the Elector's feet," he and Mama went on to Augsburg. Though he had composed several operas for Munich and had appeared there innumerable times, and though Maximilian had known him for fifteen years, he was refused because the prince thought he should first "go to Italy and make a name." So they turned up in Augsburg, the ancestral home of the family, unprovided for, but happy. Papa had told them to put up at the Lamb, in Holy Cross Street, but they stayed instead with Uncle Josef Ignaz, Leopold's brother. Wolfgang made few excursions about the town without *"das Bäsle,"* his cousin, Uncle Ignaz's homely daughter. Bäsle had a broad, plebeian nose, a rather stupidly square face, large dull eyes set too far apart, and a dumpy body. She was no beauty, but she had her points.

On the 17th of October they all had mid-day dinner with a rich young widower named Gassner. "We were entertained splendidly," which meant that the food was good, the drink excellent, and the company to Wolfgang's liking. It included a couple of broadminded church musicians, Gassner's pretty sister-in-law, and of course the delectable Bäsle. Sitting next her at table, Wolfgang could slide his hand down her forearm, run it off her fingertips onto her plump thigh, and, while earnestly discussing the relative merits of pianoforte and organ with Father Gerbl on his left, silently convey to Bäsle certain fine points of right-hand technique. This gave her a pleasant turn, but she was cleverer than her face and revealed nothing. She quietly reserved her demonstrations for the end of the day when, matters of music and moment being concluded, she would retire with Wolfgang to her room under her father's roof. Uncle Ignaz was no such surveillant parent as his brother Leopold—a state of affairs that contributed considerably to Wolfgang's advance in the naughtier arts.

After the dinner, they all went out to see Herr Andreas Stein, the ugly, interesting man who was doing notable experiments in the development of the pianoforte. Full of amiability and good dinner—always his most expansive moment—Wolfgang sat down at Stein's newest invention and "played a sonata by Beeché [a local celebrity] at first sight, rather difficult, *miserabile al solito*. The astonishment of the *Kapellmeister* and organist was indescribable. Both here and in Munich I have frequently played all my sonatas by heart. I played the 5th, in G (K. 283), at a select peasants' parlor concert. The last, in D (K. 284), goes excellently on Stein's pianoforte." Well it might, for its twelve lovely variations with the extra color lent by Wolfgang's delicate use of the new knee-pedal contraption were enchanting. "I can put it into action with the slightest touch, and when one slackens the knee-pressure a little there is no trace of an echo."

Stein had made his reputation as an organ-builder, but considered his pianoforte the vehicle of real music. The organ he thought merely an unavoidable concomitant of churches. Wolfgang finished his sonata, and before the

Mozart

murmurs of pleasure had subsided, turned around and said, "Herr Stein, I should much like to play on one of your organs." Stein was astonished. "What, an organ? Can such a man as you, a great pianist, wish to play on an instrument devoid of *douceur*, of expression, of *piano* and *forte*, one which is always the same? Is it possible?"

"Oh," Wolfgang said, "there is nothing in that. The organ is still, to my eyes and ears, the king of instruments."

Stein shook his head.

'Just as you like, my boy,' "and so we set off together. I could tell at once from his talk that he thought I should do little with the organ. . . . We reached the choir. I began to prelude; he smiled; then came a fugue. 'I can well believe now,' he said, 'that you like playing on the organ. When one plays like that!' "

Before they left the church, there was a short symposium in a reception-room, where a "certain Father Emilian, a pompous ass, a feeble-minded would-be of his profession, was very familiar. He was constantly trying to make sport with my cousin, but she made sport of him. At length, when he had got a little drunk (which happened soon) he began to talk of music. . . . I said, 'I am sorry I cannot sing with you for I am quite incapable of intoning.'

" 'That is no matter,' said he, and began.

"I made the third. But I set quite different words to it: 'Padre Emilian, O you booby you, *leck Du mich im Arsch*,' sotto voce to my cousin. We spent another half-hour laughing, and he said to me:

" 'If we only had longer together I should like to discuss the art of composition with you.'

Mozart

" 'We should soon come to the end of the discussion,' said I. *Schmecks kropfeter*. To be continued in my next."

Papa and Nannerl had some fine laughs over this and dozens of similar letters, but Leopold was secretly apprehensive. How could a young man make his fortune if, instead of pushing into the palaces of the nobility, he spent his time singing "Kiss my ——, you booby," to squiffy priests, and exchanging illicit sweets (to what full extent Papa could not gather) with his young lady cousin? Mama had been sent along to patrol him, but Leopold was perfectly aware of her limitations (she could not, for instance, guard his chastity). So Leopold fidgetted. He wrote long accounts of how he had conducted himself on his own early tours—Wolfgang to emulate him now: "I avoided all acquaintance and sought friendship with people of condition only, and among these, merely with people of a certain age, and not with youths, however high their rank." Unfortunately, he was right. Every bit of advice he gave, everything he ordered Wolfgang to do was exactly what a prudent young man should do. He was a very Polonius: "Great matters (serious opera) should be met in a great and exalted spirit."

There comes a time in every young life when the burden of parental wisdom is simply intolerable. Wolfgang was just entering this stage, but in his case the normal reactions were complicated by a loyal and tender nature. The familiar conception of temperament—the torn hair, the blazing eye, the groaning, the throwing of manuscript into the fire—is totally inapplicable to him. This quietness of spirit has led some critics to interpret his gentleness as weakness and to characterize his music as superficial. Much of the world's education in music has come from the romantics, in whose eyes rebellion burned bright and who hurled their private lives into their scores. Mozart lived before they did, in a much more objective age. Neither in his life nor in his music was he intent upon proving anything. Pleasure is the first, most obvious reaction to his work. He intended it to be so, for he believed that music should delight. Consequently, though he was mortified by Mama's fluttering presence and irritated by Papa's wise reiteration, he did not revolt from them, having no reason to revolt. His reaction was merely confused, somewhat expostulatory. That the educated mind does get something more than "pleasure" out of this boy's music may be partially the result of this inward patient struggle.

Yet the struggle was to become more and more acute during the coming year, and the first signs of this occurred in Mannheim, for which they quitted Augsburg at Papa's epistolary insistence. They arrived on the 1st of November. The leaves had fallen, the sky was gray, snow was in the air, but Wolfgang looked forward to this visit with delight. The capital of the Palatinate was the most brilliant electoral court in Germany, and its prince, Karl Theodor, was known as a good fellow, a rake, something of a wit, an intelligent patron of music—there was everything to recommend a post there—if it could be obtained. Papa overflowed with advice in this connection as in irritatingly lesser ones—how they should pack their boxes, what to eat for lunch, what to say to so-and-so, to tree their boots.

One great matter in Mannheim was the court orchestra, that same unusually fine one that Wolfgang had heard as a small boy thirteen years before on the family

Mozart

trip to Paris. Wendling was still the first flautist. He was now of interest to Wolfgang in more than a musical way, for he kept open and rather free house. His daughter was the ex-mistress of the Elector. None of the Wendlings went to church, and all of them loved their fun. Wolfgang's intimacy with Wendling was responsible for his conquering his natural dislike of the flute, and writing two flute concertos, in G and in D major (K. 313 and 314). The second in particular is a glorious example of his virtuoso style, brilliant, moving, and alive with melody.

Within two or three days after arriving in Mannheim Wolfgang had been enthusiastically received into the musical circle—Ramm, Lang, Schazmeister, Raaf, the famous old tenor, and Christian Cannabich, the orchestra conductor. Cannabich took a great fancy to Wolfgang and had him to dinner almost every day. There were all sorts of pleasurable reasons for going, not the least of which was Rosa Cannabich, the conductor's pretty daughter, for whom Wolfgang wrote some sonatas. But, while music occupied them primarily, Leopold read this one day:

"I, *johannes Chrisostomus Amadeus Wolfgangus sigismundus* Mozart, confess my fault in that the day before yesterday (and on many previous occasions), I did not come home till 12 o'clock at night; and that from 10 o'clock until the hour aforenamed at Canabich's house, in the presence of, and in company with, Canabich, his wife and daughter, Herr Schazmeister, Ramm and Lang, I frequently—not gravely but quite frivolously—made verses; and those obscene ones, about dung, excrement, and *arsch-lecken*, in thought and word—but not in deed. But I should not have behaved so impiously if the ring-leader, that is to say Lisel (Elisabetha Canabich), had not urged me on and encouraged me to it lustily; and I must admit that I enjoyed it prodigiously. I confess all these my sins and transgressions from the bottom of my heart, and, in the hope of confessing them more often, I am firmly resolved constantly to *improve on* the evil manner of life which I have begun. Therefore I beg for holy dispensation, if it can be managed; and if not, it's all one to me, for the game will go on all the same."

Papa must be given credit for holding the confidence of such a wastrel! He greeted this spontaneous confession as lightly as it was intended. But on other occasions, apparently, he lost his sense of humor, nagging Wolfgang until the poor boy wrote, in despair, "You reproach us undeservedly on many counts. We are incurring no unnecessary expense; as to what *is* necessary when travelling, you know it as well, or better, than we. . . . As to our fortnight's stay in Augsburg" (where there was no court for Wolfgang to solicit)—"really, I am almost driven to conclude that you did not get my letter from Augsburg. I am not careless, I am merely prepared for anything—I can endure anything so long as my honor and that of the name of Mozart does not suffer." In the intervals of writing these pleas to his father, and of pacifying his mother, who fretted over everything, Wolfgang went about the business of growing up.

One day, when he was arranging to have some music copied for a performance, Cannabich took him to see a man named Fridolin Weber, a poor devil who held the odd jobs of copyist, prompter, and singer at the court opera. He received a miserable pittance on which his big, shrewish wife and his children all but starved. His second daughter, Aloysia, was already a singer at the opera. Her

voice, while exceptionally clear and fine, was almost un-
trained, but her musical instinct was so sound that she had
already attracted attention. Wolfgang, usually critical in
the extreme, did not bother to analyze her singing by any
technical standards. He was simply delighted with every
note she sang, and followed all her movements, fascinated by her arch, youthful grace. Now he was to meet
her. Cannabich smiled at his eagerness, but when he
nudged Wolfgang with an insinuating remark, on the
way upstairs, he was surprised to see the boy turn a cold,
hurt stare on him. What did that mean?—from Wolfgang, who was always first when the *Dreckigkeit* began?

They found Weber with his *Frau* Caecilia and four
black-eyed daughters—Josefa, who cooked well and as
yet gave no promise of the voice which was to create *die
Königin der Nacht* fourteen years later; Aloysia, looking
older than her fifteen years; Constanze, the next younger,
given to giggling, and Sophie, a round-eyed ten-year-old.
Their father being a *Musiker*, they were often hungry
and sometimes had holes in their shoes; but by the same
token they all played or sang. There was a brief, awkward
interlude of introductions, chairs being dragged forward,
Caecilia signalling Josefa to go and make coffee, Wolfgang stammering awkward remarks to Fridolin while
throwing hasty, furtive glances at Aloysia, who was rat-
tling cups and saucers and looking very preoccupied.
Though she tried to seem cool and poised, she was not yet
the prima donna. Perhaps she sensed that young Herr
Mozart knew this, and so felt herself an uncertain girl
when he finally stopped talking to Fridolin and came
across to her. There was no reason, really, why she should
feel shy. He was only a little older . . . yet he had

reputation, they were negotiating for a place at court for him, she had heard her father say he was a fine composer. She looked up and saw Wolfgang smiling at her.

'This is a great pleasure, Mademoiselle,' he said. 'I have enjoyed your singing at the opera.'

'It was not a very big part,' she murmured.

'No,' he said, 'but it is not the part that counts, rather the way it is sung.'

Aloysia said nothing, but gave him a quick smile.

Wolfgang grasped matters with both hands.

'Would you . . . would you care to sing for me?' he asked.

'Here? To-day?'

'Why not? I am here. The clavier is there. You are—here too? *Net wor?*'

She smiled again.

'What should I sing?' Her lashes dropped over her cheeks, and the curve of her slim throat was enchanting as she turned toward the cupboard. Now it was Wolfgang's turn to be uncertain.

'I—hadn't thought—' he murmured.

'Hadn't thought? But come!' She felt surer of herself now, even a little daring. 'Have you composed no songs, Herr Mozart? No arias?'

She had broken the ice. They both relaxed. Wolfgang laughed and seized her hand, once more at ease, and strangely happy.

'Come on,' he said, drawing her to the clavier, *'was sind wir doch für Eseln!* What will you sing?'

She hesitated a moment. Then she said slowly:

'I know your De Amicis arias' (from *Lucio Silla*).

Wolfgang showed his surprise.

Mozart

'You do?'

She nodded, smiling proudly.

'Here,' she said, pointing to the chair, 'that is where you belong, sir!'

He played the first chords and the murmur in the crowded room stopped. The little girls looked at their sister with awe. Here she was about to sing the hardest aria she knew, with the composer himself, and she didn't seem to mind a bit. *Wunderbar!* So she began the first, "with those terribly difficult passages," and sang them "most excellently." Her voice was high, pure, and flexible; brilliant; above all, young. Her legato was extraordinary. One would not expect this of an inexperienced girl. Yet Aloysia brought out round, smooth tones of milky purity, something only a very fine natural singer could do. Wolfgang had never heard such exquisite freshness. He had been listening to important sopranos for fifteen years—but this was different. This was more than another lovely voice. This was someone—singing his music to him as he wanted it sung, and because he had asked her to, and because she wanted to.

From habit he played on, but he wanted to turn, to look at her, to touch her hand again. He wanted to watch every expression of her thin, mobile face; to fix her with his eyes when she rounded each phrase as perfectly as he could not have dared to hope. Then she had finished. He rose and took her hands and looked at her gay black eyes —and thought he was smiling.

'Your singing!' he stammered. 'Your singing is—it is —*ach*, Mademoiselle Weber—Aloysia——'

His eyes clouded and his lips began to tremble.

Wolfgang was in love.

Mozart

It was unlike him to make a secret of it, and he made no secret. Before he left he poured out to Fridolin his delirious joy over Aloysia's singing. But it was Cannabich, walking back through the wide, snowy streets, who had to endure the worst.

'Not only the voice, Christian—but *schön*—beautiful! And that lovely young face—those black curls—the white neck, and nice hands, and a fine high *Brust*—and—how she sings!'

Cannabich agreed. She was a nice girl, and she ought to have a good career.

'But so poor, Wolfgang. That *armer* Fridolin can't do anything for them. How can she get anywhere? You know what happens to a girl who is poor.'

Wolfgang shrank from thinking.

He parted from Cannabich at the latter's door, and hurried on through the snow to the Pfälzichen Hof, where he and Mama lodged. He ran upstairs to the little room they shared, muttering 'Aloysia, Aloysia!' under his breath. Mama was alone, wrapped in shawls, with her feet against the stove where she had a tiny fire burning. She was writing a letter, but when Wolfgang came in she put down her quill and began to rub her hands to warm them; they were blue with cold.

'Oh, Mama,' Wolfgang said, kissing her, '*liebste* Mama!'

She saw he had something to tell her; good news, perhaps!

'What is it, Wolferl?' she asked, 'what's your news?'

He was about to tell, to pour out his story of the wonderful black-haired girl. And suddenly he saw—she would laugh at him, or be angry, or reproach him. She would write to Papa. She would lament and complain, Wolfgang is in love. Papa would be furious. He would write another terrible, scolding letter. It was impossible. Slowly Wolfgang took off his greatcoat, while his lovely image of Aloysia, her laugh and her radiant voice, faded into the gray of filial submission.

'What is it, Wolfgang?' he heard Mama repeating. 'Why don't you tell me?'

He threw off his abstraction, smiled with blank brightness.

'Oh, they want me to do six trios for the concerts,' he answered, with a good show of enthusiasm, 'and a symphony. And Wendling says——'

What did Wolfgang care what Wendling said? What did he care how many concerts were given? Concerts had suddenly lost their importance. It was opera now! Voices like Aloysia's belonged on the stage. He could write anything for Aloysia. He *would* write for her. He would make his plans carefully; he would be sensible and prudent; he would give Papa no cause for worry; everything would turn out happily. He was sure of that; how could it be otherwise? He was in love! So he changed his clothes and put on the fresh shirt Mama handed him, and a new set of ruffles, and his best buckled shoes; inspected his hair and decided he could do without any more powder to-night; put on his coat, kissed Mama, and went off for the evening. She heard him humming as he ran down the stairs. She smiled a little. Perhaps Wolfgang had some really good opening afoot? He would wait and tell her when it was all settled. Perhaps. But Wolfgang was now hurrying up the street to Wendling's. He might see Aloysia there! Mama deliberated about putting more wood on the fire and ruefully chose a small piece to keep the blaze alive. Then she picked up her pen, with the ink freezing on its tip, and continued her letter to Papa: "Wolfgang is at Wendling's as usual. I am alone at home, as I am most of the time, and it is so dreadfully cold that no fire we can afford could possibly warm this room. . . . I kiss you and Nannerl 1,000,000 times. And a kiss to Bimperl."

Wolfgang's good friends, led by Cannabich and Wendling, had been trying to obtain a post for him as chamber-music composer at the court. For some days they were all busy with the plans. They would get the Elector in the right mood, at the right moment; they would broach it just so; they would take care that he heard every wonderful thing there was to hear about Wolfgang. Their mediary was to be a court attaché, Count Savioli, on whom they had Wolfgang wait with all the courtesies and attentions in his power. Savioli was cordial, careless, and a hypocrite. One day a holiday prevented his speaking to Karl Theodor; another day, a hunt; a third day, a rendezvous. Wolfgang and Mama were paying a high price for their room at the Pfälzichen Hof, and their plans all hung on the Elector's decision. Papa, of course, was kept in close touch with every development. Wolfgang's hopes were high; "I really believe I shall spend the winter here. For the Elector likes me, thinks highly of me, and recognizes my capacity. Again I beg you neither to rejoice nor grieve prematurely, and to speak of this to no one save Herr Bullinger and my sister." Bullinger, the same faithful friend of Wolfgang's childhood, was included in all the family confidences. Nannerl took such an intense interest in Wolfgang that the slightest hint of bad news from him would send her to her room in tears.

But on the 10th of December, when Mama was lonely,

homesick, ill, and wretched with the cold; when there seemed no use in the remotest dreams of Aloysia; when the skies were gray and the snow dirty underfoot, Wolfgang reported to Papa, "There is nothing to be hoped from the Elector now. I was at the concert at Court the day before yesterday, hoping to get an answer. Count Savioli definitely avoided me. I went up to him, however. When he saw me he shrugged his shoulders. 'What,' I said, 'still no answer?' 'I am very sorry,' he said, 'but it is all in vain.'" Wolfgang took the destruction of his hopes with a bow and a smile. The crystal drops of the chandeliers seemed queerly close to his eyeballs when he said, "*Eh bien*. But the Elector might have told me sooner." There was some short further discussion. "But for the rest, I am very much obliged to you, Herr Graf, for having acted so zealously in my behalf, and beg you will thank the Elector for this gracious, though somewhat tardy information, and assure him that he would certainly never have regretted it had he engaged me. 'Oh,' said Savioli, with gently twitching lips and his best bow, 'I am more convinced of that than you, perhaps, can believe.'"

Wolfgang left the Electoral palace and went to Wendling's. When he came in, calm, pale and silent, Wendling looked at him sharply. Wolfgang indicated the verdict with a shake of his head. Wendling started up from his chair, turned scarlet, and clenched his fist. '*Schwein*,' he muttered. Then he banged the table with his fist. "We must find a way. You must stay here—at least for two months till we can go to Paris together. To-morrow Cannabich returns from the hunt; then we can talk of it further."

Mozart

If this part of Wolfgang's letter grieved and bewildered Papa, the next angered him. For the gist of it all was that, his hopes of Mannheim having been dashed, Wolfgang proposed not to go to Paris at once with Mama, but to stay on in Mannheim until the 6th of March, lodging with a certain Herr Councillor, and taking his meals at Wendling's. A cheap room with board was to be found somewhere for Mama until the winter broke and she could travel back to Salzburg. And Wolfgang, with Wendling and Ramm, should go to Paris and seek his fortune with them there. The effect of this on Leopold can be imagined. He stalked the floor, clasped his head in his hands, knelt down and prayed, tossed about, sleepless, all night. He saw the destruction of all his hopes. He saw his wife neglected and disgraced by their son. He saw Wolfgang, weak and characterless, swayed by the opinions of every third-rate musician he met. Indeed, everything he saw was partly true. But he did not see a despairing youth of twenty-one, blindly groping for some solution to an intolerable situation, throbbing with the instinct to assert himself, to make his own decisions, to function free of the eternal conclave of advice and orders. Wolfgang had nothing further to expect in Mannheim; why stay another two months? The utter insanity of this inconsistency could only be explained by a knowledge that Wolfgang's heart was now fixed in Mannheim, that he had no intention of going away and leaving it there. But this (fortunately for his blood-pressure) Papa did not yet know. He wrote a long, solemn reassertion of his authority, and "the one thing I will not have is that you should lodge with some anonymous Herr Councillor while Mama lodges alone. As long as Mama is there you must remain

[91]

at her side. You shall not and must not leave her alone among strangers while you and she are together. Let the room be as small as it may, there *must* be room for a bed for you."

Wolfgang sighed over this. He might have known. Tiresome discussion had worn him out. When the "anonymous councillor," Herr Serrarius, finally offered to take in both mother and son as lodgers, to give them their fuel and light, and Mama her meals, Wolfgang to repay him by giving his daughter lessons, the harassed boy agreed wearily. He would eat at Wendling's. He had some orders for quartets and trios, the proceeds of which would pay for his travelling expenses when he finally decided what to do. He gave lessons to Rosa Cannabich and to a Dutch officer. There were ways of eking out an existence.

He saw little of Aloysia during this dreary fortnight, and that little served to increase his pangs. For Wolfgang, who had, at sixteen, stepped lightly into the garden of love, taking a kiss here and there, and more with *das Bäsle*, who had made low jokes and thought of love in terms of nibbles and pinches—Wolfgang had run into something entirely new, remote, and mysterious. He could not dream of touching Aloysia. Her fingertips were at once vibrantly intimate and a barrier against further approach. She was sacroscant. But he could hope, and he did hope.

Yet Fate was not too consistently unkind. The Princess of Orange, who had an estate near Mannheim, scolded her Dutch officer—Wolfgang's pupil—for not bringing the young genius to play for her. Wolfgang was invited to attend her, and since the princess was a fine singer, decided to take some arias with him. These Aloysia's father was already copying, with Wolfgang sitting by and making conversation.

'What a pity you aren't coming too, Herr Weber!'

'Oh, I am just a poor *Musiker*, why should I go?'

'But you could accompany—there will be lots of singing and——"

'But who will sing?'

'Oh, the Princess, and—and—maybe—' Wolfgang leaned forward eagerly. 'Oh, Herr Weber, why not?'

It took little urging. At dawn on Friday morning, the 23rd of January, Wolfgang hastened through the snow, wrapped in his heavy travelling-cloak, to the Webers'. Caecilia was hurrying the breakfast onto the table, Fridolin packing the last of the music, Aloysia tenderly folding her one court dress into a bandbox.

'*Guten Morgen, guten Morgen!*' Wolfgang cried, prancing in, 'how good the coffee smells! Come, we have only half an hour before the carriage arrives. Is all ready, Herr Weber? Here, Aloysia'—tenderly removing her hands from the heavy straps—'let me do that for you.' He thought his heart would burst with happiness. These Webers were darlings. They were so kind, so *gemüthlich* —he loved them and their shabby home. The plain, hot breakfast tasted so good. He was setting down his cup when they heard the harness-bells outside. One of the children ran to the window.

'Papa,' she cried, 'the carriage is there—ooh! Stanze, come look at the lovely *Wagen*. Oh, Papa, I want to go too—please take me, Papa, me too——'

It was a golden week. Wolfgang could hardly bear the delight of sitting the whole day long beside Aloysia in the carriage; of doing small things to help her; of gazing as much as he wanted into her smiling black eyes under the pretty travelling-hood; of holding his hands up to help her when she alighted at the snowy steps; of stepping into the background at the palace that she might shine, that her singing be all-important, that she receive all the compliments. Of course, he accounted dutifully to Papa for his time, and he tried, in a pitifully casual way, to brush over Aloysia's presence, and make her seem only a professional adjunct to the journey. But he hardly left anything to be read between the lines. "Mademoiselle Weber sang the three arias. I pass over her singing with one word—admirable! Indeed, I have recently described her merits to you; and yet I shall not be able to close this letter without writing more of her, for not till now have I really come to know her and consequently to perceive her true value. . . . Sunday, we might have supped at Court in the evening, but we did not wish to do so, preferring to be privately together at home . . . we never enjoyed ourselves better than when we were alone. . . . Mademoiselle Weber sang in all thirteen times, and played the clavier twice, for she plays not at all ill. . . . On my honor, I would rather hear my sonatas played by her than by Vogler! I waited on the Princess with four symphonies and got no more than seven *louis d'or* in silver money, mark you, and my poor Mlle. Weber only five!"

This financial blow should have sufficed to cure the love-addled young man, but on the contrary, the taste of travelling with Aloysia and her father was so memorably sweet in his hungry mouth, that he made to his aghast father this preposterous revelation:

"I propose to stay here and finish at leisure my music for De Jean, which will bring me in my two hundred florins. I can stay here as long as I like, for neither food nor lodging costs me anything. During this time Herr Weber will endeavour to get engagements at concerts with me. Then we will travel together. If I travel with him it will be just as if I were travelling with you. The very reason he is so dear to me is that, apart from outward appearance, he is just like you and has just your character and way of thinking. My mother, were she not, as you know, too lazy and comfortable to write, would tell you just the same! I must confess that I much enjoyed travelling with them. We were happy and merry; I heard a man talk as you do; I did not have to trouble about anything; I found my torn clothes mended; in a word I was waited on like a prince.

"This unfortunate family is so dear to me that my dearest wish would be to make them happy; and perhaps I may actually be able to do so. My advice is that they should go to Italy. Therefore, I want to ask you to write to our good friend, Lugiati, the sooner the better, and find out how much, and what is the most, they give a prima donna in Verona—the more the better, one can always climb down—and perhaps one could also get Mme. Ascenza in Venice? As to her singing, I would lay my life that she will bring me renown. Even in so short a time she has greatly profited by my instruction, and how much greater will not the improvement be by then? I am not anxious about her acting, either. If our plan succeeds, we —M. Weber, his two daughters and I—will do ourselves the honour of spending a fortnight with my dear Papa and my dear sister *en route*. My sister will find a friend and comrade in Mademoiselle Weber, for her reputation for good breeding here is like that of my sister's in Salzburg, her father's like my father's, and the standing of the whole family like that of the family of Mozart. True, there are envious folk as there are with us, but when it comes to the point they are forced to speak the truth. Honesty triumphs in the end. I can tell you I shall be glad to come to Salzburg with them, if only that you may hear her sing. She sings my De Amicis arias, as well as the bravura aria, *Parto, m'affretto* and *Dalla sponda tenebrosa* superbly. I beg you will do your best to get us to Italy. You know my greatest inclination—to write operas."

Leopold was transported with amazement and horror. The boy was insane. And what in heaven's name was his mother doing or thinking about? For what had she gone along—if not at least to mend her son's clothes? Not only did Wolfgang propose this fatal idea of linking his fortunes with the down-and-out Webers, but he had abandoned Paris to do so; and in abandoning Paris had suddenly decided that his real Mannheim friends, Wendling and Ramm, with whom he was to have travelled, were impossible associates—and why? *Because they had no religion!* This was the slim thread spun out by the boy in the desperate hope of catching Leopold's approval. It was all too evident what had happened. The puppy, the young ass, had allowed himself to be ensnared by these wretched people. Naturally they would encourage his passion for the girl (probably a rotten chit); naturally they would propose anything that would take them away from their low station in Mannheim. They had played on him, until he was full of holy determination to relieve the distress of this poor, deserving, "thoroughly honorable good Catholic Christian family."

Leopold sat down, "so wearied that I can only write slowly, word by word," and spent two days penning ten pages of impassioned protest; wracking the boy's emotions, drawing from his formidable armory each and every weapon with which for twenty-two years he had dominated him. Anger; sarcasm; pathos; religion; flattery; honor; terror—"it depends solely on you . . . whether

Mozart

you leave this world having been captured by some petticoat, bedded on straw, and penned-in with an attic-full of starving children"; ridicule; threats; finally a clarion call to ambition. "Those (Berne, Zürich, Holland) are places for the lesser lights, for half-composers, for scribblers, for charlatans! Name me one great composer who would deign to take so abject a step! Off with you to Paris, and that soon! Find your place among great folk— *aut Caesar aut nihil!*"

This blazing document crossed one that Wolfgang wrote Papa on hearing that their old friend, Schiedenhofen, had married—for money. And here Wolfgang gave himself away. Too plainly he was thinking of nothing but marriage with Aloysia, and dreaming himself into an idealization of marriage with a poor girl, for true love. Presently Leopold read:

"Noblemen must never marry for fancy or love. . . . It would not at all become such an exalted person to go on loving his wife once she has done her duty and presented him with a bouncing heir. . . . We common folk, though, not only ought to take a wife whom we love and who loves us, but may, can, and will do so; because . . . we do not need a rich wife; for our wealth simply dies with us, being stored in our brains. . . ."

Leopold's answering comments on Wolfgang's brains, his sweeping destruction of every particle of the hopes on which Wolfgang had built his pathetic little castle, were received with apparent humility, and with a dignity that spoke well for Wolfgang's rapidly increasing poise. "In the last letter, I discussed my mother's homeward journey, but I see from your letter of the 12th that this was quite unnecessary. Not for a moment did I suppose you would ever do anything but disapprove the journey with the Webers, for I, myself" (a pitiful attempt at retraction) "never entertained the idea *in our present circumstances. . . .*"

Papa's next letter continued in ironic, angry vein. Between painful scenes with his mother, these letters to read, and hours when he sat with Aloysia, dumb, miserable, and ashamed, Wolfgang fell ill. "I have been confined to the house for two days and have been swallowing *Antispasmotisch,* black powder, and elderberry tea to induce sweating, because I have had catarrh, cold in the head, headache, sore throat, eye-ache, and ear-ache. . . . I cannot write much, I fear I might get headache again; and besides I am not at all in the vein for it—one cannot write all one thinks; at least I cannot. . . . Pray believe anything of me—what you will—only nothing evil. There are people who believe it is impossible to love a poor girl without forming evil designs upon her; and that pretty word, *maîtresse,* whore in our tongue, is too pretty for me! I am no Brunetti, no Misliwetceck!—I am a Mozart—a young, right-minded Mozart, so I hope you will forgive me for occasional excess of ardor. . . ."

Wolfgang had given up hope. There was nothing to be done against such opposition, nothing to do when Mama cried and complained, but assure her that he was still her dutiful, loving son; that they would go to Paris; that he would work hard until their departure in March, preparing sonatas, arias, and quartets in the French taste; that she must not worry about Aloysia (Ah, Aloysia, can I ever forget you?); that he would not hurt his dear, blessed Mama and Papa for a hundred singers. Then he would kiss her hands, wrap himself in his cloak, and go haltingly down the stairs and out of the house, making his way to the Webers', where the whole family gathered round with affectionate clamor as soon as he came in. He had talked it over with Aloysia. She would hear from him soon. He was sure to get a fine appointment; only be patient, give him a little time; they would still be happy.

The last day came, a black March evening, with a wild wind blowing, treacherous slush underfoot, and cruel clouds racing across the dirty sky. Wolfgang walked to the Webers'. He tramped upstairs wearily, knocked, and entered as Caecilia called *Herein!* She bustled in from the kitchen and took his wet cloak, pulled a chair to the stove and urged him to sit down and rest. He shook his head.

'Where is Aloysia?' he asked.

'In the bedroom,' her mother said; 'go and call her, Sophie.'

Wolfgang waited, gazing dully through the open door at the next room where Caecilia and the little girls were setting the table for supper. Aloysia came in. She was pale, and her eyes were heavy. Wolfgang kissed her hand silently. Holding it tightly, he turned it over and pressed his lips to the palm. He looked uneasily around the room. Aloysia went and quietly shut the door.

'Sing?' Wolfgang indicated the clavier with his head.

She nodded. He sat down, she stood behind him, looking over his shoulder at the music neither of them saw. Once again her young voice floated out to melt into the music that was his heart. Through the painful throbbing in his throat, Wolfgang tried to take up the tenor. Twice he opened his lips; no sound came. Aloysia's hand dropped lightly on his shoulder; he reached up and clasped it. The song died. He rose, and took her in his arms.

Mozart

'Aloysia,' he sobbed, burying his face on her white neck, 'I love you so!'

He covered her face with kisses. For the first time, and with passion that seemed to sense it was the last too, he drained her lips, closed her eyes with his mouth, and buried his hands in her loose black curls.

'You will wait for me, my darling?' he begged. 'Say you will wait for me!'

She nodded.

'Remember I love you, Aloysia. I want you. I want to marry you. I want you to sing for me—always. You want it too, *meine Geliebte?*'

Again she nodded.

She was very young. She had nothing to say, but she reached into the pocket of her skirt and pulled out a little silk purse.

'I netted it for you,' she murmured, *'für Andenken.'*

He pressed it to his lips, then dropped on one knee and took her hands. Looking up at her, he said:

'I love you, Aloysia, and I will be true to you. God bless us both.' He covered his wet eyes with her fingers.

The door opened and Fridolin Weber came in. Wolfgang rose and they embraced silently. Weber took a thick roll of papers from under his arm.

'Here, Wolfgang,' he said, 'I have copied all your Mannheim compositions for you—all ready to play in Paris.' His voice broke. 'And here is some extra music-paper I thought you might need, and here is—something French—' Turning away his head, he thrust into Wolfgang's hands a copy of Molière's comedies. On the title-page he had written, *"Ricevi, amico, le opere del Molière in signo di gratitudine e qualche volta ricordati di me."*

Mozart

Now all three were weeping, reaching for their handkerchiefs. Caecilia came in, with the little girls.

'Don't go away, *lieber* Wolfgang,' they cried in chorus. Fridolin said:

'You have been a good and true friend to us, and we all love you dearly.'

'*Ja, ja,*' the children cried, '*alle, alle.*'

Wolfgang looked about for Aloysia. She was in the corner, with her head bowed. He went to her and kissed her hands again.

'*Addio,* my darling,' he whispered. Holding his manuscripts, he reached clumsily for his hat and cloak. Caecilia protested:

'But what are you doing, Wolfgang? You will stay to supper! Your last evening!'

He shook his head.

'I can't. Mama is waiting for me.'

Caecilia wailed with disappointment:

'*Aber Du musst hier bleiben, wir haben Kartoffelnklösse mit——*'

But Wolfgang was on his way downstairs, Fridolin stumbling along with his hand on his shoulder.

'Good-bye, dear Wolfgang, *lebt wohl,*' he said over and over. Wolfgang pressed Weber's hand for the last time, gathered his cloak over the new manuscripts, and stepped into the slush. He bowed his head and walked quickly toward the corner. Just before he turned it and passed out of sight, he heard Fridolin's voice calling from the step—

'*Adieu,* Wolfgang. . . . *Adieu.*'

VII

1778

WOLFGANG was in no frame of mind to be tender with his mother. For nine days and a half they sat side by side in the airtight coach, speaking as little as possible, silently sharing their bread and meat and cheese, and the bottle of tepid drinking-water. Wolfgang's expression implied that he thought his mother a gaoler, the agent of his father's insanely despotic will. Mama made it plain that he was little better than a small boy being led away in disgrace from the scene of his misbehavior. Her obvious relief at his escape from the unthinkable danger of Aloysia was salt in his raw wounds. His brooding grief, the moments when he turned away to press a crumpled object to his lips, made her quiver with irritation. The weather was good for early March but occasionally there were stretches of road sheeted with ice, where the horses slipped and staggered, or went down with terrifying lunges that threatened to overturn the coach. Mama would blanch and put her hand to her heart, and when Wolfgang moved instinctively to reassure her, two pairs of blue-gray eyes would meet, turn cold, and drop for shame. By the next day it would have thawed, the road disappearing in great sloughs of slippery mud. Here the horses balked, the postilion swore and shouted, forced them to this side and that, the coach swaying crazily behind. The beasts reared and snorted, the whip snapped their steaming flanks; they bent their heads and plunged. Their hoofs went down, they grew wild on losing their footing, the yellow mud engulfed their legs. Behind them the coach lumbered leadenly as the wheels sank in to the hubs. Then came a long, maddening delay while the whole mess was extricated from the mire and another ten feet of road negotiated. Twitching with impatience, Wolfgang would let down the glass and thrust out his head in the same futile concern with which every traveller meets delay. Mama would snap behind him:

'Wolfgang! Shut that window. Do you want me to catch my death of cold?'

So they came to Paris. "Yesterday, Monday the 23rd, at four o'clock after noon, we arrived, thank God, safe and sound. . . . Never in my life have I endured such tedium! You may imagine what it was like to leave Mannheim and with it so many good friends, and then to be compelled to exist for nearly ten days not only without those good friends, but without anyone, without one single soul [sic] with whom to converse or associate!" Naturally they went to the musical quarter on the edge of the fashionable St. Honoré district, and took temporary rooms. Within a few days, they settled in the Hôtel des Quatre Fils Aymon in the rue du Gros Chenet, now the rue Sentier, between the rue de Cléry and the rue des Jeneurs, near the Boulevard Poissonnière. To-day the street is a shabby wholesale-mercantile centre, and the Quatre Fils Aymon, a sort of warehouse. The court through which Wolfgang picked his way, hopping over dirty puddles and heaps of refuse, echoed in those days to a dozen kinds of musical practicing. To-day it is filled with tradesmen's carts, bales, and boxes; yet the flat gray walls, the mansard roofs, gabled casements, and chimney-pots have never changed. It was here that Mama was to be ignored even more than she had been in Mannheim, until her heartache for Papa and Nannerl and home became so acute that it had to be concealed. She wrote cheerful letters, spreading one pathetic trip to an art gallery over much space, that they might think her well amused and contented. She spoke of their lodgings with such apparent enthusiasm—"we pay one *louidor* a month and have two rooms on the street side, near the *Noblesse* and the theatre . . . quite clean, not very dusty, with good air"—that Papa could not visualize the miserably dark attic chambers, too small to hold a clavier for Wolfgang, in which she sat all day "as if under arrest." She did not go so far as to hoodwink him about the food; nobody could, whose diet was "first, soup with butter, which I don't like, second, a piece of bad meat, third something like a calf's foot in a messy broth, or a piece of liver as hard as a stone. . . ." Wolfgang fared better because he was frequently invited out to dine—he only managed to have his mother included on a few occasions. After six or eight weeks of this life, Mama gradually abandoned the pretense, and by May, "I have had, for three weeks, toothache, headache, earache, and sore throat, though I am a little better now. . . . If Graf Wolfegg comes to Paris, will you send me by him some black powder and some digestive powder." She was uneasy without the familiar home remedies.

Mama unpacked Wolfgang's best clothes at once, and set to work with brush and needle to turn him out at his finest. The first call he made was of course on Grimm, now a Baron and a power in the artistic world. In the rue de la Chaussée d'Antin was the handsome *hôtel* in which

A Paris letter from Mozart to his father. Courtesy of the
Preussische Staatsbibliothek, Berlin.

he and Madame d'Épinay had their joint menage. Such arrangements were the rule rather than the exception, and one expects no comments from the French. But to find Mama Mozart taking it as a matter of course is something of a surprise, though she could not well have protested Wolfgang's presence in the household, in any case, since his whole fortune depended on Grimm's support. But Wolfgang's love for Aloysia was now so intense that he seemed actually blind to seductive wiles, whether these should originate with Madame d'Épinay or any woman else. He was, indeed, quite safe from amorous intrigue of any kind, for though he may have seemed to maternal eyes the glass of (provincial) fashion and mould of (German) form, he compared quite laughably with the Parisian dandies. He was, of course, unhappy, which took all the animation from his face, and made him look dull and homely. He was preoccupied, listless. "I am tolerably well, thank God, but my life often seems to be without rhyme or reason. I am neither hot nor cold—and take little joy in anything. My chief support and encouragement is the thought that you, my dearest Papa, and my sister are well, that I am an honest German, and that if I may not always speak I may at least *think* as I will!"

Outwardly he displayed a gloomy resolution to obtain at any price a fine appointment in Paris, almost as if to fling it at his father; yet secretly he was filled with enormous indifference, with contempt for the scraping and smiling and lying which his mission exacted of him. He was miserable about his mother. He knew it was brutal to leave her shut up in her little black hole all day, but at the same time her presence irritated him, a constant reminder that he was not free. These conflicting emotions left him depressed; he became uncertain and awkward pursuing the tenuous threads that might lead to something worth while. Assurance, gaiety, flippancy would have had more favorable effects on the French. This sad-eyed young man was the embodiment of everything that bored them, even though he could and did write music that pleased. Except for his piano-playing, which was too academic for their taste, there was nothing about Wolfgang that could by any stretch of the imagination be called sensational. Paris loved diversion, marvels, surprises, as it always has. Fourteen years earlier he had been the ideal entertainment for this public—a six-year-old in miniature court clothes playing sweet minuets on gilt harpsichords. Now, his playing demanded attention, but he himself had no trivial charms. The contrast did not escape him; "the French have no longer the *politesse* which distinguished them fourteen years since; their manners approach rudeness and their arrogance is abominable."

He had a few consolations. Wendling, and Ramm the oboeist had come on from Mannheim according to their original plan, and Wolfgang was pitifully glad to see them. No longer were they unworthy of his company because of their irreligion. They were real friends, and he blushed to think of his childish excuse for not travelling with them. Raaf, the Mannheim tenor, was in Paris also, and Wolfgang was happiest with him because he admired Aloysia's singing, had given her lessons, and was the one sympathetic soul to whom the boy could turn and pour out his heart. Wolfgang was none too sure of Aloysia. He wrote her shy, longing letters which she seldom answered. She had been studying the stage under Marchand, director at the Mannheim opera, and was already developing the character of a prima donna. In three or four months a girl of sixteen, talented and shrewd, may mature quite unbelievably. Wolfgang could not see the change, but he was disturbed at her silence, and no doubt something of her metamorphosis could be discovered between the lines of her father's letters, which came to Paris like blessed messengers. One of these, however, was extremely disquieting—Karl Theodor (having succeeded the deceased Bavarian elector, Maximilian), was moving his court to Munich, and Fridolin, among other musicians, was planning to follow him thither as soon as he could raise the money. So Mannheim was to be deserted! Even so, Munich was much nearer Salzburg (though farther from Paris) than Mannheim had been. Hence Wolfgang pleaded futilely with Papa to do what he could for the Webers. And alone in his stuffy attic he clung with empty arms to his darling illusion of marrying that girl. He was afraid to speak it out, and yet he could think of nothing else. After months of hiding it in his heart, "I have something in my mind for which I pray to God daily; if it is His divine will, it will come to pass; if not, I am content. I have at least done my best" (in obeying Leopold). "If all goes well, and things turn out as I wish, then you must do your share, or the whole business will fall through; I trust to your kindness to do it. Do not attempt to discover my meaning, for the immediate favor I beg of you is to let me keep my ideas to myself until the right time comes."

Papa had provided his son with a list of fifty-three names, addresses, and explanatory data. These people Wolfgang was supposed to besiege in their houses, demanding opportunities to play or introductions to powerful potential patrons. Among them Papa had included M. le Comte de Rohan-Chabot, M. le Duc de Chartres, M. le Prince de Condé, M. le Prince Conti, Mme. la Duchesse d'Aiguillion, Mme. la Duchesse de Mazarin, le Prince et la Princesse de Turenne—the greatest names in Paris, the very sight of which floored the poor boy, for these people were less apt to remember him than a pet falcon of ten years ago. Marie Antoinette, out at Versailles, was as unaware of his existence as if she had never seen a pudgy little boy at Schönbrunn, much less played with him and picked him up from the floor. The great days of Versailles were long over; the amplitude of Louis XV's court had dwindled. Little Louis XVI alternated between his beloved machines in their outhouses, and admiring attention to his wife whom he had hitherto ignored. After seven years of frivolous sterility (when she had not, apparently, been able to compete with the machines) Marie Antoinette was at last *enceinte*. Leopold construed the coming heir of France in terms of Wolfgang's fortune; "there are sure to be grand festivities when the child is born; you may get something to do, and make your fortune; for in these cases everything depends upon the pleasure of the queen." As it turned out, Wolfgang left Paris before the Dauphine was born. He was so convinced of the futility of approaching the queen that he abandoned all attempts to obtain the necessary letters.

Instead, he stayed close to Grimm in pursuance of Leopold's expressed policy: "Life in Paris is very different from life in Germany, and the French ways of expressing oneself politely, of introducing oneself, of craving patronage, etc., are quite peculiar; so much so that Baron von Grimm used always to instruct me as to what I should say, and how I should express myself. Be sure you tell him, with my best compliments, that I have reminded you of this, and he will tell you that I am right." Perhaps so; but Wolfgang was no such docile pupil as Leopold. His gorge rose at French ways of "craving patronage, etc.," and he was quite capable of being blunt, tactless, impatient, or sarcastic. None of Leopold's smooth, conciliatory manner had found its way to Wolfgang—he loathed the memory of his father bowing, smirking, rubbing his hands, making empty compliments. Nevertheless, a career must be had. He stifled his delicacy and set out on his miserable rounds of the fashionable houses.

His first call was to the Duchesse de Chabot, through whom he hoped to obtain the good offices of the Duchesse de Bourbon. He left Grimm's letter of introduction at the Chabot *hôtel*, and received no answer except that he might call after the lapse of a week.

"So I presented myself. On my arrival I was made to wait half an hour in a great ice-cold unwarmed room, unprovided with any fireplace. At length the Duchesse de Chabot came in, greeted me with the greatest civility, begged me to make the best of the clavier since it was the only one in order, and asked me to try it. 'I am very willing to play,' I said, 'but momentarily it is impossible, for my hands are numb with the cold,' and I begged she would have me conducted to a room with a fire. '*Oh, oui, Monsieur, vous avez raison,*' was all the answer I received, and thereupon she sat down and began to sketch in company with a party of gentlemen who sat in a circle round a big table. There I had the honor of waiting fully an hour. The windows and doors stood open, and not only my hands, but my whole body and my feet were chilled. My head also began to ache. *Altum silentium* prevailed, and I did not know what to do for cold, headache, and tedium. I kept on thinking, 'If it were not for M. Grimm I would leave this instant.'

"At last, to be brief, I played on the wretched, miserable pianoforte. Most vexing of all, however, Madame and her gentlemen never ceased their sketching for a moment, so that I had to play to the chairs, tables and walls. Under these vile conditions, I lost patience. I began to play the Fischer variations, played them half through, and stood up. At once I received a host of compliments. I said, however, what was quite true, namely, that I could not do myself justice with that clavier and should be very glad to choose another day when a better clavier would be available. But she would not consent to let me go; I must wait another half-hour until her husband came. He sat beside me and listened with close attention, and I—I forgot cold and headache and in spite of all played the wretched clavier as—I do play when I am in the vein! Give me the best clavier in Europe with an audience who understands nothing, desires to understand nothing, and does not feel with me in what I play, and I would have no joy in it!"

Seething with rage, conscious of his own awkwardness, yet determined to see it all out, Wolfgang allowed Grimm to continue giving him letters to the great houses, but the difficulties in the way of building up such a clientele were prodigious. "The distances are too great for walking—or else the roads are too dirty, for the filth of Paris is indescribable. As to driving—one has the honor of expending four to five livres a day, and all in vain—people return your compliments, and there is an end. They bespeak me for such and such a day, I play, and they say, '*O, c'est un prodige, c'est inconcevable, c'est étonnant!*'—and so—'*adieu*'!" However, there was the whole field of concert and opera still to be attacked, and Wolfgang thought himself more fortunate there, for Wendling and Ramm had

obtained positions in the orchestra of the *Concerts Spirituel*, founded in 1725, which were given in one of the
halls of the Tuileries. The director, Jean Le Gros, was
suave, evasive, untruthful, and stingy. Almost as soon as
Wendling presented Wolfgang, he asked him to write
four choruses. Though hurried, Wolfgang remembered all
Leopold's admonitions about writing in the French taste,
and he had not heard the fine choral work at Versailles
in his childhood for nothing. But what was his astonishment to find that only two of his choruses were sung at
the performance. He was thoroughly irritated and ready
to break with Le Gros, but some half-explanation was offered, and Wolfgang was pacified with an order to write
a *sinfonie concertante*. Again, "I put out all my powers,
and the four *concertanti* were in love with it. Le Gros had
it four days for copying, but I always found it lying in the
same place. At length, on the last day but one, I could
not find it, but searching under a pile of manuscript, discovered it—hidden away. I did not do anything at once,
but said to Le Gros, '*Apropos*, have you sent the *sinfonie
concertante* to be copied yet?' 'No, I had forgotten it.'
Since I naturally could not order him to have it copied
and prepared, I said no more. The two days went by on
which it should have been performed at the concert. Then
Ramm and Punto came to me in a great heat and asked me
why my *sinfonie* had not been given. 'That I do not know,'
I said, 'it is the first I have heard about it. I know nothing about it.' Ramm fell into a raging passion and abused
Le Gros in French, saying it was most unhandsome of
him, etc. What vexes me most in the whole affair is that
Le Gros said no word to me about it—kept me in the
dark."

Mozart

Now Wolfgang consigned Le Gros to hell, and going home, climbed the dark stairs, flung himself on his bed and wept into his pillow. What was the use of having a greater talent than any of these vermin, of being willing to work faithfully and hard, of being decently in love with a pure girl, of living like an honest man and saying one's prayers like a good Catholic? He lay long in the lonely dark; finally rose, washed his burning face, and sat down to finish his letter to Papa. "Well, I am here, I must support it for your sake, but I shall thank Almighty God if I escape with taste unvitiated. I pray God daily to give me grace to endure here steadfastly, to do honor to the whole German nation, putting His glory first, and to grant me fame and money that I may be able to help you out of your present embarrassed circumstances. . . . But I pray you, dearest Papa, to do your best in the meantime to make it possible for me to revisit Italy, where I may be recalled to life after this experience. . . ."

Leopold did write to Padre Martini in Bologna to solicit suggestions, if not a possible position for Wolfgang. But nothing came of it. Indeed, Mozart never saw Italy again. Dreams of Naples and Capri, of blue water and laughing brown faces, of real music-lovers who would appreciate to the full his dearest wish of becoming an opera composer, were crowded away by the realities of Paris; by hateful squabbles, intrigues, disappointments and mortifications; worst of all by lessons, which he must now undertake if he and Mama were to subsist, much less ever get home. He made friends with the Duc de Guines, who was a fine flautist, and whose daughter played the harp well. At the Duke's order Wolfgang wrote his concerto for harp and flute (K. 299), that lovely thing for the

Mozart

two instruments he actively disliked. He was to teach Mademoiselle de Guines composition, and after getting over his initial impatience at her lack of inspiration—"do you think everyone has your genius?" Papa wrote—he tried a little French tact and subterfuge. "I said she should make something of her own, only the first part, the melody. She thought for a quarter of an hour and produced nothing. Then I wrote four bars of a minuet and said, 'See what an ass I am! I have begun a minuet and cannot finish the first part. Pray be so kind as to do it for me.'" So he tricked the stupid girl into composing a little trash. But within a few weeks she was betrothed. The lessons stopped and Wolfgang lost another source of livelihood.

Leopold was none too pleased with him, and thought him crazy when he evaded an offer for a position of organist at Versailles, with a salary of 2,000 livres and the condition that six months of the year were to be spent at Versailles. Wolfgang never seriously entertained the idea of accepting this. To his relief, Grimm assured him that he was right, which was the only way of convincing Leopold. Papa set down in careful order every possible advantage to be derived from the position, and forwarded the whole composition to Wolfgang, who was thereby thoroughly annoyed. He answered briefly, "My inclination has never been toward Versailles; I took the advice of Baron Grimm and others of my best friends, and they all thought with me. It is small pay. I should have to waste half the year in a place where nothing else could be earned, and where my talents would be buried. For to be in the royal service is to be forgotten in Paris—and then only organist! I should like a good post extremely, but nothing less than *Kapellmeister*, and well paid."

Mozart

Leopold consoled himself with the thought that Wolfgang was a constant guest in the Chaussée d'Antin, where the presence of the most dangerous French thinkers, and with them their mistresses and sometimes their bastards, was not sufficient to prevent his hoping that Wolfgang would come to good fortune through Grimm and his intimates. Grimm's quarrel with Rousseau, who died during this year, was of course long past, but Madame d'Houdetot, d'Épinay's sister-in-law, had been Rousseau's mistress, and filled the place with the seer's opinions. Now, at fifty, she was having her passionate platonic affair with the idol of Paris, the American commissioner, Benjamin Franklin, who was of course totally unaware of Wolfgang. Diderot was often at Grimm's house too, and his intimate d'Holbach with him, and the Abbé Galiani showered his snuff and his *mots* all over the dinner-table. The very fact that the great Voltaire was too ill to go anywhere kept him in the forefront of these brilliant minds, and made the house the stronghold of his *devotes*. Every day during his last illness a bulletin was issued from the front door of the Grimm *hôtel;* and every day the conversation at the long dinner-table was guided by Madame d'Épinay, with her wide, brown-eyed smile and thin gesturing hands, into a series of eulogies of the dying genius. To-day he had had a relapse and someone had actually got a priest into his chamber; but the feeble nerves no sooner sensed the cassock and tonsure and oily smirk nearby than they whipped the old man to shaking his bony fist and ordering the servant to throw the *cochon* out into the kennel—*et apportez-moi du café*—. Wolfgang was sincerely shocked. If he had known any Germans of equal brilliance, or come under the influence of an Austrian agnostic, he might have delighted in the play of their wonderful and outrageous minds; but these people were French, and that finished them with him.

He sat at the table with his head bent and his eyes on his plate; sullen, awkward, resentful of these superficial infidels; horribly conscious of his dependence on Grimm, who was beginning to show that he was not altogether enjoying his rôle of godfather to this doggedly German bumpkin. Everything combined to put Wolfgang in the most unfavorable light. Where was the happy, graceful youth of Naples, the mischievous devil of Augsburg, the romantically tender artist of Mannheim? There was no trace of them in this pale, silent, colorless young man, with his slow-moving eyes and his air of *malaise;* nor in the nervously compressed lips; nor in the lean lines of a face that accentuated a large skull and a bit of flabby skin above his neckcloth. The wounds made in his spirit by this Paris experience would all heal with time. But one scar remained until his dying day, one he never missed an opportunity to point to with almost morbid intentness: a hatred for France, its people, and everything French, with two surprising exceptions—the language, *when written,* and Beaumarchais's *Figaro,* whose enchantment of him he made immortal.

He left Grimm's house one hot afternoon, the 19th of June, and reached home to find his mother, who had been ill the week before, again in bed. Forgetting his tedious walk in the sun, he threw off his coat and knelt by her bed. He took her hands; found them hot and dry. She looked at him dully, but for the first time in months without resentment.

'I feel very ill, Wolferl,' she said.

Mozart

He put his hand on her forehead, found that she had a high fever.

'I shall send out for a physician,' he said.

Mama shuddered and said:

'No, I will have no French poisoner. Don't send for anyone . . . I will be all right.'

Wolfgang pleaded but Mama would not hear of a doctor. Next day he was alarmed to see her worse, and again begged vainly for a doctor. Finally they agreed to wait until the daily visit of Haina, the kind German neighbor who with his wife had been Mama's only company for weeks. He might be able to find them a German physician. But this was the day that Haina, not knowing how ill she was, had put off his visit; Wolfgang waited hour after hour; by evening he was very nervous, moving uneasily from the bed to the window, then to the door; no one came. After two days of suspense, when he would no sooner have formed a desperate resolution to go out himself and get help than she would call weakly, 'Where are you going, Wolferl?' Haina appeared. He was greatly upset and went at once to look for a German doctor. Wolfgang took up his bedside post again, terribly frightened, yet forcing himself to be calm. He bathed Mama's forehead, moistened her lips, made her as comfortable as he could, repeated the prayers she asked for. Haina came back in the evening and asked her how she felt. She looked at him strangely, tapped her ear weakly with her hand, and slowly shook her head. She had not heard. Wolfgang's heart jumped. He took her hands and bent over her.

'*Liebste Mama*, did you not hear Herr Haina? Can't you hear me?'

Mozart

She stared at him a moment, closed her eyes, and sighed. She had really lost her hearing.

Wolfgang now ". . . went about as if bereft of my senses; all I could do with a good conscience was to pray continually to God to order all things for the best for her." He spent a night of poignant anxiety, lying dressed on his bed with his watch in his hand, waiting for the hours to go and morning to come, bringing the doctor. Every little while he got up and went to Mama, turning her pillow and fanning the flies away. The heat welled up around them in a fetid fog. The little room reeked, gusts of hot wind from the street brought in all the nauseating smells. By the time the doctor came, Wolfgang had been five days alone with his mother, watching her grow visibly worse each hour. The old German, whose seventy years destroyed the last shred of Wolfgang's confidence, gave her rhubarb powder mixed with wine. Helplessly the boy stood by and protested that wine was heating, that his poor Mama only wanted a little fresh water.

"Oh, by no means," the old quack said scornfully, "wine does not heat, it merely strengthens. Water heats." Then he put on his hat and tramped out.

Haina got a neighborhood woman to come in and nurse Mama while Wolfgang waited another forty-eight hours. She grew steadily worse. The doctor came again, looked her over, and said to Wolfgang, quite unexpectedly, "I fear she will not last out the night. Should she be taken with pains and have to leave her bed, she might die in a minute—so see that she has an opportunity to make her confession." Wolfgang grasped a chair as the humid room began to sway round him. Then he begged the nurse to watch his mother closely and ". . . ran out, to the end

[118]

of the Chaussée d'Antin, beyond the *barrière*, to seek out Haina, for I knew he was at music with a certain count. He told me he would bring a German priest next day. On my way back I stopped for a moment in passing to call on Grimm and Madame d'Épinay." When they saw the wild-eyed boy, streaming with perspiration and covered with dust from his chase, ". . . they were quite distressed that I had not spoken to them earlier, for they would have sent their own doctor at once. . . ." Wolfgang ran home and found his mother unchanged. He sat down for a moment and held his throbbing head while he tried to think how to tell her, without frightening her, about the priest. Then he leaned over her and said as loudly as he could, "I met Herr Haina with a German priest, who has heard much of me and is eager to hear me play, and they are to come to-morrow to pay me a visit."

Mama smiled feebly. She had caught the word "priest" and was now so ill that it was no alarm, only a comfort. Next day there was no need to carry on Wolfgang's heart-rending pretense. The priest heard her confession, gave her the Sacrament and extreme unction. Immediately afterward, Wolfgang was overcome with horror to hear her scream and see her strike out wildly with her hands. She had become delirious. For three days more he crouched in the dark, hot, poisoned room, holding his mother's hands while she tossed and wailed. In the black silences between her spells of frenzy, when he saw her growing weaker, he put his head down on the edge of the bed and desperately relived every moment of the past months when he had neglected her, left her alone, spoken shortly or rudely to her. Every bitter word and cruel action came back to weave itself into a terrible tapestry of remorse that spread like a pall over his brain.

Mozart

'*Ach, Mama,*' he sobbed, pressing his lips to her hands, '*liebste, selige Mama, bitte verzeihe mir!*'

On the third day of this suffering, when his senses had been racked into stupor, he saw her fall into convulsions, and then lose consciousness. "I pressed her hands and spoke to her, but she saw me not, heard me not, nor seemed sensible of anything." Wolfgang fell on his knees and began the prayers for the dying, after which, "I prayed to God for two things only, a happy death-hour for my mother, and then for myself, strength and courage." After five hours, at twenty-one minutes past ten on the night of July 3, she expired. Wolfgang still knelt by the bed and prayed, oblivious of Haina and the nurse who were waiting uneasily to see what he would do. Finally he rose, crossed himself, made the sign of the cross over his mother, and went quietly into the other room, where he lit a candle and sat down.

Wolfgang had aged years in the past fortnight. He now wrote Leopold a long, tender letter, a noble message of loyalty, tact, and fortitude, in which he made the supreme effort, first of a necessary lie, telling only that his mother was gravely ill, then going on to write pages of the sort of news his father loved to hear; how he had become reconciled with Le Gros and written a symphony (the "Paris" in D, K. 297) for the *Concert Spirituel,* how it was successfully performed, with all the details of score and reception; how he hoped to find an opera to write. Toward the end of the letter his bitterness about Paris and the strain of the past weeks burst out ". . . in a piece of news for you which you may have heard already, namely, that that godless arch-rascal, Voltaire, has died like a dog, like a beast." He closed with expressions of the calm faith that carried him, a trusting Catholic, through this and many future trials; "let us submit ourselves steadfastly to the Divine Will, fully convinced it will be for our good, for He does all things well."

It was now two in the morning, and many nights since he had rested. He began a letter to the Abbé Bullinger in Salzburg, telling of Mama's death, then: "Let me beg you to do me one friendly service, to prepare my poor father very gently for this sad news! I have written to him by the same post, but only to say that she is very ill. . . . Do what you will, use every means—only ease my mind so that I need not be apprehensive of a second blow." When he had finished, he sealed both letters and put them aside to take to the post the first thing in the morning. Then he blew out the stump of his candle and went back to watch by the corpse.

VIII

1778

DESTINY lights her fires upon strange hearths. Only she would dare to place the precise musical tools, the instinctive knowledge of a master, in the hands of a boy who was to live but one week of his first twenty-two years unsurveyed by parental eyes. At twenty-two Wolfgang had never yet belonged to himself. Whether as a baby at the keyboard with Papa's finger beating time, or as a young man in love scourged by Papa's letters, it made no difference. He was treated as a child, and he accepted the treatment with a submissiveness that has startled all students of his music.

For Wolfgang's music was technically mature, almost from the beginning. No amount of "living," whether in the eighteenth or in the twentieth century, could materially improve upon the wondrous structure of the "Haffner" Serenade in D major (K. 250), and particularly of its second Andante. It is not his mastery of sound and form which has enabled glib critics to characterize him as a superficial minuetist, but a quality of emotion; a quality which has its source in Papa's finger rather than in Wolfgang's mind, and is therefore certain to be misunderstood without some scrutiny of his life. Leopold created him a perfect musician, turned him loose upon the world a sophisticated child. But, strictly speaking, Leopold never did release him; for three years after the Paris tragedy Wolfgang lived in lingering obedience to his father, in a kind of artificial reflection of his boyhood emotions. He had then only ten years to exist in his own right as a musician, and according to his own wisdom as a man. In the end he never grew up to his talents. Ten years were not enough.

Meanwhile, Destiny's initiation was both harsh and crude, among the realities of Paris, in the sordidness he hated most of anything he had ever encountered. First of all he needed money, and at once. He who had never been aware of death had to find money for medicines, for the crude German doctor, for the nurse; for—how his soul shrank—the expenses of shroud, mass, and burial. He crept to Grimm and borrowed a pathetic little sum; it was not enough, he had to go back for more. Haste was vital. The heat and filth made it necessary to bury his mother at once. But—how did one bury one's dead in a strange city?

'Ah, Herr Haina,' he groaned, staring with black circles round his red eyes at the kind-hearted friend, *'was macht man hier für—für Sarg—und Grab—und—'* Wolfgang's words were swallowed in a sob, and Haina tried clumsily to comfort him.

Nor did his mother's death give him any immediate sense of liberation. On the contrary, he held her the more closely in his heart, and the first effect of his loss was to tighten the bonds between him and his father. Soon after the burial he sat down to write to Papa and Nannerl, giving them the whole truth in all its details, with many tender prayers that they take comfort and remember "how much happier she is now than we, so that I could have wished in that moment to journey with her." In this vein he met the exactions of the tragedy with remarkable poise. His mother's death was the will of God, and as a true

Catholic he took refuge in submission, resignation, and obedience. Wise indeed were the minds that ordained pater nosters for beloved souls, to be followed by rational attention to the duties of living!

Somehow, it was over. Grimm saw that the distracted boy should not stay in the hole where he had had his terrible experience, and spoke to Madame d'Épinay about it.

'*Qu'il vient ici,*' she said. 'He won't be in Paris much longer, will he?'

Grimm thanked her. Of course the boy would not stay any longer now; he ought to get back to his father as soon as possible.

So Wolfgang, dazed and unable to plan, found himself in the house in the Chaussée d'Antin, resigned to a new consideration of the same old problem: what should he do? What about a post? Where could he find a patron? Grimm, not at all to his surprise—for he had sensed a growing reluctance on the Baron's part to continue sponsoring such an unwieldy protégé—implied that he had nothing further to expect in Paris. Leopold had written several times to Grimm—long, submissive letters, overflowing with superfluous thanks, and with unnecessarily detailed eulogies of Wolfgang's talents. Grimm had no doubt of Wolfgang's talents, so the redundance of Papa's letters was annoying. And he did have a very clear conviction that this boy belonged elsewhere than in Paris—if he belonged anywhere. He answered Leopold:

"He is too *sincere*, not active enough, too susceptible to illusions, too little aware of the means of achieving success. Here in order to succeed, one must be artful, enterprising, and bold; for the sake of his fortunes I could wish he had half as much talent and twice as much of the qualities I have described, and I would be less embarrassed for him. In short, there are only two avenues open to him here. One is to give lessons on the clavier, but always remembering that pupils expect one to be a charlatan. . . . I doubt if his health would stand chasing to all the four corners of Paris. . . . And this would not suit him because it would prevent his composing, and he would rather do that than anything. He could acquit himself of it well, except that the greater part of the French public does not know him; here everything is given to recognized names. Therefore . . . it would be extremely difficult for your son to succeed. . . . You may see, my dear Sir, that in a country where all the mediocre and detestable musicians have made immense fortunes, your son could not manage at all. I give you this faithful account of the truth not to distress you, but so that you may decide upon the best course to follow. It is unfortunate that the death of the Bavarian Elector has prevented your son from returning to Mannheim."

Unfortunate, perhaps. Yet those wonderful Mannheim days were dead forever, Karl Theodor having moved bag and baggage to Munich, followed by the court and also by the Webers. Mannheim offered him no way out of Paris. Wolfgang knew this perfectly well, yet his heart was set on Mannheim, it seemed to him a magic city where everyone was always happy. He would return to Mannheim; for nothing, however, but the memory of black eyes under a red hood, awkward hot young hands, trembling lips. . . . But, on the other hand, Aloysia had moved to Munich. So he must go to Munich. This emotional morass was not simplified by a kind of fierce desire to remain in Paris, which he hated, but where he was at least removed from Leopold's unremitting dictation. He distracted Grimm with these vague plans. He drove his father almost mad with wandering letters which would set down every angle of the problem in one paragraph and contradict them all in the next. Only to Aloysia could he write without equivocation:

"Carissima amica, I hope you are well! Do please take care of yourself, for good health is our most precious possession. I am well enough, not having any special trials at the moment, but my soul is without peace or repose. This cannot be otherwise until I have received the consolation of knowing that your talent is being recognized as it deserves. But the greatest happiness and deepest peace will not be mine until the day I have the unspeakable joy of seeing you again—and embracing you with all my heart! Oh, how I yearn and pray for this, and for nothing more! My only comfort and refuge is this longing for you; I beg you to write me. You cannot possibly imagine what joy your letters give me. Do write me each time you see Herr Marchand, and give me a short account of your dramatic studies; I have been so eager for you to pursue them. *Basta!*—you know that everything that concerns you is vitally important to me! The fondest farewell to you, dearest friend! I long so desperately for a letter from you—oh, please do not let me wait and languish in vain. In eager hopes of your answering soon, I kiss your hands and embrace you from the depths of my heart; I am now and always will be your true and devoted,

W. A. M."

But to her true and devoted, Aloysia was now very cold. No letter from her, during his stay in Paris, is in existence—at best there had never been more than a few cherished little pages. Now came the news of her appointment at the Munich opera at a salary of 1,000 florins. With Fridolin's new stipend this gave the Webers an income of 1,600 florins a year and made ridiculous any further efforts of Wolfgang on their behalf. He had seen his fledgling take flight from his heart; instinct should have told him that it was permanent. And perhaps his indecision would have been cleared up altogether had he not shut his eyes to the obvious conclusion to be drawn from this sudden affluence of Aloysia's. Large salaries were not paid to seventeen-year-old novice sopranos merely for their voices. The minister of war, Count Hadik, had become Aloysia's "protector." Either Wolfgang did not know this (since Fridolin would take pains not to tell him) or else he refused to face its implications. He gave the credit for her success to Cannabich. Had he faced, or known, the truth, his life would have been simplified at once.

Meanwhile, driven to desperation, Papa had finally taken Grimm's letter to heart and had abandoned all hope of a Paris career for Wolfgang. He approached his own patron, Archbishop Hieronymus, with tactful reminders of his son's prowess, and rather to his surprise received an offer. This he communicated with joy to Wolfgang. At a salary of 500 florins Wolfgang was to become assistant *Kapellmeister;* "we shall receive, then, a yearly official salary of 1,000 florins a year. . . . All depends now on whether you believe I am still in possession of my mental faculties, whether you think I have served your best interests—and whether you want to see me dead or alive! . . . the Archbishop declares that he will give you leave to travel where you like for the purpose of writing operas; he said, in excuse for having denied us leave last year, that he could not tolerate people going about the country begging! In Salzburg you will be midway between Munich, Vienna, and Italy. It will be easier for you to get an opera commission in Munich than to get an appointment there, for where are there German composers to be found? And how many?"

Leopold had done a piece of his craftiest work. He had put a pink sugar roof on a castle intended to house Wolfgang's two dearest dreams—Aloysia, and the composition of opera. "You will find amusement enough here, for when one has not to look at every kreutzer, it makes many things possible . . . all the balls at the Town Hall . . . the Munich theatrical company, to remain here the whole winter . . . our quoit-playing every Sunday . . . society. . . ." He gave this structure plausibility by grounding it on Karl Theodor's intention to found a German opera in Munich, which is close by Salzburg. Wolfgang could not possibly escape the glamour of the statement that "the prince and the whole court here are wonderfully taken with Mademoiselle Weber and are absolutely determined to hear her; I will manage better for them if they will follow my advice. You must speak the word for her here, for there is another singer needed for the operatic performances." With this *volte face* from a few days before ("tell me, how, being in your right mind, you are for a moment able to entertain the idea that *you* would be the person capable of making these people's fortune?") Papa thought to insure the return of his bewildered son, was even ready to hint that he would share his home with Wolfgang and Aloysia if they should marry. This was news indeed.

But Papa's glowing plans soon burned to ashes; for was not Aloysia launched on a glamorous career and had she not cast Wolfgang aside? Thus the whole miserable round of speculation and indecision was begun again. Where should he go? To whom should he fly? He writhed at the thought of Salzburg. He was in fact emotionally tired. His mind was misty and uncertain—he had never been this way before and he did not understand it. Now already five weeks had gone by and he was still quartered with Grimm, waiting only to be paid for five piano sonatas, which were in the hands of the engraver, among them the heartrending, youthfully tragic A minor (K. 310). Grimm and Madame d'Épinay were frankly tired of his sighs and his drawn face. Madame had installed him in *"das Krankenzimmer,* where they put any member of the household that falls ill," and in that little hole, with no outlook of any kind, without even a chest to keep his clothes and manuscripts in, he sat and stared at the bare walls and wrestled with his troubles. His French debtors had apparently no idea of paying him; Le Gros and de Guines both owed him money for which he danced vainly on their doorsteps every day; and he owed Grimm money which he was not allowed for a moment to overlook.

All his sensibilities rose in pitiable defiance. "M. Grimm is fit to help children, perhaps, but not grown men. . . . Only do not imagine that the man is what he used to be. If Madame d'Épinay were not here I should not be in his house. And he need not be so proud of his hospitality, for I could have stayed in any one of four houses . . . he is quite unaware that had I been remaining here I should have gone to a less primitive and stupid house . . . where they can do one a favor without constantly casting it in one's teeth! . . . I only regret that I cannot remain here to show him that I do not need him—and that I can do as well as his dear Piccini, though I am only a German!" The sour reference to Piccini was, of course,

Mozart

Wolfgang's comment on the famous Gluck-Piccini musical war in which all Paris was engaged. The feeling ran so high that all other composers, including Mozart, were ignored; and as he knew quite well how trivial the whole thing really was, he felt the artistic injustice bitterly.

He had ordered a suit of conventional mourning in the French style, a red frock-coat with black buttons and bands of crape. One afternoon in late September he was encumbering Madame d'Épinay's salon with his morose presence, when Grimm returned from an errand and entered the room with a firm tread, glancing about quickly for his mistress. She caught his look; as she arranged the tea-cups, she raised one eyebrow in question. Grimm compressed his lips, nodded very slightly, and turned, with a frown, toward Wolfgang, who was sulkily turning over some music in the corner. Grimm settled his waistcoat and rearranged his sword. Then he cleared his throat and walked across to Wolfgang. Madame addressed herself to the circle of wits waiting for their tea. The sharpest brain in Paris could not have told that she was attending to every word that passed in the corner. Grimm bowed, and Wolfgang, always conscious of his manners, returned the salute politely.

'A very good day to you, *M. le Baron*,' he murmured.

'A good day to you,' Grimm answered, 'and surely you have been out to enjoy the fine air?'

'Yes,' Wolfgang said, 'I have been out—to the *hôtel* de Guines.'

'Ah,' Grimm replied, raising his eyebrows, 'and you saw *M. le Duc*?'

'No,' Wolfgang said shortly, 'I saw his housekeeper. *M. le Duc* is out of town.'

'And the housekeeper——?'

'Did not pay me the money *M. le Duc* owes me.'

'A pity,' Grimm sighed, 'a great pity. I begin to fear *M. le Duc* misunderstands the imminence of your departure from Paris.'

Wolfgang peered at him.

'My departure? Imminence?'

'Mais oui, Monsieur, certainement. Votre père vous attend à Salzbourg, n'est ce pas?'

'My father does indeed expect me—after I have concluded my affairs here and elsewhere. But I have not decided upon a date of departure.'

'Tiens!' Grimm exclaimed. 'But why should you disturb yourself over a so-irritating trifle? I have anticipated your requirements, *mon fils*, in accordance with the expressed wishes of your dear father.'

Wolfgang moved his shoulders uncomfortably.

'My father has not fixed upon a date for my departure so far as I am aware.'

'But you are mistaken, *mon cher*. Your father has asked me to facilitate this complicated matter for you; I assure you it has been no trouble at all, not,' raising his white hand protestingly, 'the slightest bother, dear boy, busy as I am——'

Wolfgang scowled.

'I am afraid I do not understand you, *M. le Baron*.'

'But it is so simple,' Grimm protested, spreading his hands and smiling. 'Why, it is nothing—see!' and reaching into his square pocket he took out some papers with official stamps and seals. 'See,' he said gaily, 'here is your ticket to Strasbourg by the fast diligence, and here is your——'

Mozart

'Ticket? Diligence? Strasbourg?'

'*Certainement, mon brave!* It has been a privilege, *j'en vous assure*, to execute this small matter for you. Everything is arranged, you have but to——'

'To pay for this?' Wolfgang asked. 'What about money?'

Grimm dropped his hands jauntily on Wolfgang's shoulders. 'Nothing! *Riens du tout!* It is all paid—a mere *bagatelle . . .*'

"But you do not pay for my ticket,' Wolfgang stammered. 'I cannot allow you to undertake——'

'Nothing, nothing,' Grimm cried. 'My pleasure, to do some trifling courtesy for my good friend, your dear father.'

Wolfgang was silent for some time. Grimm took snuff, brushed his waistcoat, flicked the tips of his fingers with the diligence tickets.

'The—diligence,' Wolfgang said finally, 'it goes——'

'The *express* diligence, *cher* Wolfgang,' Grimm insisted gaily. 'The fastest, the best to Strasbourg. In five days you are there, in no time you will be in your dear father's arms!'

Wolfgang was silent again. He closed his mouth tightly and swallowed. Then he said:

'This diligence, *M. le Baron,* when does it go?'

'Ah!' Grimm answered joyfully, 'that is the best news of all. It goes next week, Wolfgang, next Sunday. Only think how soon your dear father's sorrows will be over!'

'Next week,' Wolfgang cried aghast. 'Sunday? *Aber, Herr von Grimm, 's'ist unmöglich!* I cannot be ready. My sonatas! My concerto! I have not been paid. I have not corrected the proofs. I cannot go next week, Monsieur,' he said, drawing himself up and bowing. 'I thank you with all my heart, but I shall have to decline your most courteous and generous offer.'

Grimm turned aside and frowned. Madame caught his eye, and imperceptibly shook her head. He saw her bony fingers tighten on the arm of her chair. He turned back to Wolfgang with a warm smile.

'Ah, now, come, come!' he cried. 'Those things will all be taken care of. Surely you will not allow such details to detain you from your poor old father who mourns your absence for so long. Do not worry your head over so many things, dear boy. *Tout cela s'arrange. Ne vous dérangez pas trop!*' he said with a comfortable slap on Wolfgang's shoulder. '*Soyez tranquil, mon fils, et maintenant*'— with another courtly bow—'*allons prendre une tasse de thé avec notre chère Madame, n'est ce pas?*'

Fourteen days later, in Nancy, still some thirty-three leagues from Strasbourg, Wolfgang took time to sum up all the proofs of Grimm's devotion, beginning with apologies to Papa ". . . for not having announced my departure to you from Paris, but the whole business was hurried so much beyond any conjectures, wishes, or opinions of mine as I cannot describe to you. . . . Can you conceive that M. von Grimm actually pretended to me that I was to travel by the diligence and get to Strasbourg in five days, and that it was not until the last day that I knew that it was another coach altogether, which travels at walking pace, never changes horses, and takes ten days! You may imagine my wrath! . . . When I got into the coach I heard the pleasant news that we should be twelve days on the road. Now you can see the great wisdom of Baron von Grimm! He sent me by this slow conveyance simply to save money, not considering that the actual expense would nevertheless be greater because one would have to stay at so many more inns! . . . Of course he has spared his pocket but not mine, for he paid for the fare but not for board and lodging. If I had stayed another week or ten days in Paris I should have been able to arrange more fitly myself.

"Well, I have endured a week in this coach, but I could endure no more, not because of the shaking, for the vehicle is well hung, but for want of sleep. We are on the road every day by four o'clock, and so have to rise at two. Twice I have had the honor of rising at one in the night, as the coach was to leave at two o'clock. You know I cannot sleep in a coach . . . however, I have had the good fortune to fall in with a man that I like, a German merchant . . . he too grew weary of the coach so we have both left it and to-morrow have a fortunate and not costly opportunity of reaching Strasbourg. . . . I have one thing more to ask you. May I have a great coffer in my room so that I can have all my possessions by me? I should very much like it if I could have the little clavier which used to belong to Fischetti and Rust upon my desk. . . . I am not bringing you many new compositions as I have made very few. . . . I am bringing no finished work with me save my sonatas—for Le Gros bought the two overtures and the *sinfonie concertante*. He thinks he has them all to himself, but it is not so—they are still fresh in my head and as soon as I am home I shall write them out again!"

Wolfgang's burning indignation had other root than any vast desire to get home to Leopold. Grimm had tricked him, abused his honor and his intelligence, and betrayed him in the name of friendship. Wolfgang had not felt ready to leave Paris, and he was deeply mortified at the way he had been hustled off. But once on his way, the tension began to lessen. A change of scene was doing him good, and though he had to worry about money, he was alone, and the absence of prying eyes and didactic tongues immensely soothing. When he reached Strasbourg with his merchant friend his money was low and he decided to give a small concert to replenish his purse. "I played entirely alone, and took no music with me, to be sure of losing none. In brief—I made three louis d'or; but the chief thing was the *bravo* and *bravissimo* that resounded on all sides. . . . Prince Max of Zweibrücken honored the room with his presence. . . . When this was over I wished to take my leave but was persuaded to wait until Saturday and give a grand concert at the theatre, at which my receipts were the same, to the amazement, the shame and the disgrace of Strasbourg. The manager, Villeneuve, gives the worst character to the inhabitants of this abominable city. . . . The expenses of the orchestra, which was very bad and very dear, the lights [candles], the printing, and the numerous attendants at the entrances, caused a heavy deduction. . . . Everyone present complained loudly of their townsfolk's negligence, and I frankly told them that if I could reasonably have expected to meet such a meagre audience, I would much rather have given the concert *gratis* for the pleasure of having the house full . . . upon my word, nothing is more dismal than a grand entertainment of eighty covers and only three people to dinner . . . and then it was so cold! I soon warmed myself, however, and to show *Messieurs* Strasbourgers that I did not take the thing to heart, played a good deal for my own amusement—a concerto more than I promised."

For the next six weeks Wolfgang pursued a very leisurely course across Germany. The slowness of his trip and his evasive reports of his movements were largely due to a tremendous reluctance to confront the realities of Salzburg, and they do not correspond at all with his intense eagerness to reach Aloysia in Munich. They are, however, a revelation into that mysteriously tenebrous chamber, a young man's heart. He burns for some object of desire, and he will do a hundred circuitous things before he bestirs himself to possess it. If he does attain it, he may turn in a moment from his enjoyment, and run from the thing he loves as if from the plague. He loves it no less, but rather too much; and his is a most penetrating mind before he realizes that he is deliciously stimulated by his own perverseness. Wolfgang experienced these sensations without any recognition of their quality. He only knew that the whole question of Aloysia was an uncertain one. He put out feelers in every established quarter of his life, as if to assure himself of as much ballast as possible before embarking on the very doubtful seas ahead. Mannheim, for that reason, was a haven, and the house of Frau Cannabich, who had not yet gone to join her husband in Munich, the happiest possible atmosphere. "Thank God I am in Mannheim once more! . . . Since I have been here I have not once dined at home—there is a regular scramble for me. In a word Mannheim loves me as I love Mannheim." This, after months as a wretched, importunate hanger-on in a hateful foreign country, was pure paradise.

He ignored Leopold's irritated prodding and pushing.

Mozart

He would stay in Mannheim six weeks or two months—on an incidental chance of making forty louis—and proceed when he felt ready, though he did not couch his declaration so flagrantly. One by one the light threads that had spun the webs of his former pleasures came back to his hands. Bäsle caught him with a letter. Never particularly shy, she joyfully anticipated his arrival in Augsburg and the resumption of their *Unartigkeit*—to which, of course, she attached all the significance that he did not. Wolfgang had no idea of stopping at Augsburg. Once he left Mannheim, and gave himself up to the joy of hurrying to Aloysia in Munich, he made good time, and abused his poor cousin's devotion most shockingly. He lied to her; he cajoled her with the usual assortment of ill-savored remarks; and he kept her in the dark about Aloysia. "I should have liked to have come to Augsburg, only—his Grace the Prince-Bishop"—(on whom Wolfgang had until now not wasted a thought)—"has not given *leave*, and hate him I *dare* not, however I *grieve*, for to do so would be to break Nature's and God's *law*, and she who thinks otherwise is naught but a *whore*. . . . Consequently, so it is! . . . If you care to see me as much as I care to see you, come to the noble city of Munich. See that you get there before the New Year. I will then look you up and down, escort you everywhere, and if need be, criticize you. But I am sorry for one thing—I cannot give you lodging, for I am not to stay at an inn but to lodge with—well, whom? I should very much like to know! Well, joking aside, that is the very reason why I shall need your presence so much. Perhaps you will find you have a great part to play. . . ."

Anyone choosing to read between the lines can see what

Mozart

Bäsle did not—that Wolfgang was at last in a hurry to get to Munich, that he expected to lodge with the Webers there, that he might marry Aloysia at any moment, even by New Year's, and that Bäsle would not be an unwelcome participant in the wedding festivities. Then, lest she take umbrage at his evasions, he plunged in detail into the respects he would pay her "in my own exalted person, *ihnen den Arsch petschiren*, kiss your hand . . . embrace you . . . quiz you up and down, pay every farthing I owe you **** [sic] and perhaps too—? Well, adieu, my angel, my darling, I can scarce await your coming. *Voltre sincere cousin*, W. A. P.S.—Only write to me at Munich, Poste Restante, just a short note of some two dozen pages, but do not say where you will lodge in case I should find you and you me." By which it may be seen that the dark pall of Parisian gloom was beginning to wear away, the wounds to heal, and Wolfgang to recapture some of his own impudently light spirits, which were presently to stand him in good stead on a critical day.

That day was Christmas. The bishop of Kaisersheim had invited Wolfgang to travel the short distance to Munich with him, and the coach clattered into the snowy streets of the capital as the bells were ringing *Adeste Fideles*. Though every other sound was drowned by the clamorous repetition of "Aloysia" in his ears, Wolfgang made quiet and polite replies to the bishop, without an idea of what he was saying. He gave no sign of the rioting pulse that pounded his temples. He clasped his hands tight to hide their trembling, and vacantly turned his eyes to his host when this seemed to be expected. Would they never arrive? He had thought it but a short distance! He thought he had sat in that coach, pulling one watch and then the

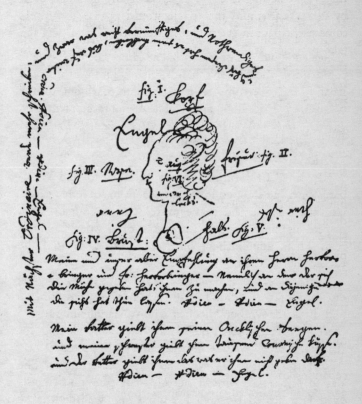

Part of the letter to Bäsle quoted on page 148. Some of it is unprintable. The features of the subject are all numbered and labelled, and the portrait surrounded by many repetitions of the word "*Engel.*" Courtesy of the *Preussische Staatsbibliothek*, Berlin.

Mozart

other from his waistcoat pockets, as long as he could remember. If one of the horses slipped or stumbled, he started up terrified; he was not afraid, but what if they should be late? The Webers were expecting him. He had written Fridolin. Why, he could not be late! But all things end, and at last the moment came when Wolfgang could grasp the bishop's hands, thank him warmly and hastily, and overcome with excitement, fall out of the coach into Fridolin's arms. They embraced tenderly. *Lieber, lieber* Wolfgang! *Liebster, bester* Fridolin! Wolfgang heard himself murmur:

'Aloysia?——'

'Upstairs,' Fridolin indicated with his head, and Wolfgang flew. He stopped in the anteroom to leave his greatcoat and tricorne and heavy mittens, to smooth his hair, inspect his hands, and brush specks of powder from his coat. Then, admonishing himself not to be a fool, he turned the handle of the salon door.

There was a crowd inside; court musicians, singers, orchestra players, come to pay their holiday compliments and drink the Webers' health. Many Mannheimers were there. Wolfgang stood quietly by the door, looking for Aloysia. There! Why—she was taller! He peered at her. And the girl, *his* girl?—who was this—this stranger? She was so *poised*—so sure of herself— A tremulous moist-eyed face floated through his mind and vanished as he gazed stupidly at this Aloysia, cool, sharp, cutting the chorus of repartee with a high, glassy laugh that he had never heard before, accenting the talk with knowing gestures of her thin hands. Wolfgang stared hard at the hands. His brain twisted, uncomfortably remembering; he frowned, and presently knew. Those were French gestures, invidious, familar. He knew them all. They were

so *recent;* had he seen them yesterday? Last week? Of
course! Madame d'Épinay had such hands, and used
them so. Wolfgang felt cold. Marchand's lessons had not
been wasted on Aloysia. Wolfgang still stood clumsily,
with his hands hanging by his sides, and studied her in a
half-daze. Black curls in delicately sophisticated disarray,
round white bosom, higher than he remembered, sweeping
out of the low square decolletage of her new brocade
gown; her face thinner, but firmly outlined, marked
definitely by he knew not what. And lovelier. Lips redder
and riper; eyes slanting into disturbing shadows. Wolfgang moistened his lips and ran his forefinger inside his
neckcloth. She had not seen him, she was holding court,
matching flippancies with her circle of admirers.

Presently he thought, I am a fool. Why am I standing
here like a lout? Ass! He straightened his shoulders,
tugged at his waistcoat, and advanced to the edge of the
circle. He murmured an apology to a large blue elbow.
It moved aside, and Aloysia, preoccupied, found her hand
taken by a queer little man in a long red frock-coat with
black buttons and silly bands of crape. He lifted his face,
met her black eyes twinkling with laughter in which he
had no part. He hesitated an instant, waiting for the softening recognition that did not come. Aloysia!—he bent
his head and pressed his lips to the hand—hard and little
and thin and white—whose cold fingertips were all he
held. It lay absently in his as he kissed it. When he finished his bow and raised his head to look at her again,
she turned to a tall, horse-faced fellow at her side, and
said:

"Look, my friend, aren't you jealous of my new cava-
lier? Did you ever see such an imposing *livery?*"

The boor's guffaw joined her cascade of laughter, to

jar on Wolfgang's ears. His head jerked; he drew himself up. There was a slight movement of his mouth. The lids drooped over his dim gray eyes, and from under them he fixed her with a cool, lazy stare. If his heart pounded he gave no sign, but his lips curved into a fine, deliberate smile. He brought his heels together for a sweeping bow, turned, and sauntered to the clavier. He sat down, comfortably disposing the tails of his red coat, and gave himself time to observe that some of his old Mannheim friends were watching, uneasily. Then he played a few notes and began to sing. Everyone knew a popular doggerel tale of the hero Götz von Berlichingen, and recognized the line *"Leck mir das Mensch im Arsch das mich nicht will."* (Any fellow who doesn't like me can —— my ——.) Incredibly odious taste, of course; much worse than Aloysia's vulgar brutality. But typical eighteenth-century, and typical middle-class worldling. The light tenor warbled it coolly, and gasps of surprise met growls of approval in the corners of the room. Wolfgang finished his song, rose, and strolled across to greet Cannabich, who embraced him ecstatically.

'And now, *lieber Freund*,' Wolfgang said, taking his arm, 'do I or do I not see punch in the corner over there?'

IX

1779–1782

SO ended Wolfgang's romance. So he finished with
boy's dreams, calf love, heartache. One year of his
life had been occupied with hazy visions, inchoate
longings, distant adoration. Now he became the real Mozart; sensitive and cynical, humorous and loyal. So much
was he the son of his age that the mere body of Aloysia
could not torture him with reminders of his unhappy passion. She was attractive and amusing. Good: that made her
a pleasant friend. And so utterly was Wolfgang the musician that his clear mind could always divorce the instrument from the player, the voice from the personality.
Aloysia had a magnificent voice and was a superb singer.
Excellent: there was no one for whom he would rather
write. Some have said that he did not feel his love deeply,
that it was not sincere, that he could not have taken his
dismissal as he did if he had truly suffered. That judgment is too easy, based on ignorance of the things Wolfgang had learned in this past bitter year. He had had his
heart torn and slashed in the one city where a man must
learn to endure such torture with grace, wit, and poise; in
Paris. He had not practiced his lesson there, but in Munich
he showed that he had learned it.

Wolfgang was the complete musician, with the typical
musician's attitude. This is a sort of laziness in respect to
emotion and the personal depths of life that has very few
parallels. The lady-killing violinist with soulful eyes and

a dangerous reputation is largely a figment of playwrights. The typical great musician is much more apt to settle down by the side of any woman who can make him physically comfortable, satisfy all his creature needs, and remove personal and emotional irritants from his consciousness, leaving him free to function in an ideational world of his own. There have been very conspicuous exceptions to this rule, but even more decided proofs of it. From old Bach with his twenty children to the half-dozen outstanding virtuosi of the twentieth century, it is seen to be true. Of course musicians are no more monogamous than other men. But they are not apt to succumb, in daily life, to the involutions of romantic love, to distress themselves with its phantasmagoria. They know such emotions—and they put them into their music. They have not much left over to waste on the world. Moreover, the true musician is an excessively hard worker, trained from his earliest youth to spend most of his waking hours in severe labor. He cannot indulge in loves that consume thought, time, and energy. He must practice six or eight hours a day, or if a composer, must subject himself to the most stringent mental discipline. When he is finished, he appreciates the consolation of a simple, comfortable woman who expects nothing of him as an idealistic lover. This digression is concerned only with the great in music, and with the male among the great. Singers, particularly women, are of another breed entirely.

Wolfgang grew into this habit of mind as he matured, and he did not begin to enter maturity until he had the benefit of his Mannheim and Paris experiences. Then he found himself clinging to the things that gave him real comfort and peace; simple friendship, straightforward physical love, homely human loyalty. He was very strongly sexed, very intense, very demonstrative. He had women, sometimes in gaiety, later in sordid despair. But he never had a moment of romantic passion for a woman after Christmas Day, 1778. He did not trouble to analyze this. "I loved her in very truth," he said of Aloysia, and repeatedly he said and proved that he loved his wife. But the difference in these loves is one of the differences in his music, before and afterward.

Friendship was always dear to him, and he was sentimental, like all true Germans. It was for friendship that he remained with the Webers in spite of Aloysia. Fridolin Weber loved him dearly. Caecilia, while of lower character than her husband, and not above eyeing Wolfgang opportunistically, had been kind and motherly. The little girls surrounded him with affection and gay prattle, always indispensable to him. Shortly he realized that little Constanze, lively, playful, and fond of him, was a sweet girl to have around. She was now sixteen. Even if he had wanted to, Wolfgang had neither the time nor the social and emotional energy to look any further. The Webers held out their arms and Wolfgang sank into them.

After Aloysia's shameful treatment he stayed on in Munich near the family. It never occurred to him to run away and nurse his bruised heart. Munich was filled with his best friends, all moved from Mannheim. It boasted the best orchestra in Europe. Karl Theodor, now Elector both of Bavaria and the Palatinate, might wake up and give him some splendid appointment. Wolfgang was quite untouched by his standing obligation to Hieronymus in Salzburg. It was a gay season, with many operas being produced at the court theatre. Aloysia was making a re-

markable reputation for herself, and Wolfgang helping
her by writing anything in the way of arias that she asked
for. He took a text from one of Gluck's operas, and
wrote her the noble *Popoli di Tessaglia* aria (K. 316),
which made demands that she met in a really extraordinary way. From the most difficult sostenuto to dazzling
coloratura, she acquitted herself splendidly. Wolfgang
was delighted. They fell at once into an easy, friendly relationship which disregarded their former intensity and
her present obligation to Count Hadik, her protector.
When he had learned about it, Wolfgang had found himself able to contemplate the Hadik situation quite calmly.
It was, after all, a natural thing for a worldly, ambitious
girl to have done. Wolfgang's calmness, like the frigid
control with which he had met Aloysia's crude rebuff, was
an enamel, a stylized shell applied with all the precision of
eighteenth-century manners to cover real emotion. There
had been before, and there was shortly to come again, an
age of emotional exhibitionism when broken hearts were
fashionable; but in Mozart's time, while it was all right
to be frank about the body or the brain, the heart and its
ills were considered neither pathetic nor divine. And Mozart had something that the solemn writhings of the Romantics precluded—a sense of humor, as well about his
personal life as about the world he knew. Picture Shelley
with his fantastic menages if he had had one ounce of
Mozart's sense of the ridiculous! or Wagner! It may be
cruel but it is surely true, that a broken heart on display
has definitely laughable aspects; so Wolfgang could feel
for Aloysia, yet laugh at himself and her, and write some
time later, "I was a fool about Lange's wife, but who is
not when he is in love? . . . A good thing for me that

her husband is a jealous fool, and never lets her out of his sight, so that I seldom see her." This was not yet, of course, the case. But many years later, when Wolfgang had long been dead, the withered old lady said to someone who protested her youthful folly, "I did not know, you see. I only thought he was such a *little* man."

But if Wolfgang had grown up, Leopold did not and would not realize it. He stormed and fussed in Salzburg, and wrote peremptory letters ordering his twenty-three-year-old son to return at once. Wolfgang used every possible excuse for prolonging the Munich visit. He had to hear Gluck's *Alceste*. He had to wait for a present from the Elector. He had to find a way of getting in touch with Bäsle. Of course he turned to her as soon as his hopes of Aloysia were dashed. His long spell of voluntary, idealistic restraint was over, and he was eager for a little relaxing play. He told Papa he wanted to bring his cousin with him, and would wait until she could arrange it. But Leopold ordered him to come home with a merchant named Gswandner, who was leaving Munich on January 13, and then said, "If my niece wishes to honor me with her presence, she can come by the post-chaise on the 20th." Wolfgang made better arrangements than that. He left in the diligence on the stipulated day, and took Bäsle with him.

In spite of Papa's passing irritation, Wolfgang was received as only his aging, agitated father could receive him—with tears, kisses, and the deepest emotion. Nannerl was overcome. It was bitterly hard, even six months afterward, to see Wolfgang arrive without Mama. But Theresa the cook had consumed her grief in hard work, and stuffed Wolfgang on roasted capons and all his other favorite dishes. Bäsle made a long visit, during which she consoled him with small sweets that helped him forget the bitter dose he had had to take. When she went home to Augsburg, leaving an indefinite situation behind (that Wolfgang had no idea of terminating in marriage, though Papa would have been willing), she was again made the recipient of astonishingly smutty letters. Most of them were sheer nonsense, intended as that and nothing else. One ended in a *"Zärtliche Ode"* (a tender ode) addressed to Bäsle's portrait. *"Finis coronat opus,"* the genius appended, and signed himself "Lord of Sowstail." Then followed a caricature which is anything but flattering to a lady already known to be so plain.

This was by far the lightest of Wolfgang's occupations. He was now a regular employee of the archbishop, on full salary as court organist. This meant that he must take his place at the musicians' table at court with the whole pack whom he so intensely detested. There were the profligate Brunetti, the violinist; Ceccarelli, the *castrato*, an excellent singer but a loathsome character; and numbers of nondescript players so coarse and ignorant as to revolt him. There were also valets, lackeys, cooks, and other domestics at the same table. Wolfgang had never felt so degraded. He would have sunk into a chasm of despair, except that he never seriously considered staying on with Hieronymus and he felt he was merely biding his time. He kept in close touch with Munich and was ever alert for news of possibilities elsewhere. Meanwhile he did all that was expected of him, and more. He wrote quantities of church music, many symphonies, and much piano music which, of course, he played himself. He took part without much enthusiasm in the usual Salzburg amusements. During this time a travelling theatrical company came to town and set up in the theatre for a few performances. Wolfgang met the director, a clever, rough-and-ready character named Emanuel Schickaneder. Together they made a few gestures in the direction of a fairy opera with an Oriental setting. It came to nothing, but the idea, still in the brain of Schickaneder himself, re-entered Wolfgang's life in time to produce *Die Zauberflöte*.

Wolfgang had parted from the Webers in Munich assuring them that he would see them there soon again, but to his surprise the whole family turned up in Salzburg about this time. He was overjoyed to see them. What were they doing?

'On our way to Vienna, Wolfgang. Aloysia has an appointment.'

'Where?'

'At the National Theatre!'

Wolfgang's eyes grew big. That was a fine thing for Aloysia. He did not make too many inquiries about how she had received her appointment; it had been through Hadik's influence, of course. He could not help wishing that he and the Webers might all some day be together in Vienna, in the national capital where one could get true recognition, and where the good young Emperor Joseph was doing his best to organize a real German theatre. He had just dismissed an Italian company, and was now known to be seeking German singers, musicians, and composers. Wolfgang could not overlook this. Until the Webers left for Vienna he spent most of his time with them, and gradually found himself seeing more and more of little Constanze. She was not as talented as Aloysia and Josefa, the eldest, who had a fine voice. But she was bright. Wolfgang gave her a few clavier lessons and was

Mozart

delighted to see how quickly she learned, and how much pleasure she took in his company. She was an easy girl to be with. She seemed to understand all his little ways of speaking and to know what his demonstrative gestures meant. He parted from her with great regret.

'But we will meet soon, I'm sure, Constanze!'

'Where?' she asked shyly.

'Oh, I don't know . . . wait and see!'

The Webers had not long been gone when Wolfgang heard some sad news from them. Fridolin had fallen ill as soon as they arrived in Vienna. Aloysia had made an instantaneous success at the new theatre, and was drawing a good salary, but, complained Caecilia bitterly, the cruel spoiled girl had run off to lodgings of her own with all her money and left them nearly penniless. Fridolin had grown weaker, and, within a few days, died. Wolfgang was much upset. He went on to read that Caecilia, not knowing what else to do, had taken large lodgings with rooms to spare that she would let to paying guests. She had the capable Josefa and the two younger girls to help her. If any of his friends were coming to Vienna, would he try to send them there to lodge with her? It was hard for a poor, hardworking woman—to lose her husband and have her only salaried daughter abandon her. Aloysia was a bad heartless girl, as he should know well—she would be punished, indeed she would. He would not forget about the lodgings, would he? In the house *Am Auge Gottes*, on the Petersplatz.

Shortly after that there was more news of Aloysia. She had taken up with an actor, a tragedian at the German theatre named Josef Lange. Wolfgang deduced that Hadik, having spent enough time and money and grown

Mozart

tired of her, had given permission; anyway, she had decided to marry Lange. But Caecilia was not going to be duped out of any more rightful money! Aloysia was still a minor, in spite of her fine ways and her turned head, and could not marry without her mother's permission. And what had Caecilia done? Why, refused to let Aloysia marry Lange unless he paid down some of the money for the debts incurred by Aloysia's leaving them all to starve. So Caecilia had gotten nine hundred ducats from Lange, and then allowed the marriage to take place. That was very smart of her, wasn't it, Wolfgang? But very clever! Wolfgang found himself not caring much whether it was clever or not. It seemed to him a bit crude. Anyway, it was up to Lange to do the worrying now. Wolfgang had more pleasant things to think about.

His good friends in Munich had not ceased their efforts to get him an appointment at the Electoral court, and failing that had managed to have him commissioned to write the new opera for the carnival season of 1781— early winter. They sent him the good news in the fall, and he started work at once. The subject was to be *Idomeneo, Re di Creta* (K. 366)—a variant of the old Iphegenia or Jephtha legend, changed so that *Idamante*, the king's son, should be the intended sacrifice. The Abbé Varesco, one of Hieronymus' chaplains, wrote the libretto, and a dull one it was. But no libretto could have been so dull as to damp Wolfgang's enthusiasm. He was thrilled. It was his first big *opera seria*, and is indeed the earliest Mozart opera still ever to be currently given. It is strongly under Italian and French influences—French as typified by Gluck's *Alceste*—and consequently of a stiffness and formality that were swept away in Wolfgang's next opera, never to appear again. There were various handicaps to a vital score for *Idomeneo*, chiefly the limitations of the singers, who could not manage the difficult music. In 1931 it was rewritten by Richard Strauss and presented in Munich for the one hundred and fiftieth anniversary of its première. But it is still far from a perfect or a thrilling score.

Nevertheless, Wolfgang left for Munich in November, overflowing with vitality and joy. He had obtained leave from Hieronymus without any trouble, and he worked very hard on *Idomeneo*. For the first time he showed a masterful grasp of the requirements of opera, and a sureness of touch in dramatic point of view that vindicates his conviction that he was first of all an operatic composer. He wrote Leopold the most detailed letters, entering every fine point of the score, the orchestration, the recitative, the rehearsal routine. For his part, Papa tendered the usual flood of advice, always with one eye to the main chance. "I recommend you to think when at work not only of the musical but also of the unmusical public. You know that for ten true connoisseurs there are a hundred ignoramuses! Do not neglect the so-called popular, which tickles long ears."

The première was early in January and was splendidly received. Many thought the opera "new and strange," a reaction accounted for by the orchestra music, which is really the significant part of the score. Wolfgang had had the magnificent Mannheim orchestra to write for (by way of contrast to the singers), conducted by his beloved Cannabich. He had lived up to the opportunity. After the opera was launched, and he might normally have gone back to Salzburg, he continued to stay in

Mozart

Munich, blissfully happy among his best friends. But in March came peremptory word from Hieronymus. The Archbishop was going on a state visit to Vienna and taking part of his retinue with him. Leopold was not to go, but Wolfgang was ordered to leave Munich and meet the Salzburg staff in the capital. He obeyed at once; this was certainly much better than going back to oblivion to play the cathedral organ.

He had not been in Vienna for eight years—not since the summer of 1773 when Papa had taken him there on a short visit the result of which was infinitely more significant than would have been the appointment that Leopold had sought and not obtained. For Wolfgang had then met Joseph Haydn, had heard his symphonies, and had from that time begun to consider "Papa" Haydn his true master. The year before, *Lucio Silla*, Wolfgang's last opera presented in Italy, had failed. Coming when it did, at the peak of his formative years, and followed by the new Haydn influence, that failure caused Mozart to turn from his Italian hopes and become the truly German composer who nevertheless gave Italian style and song their due. Much as he had loved Italy, and eagerly as he longed for it after the Paris fiasco, Wolfgang sensed through the deep, earthy vitality of Haydn's music that it was to the German world that he himself belonged. And when he finally reached Vienna, which he was hardly ever to leave again —the beloved Vienna warming to its ineffably beautiful spring—he knew, quite certainly, that this was his home. Everything he cared about and hoped for was centred in this one enchanting place. No other ambition was thinkable compared with the urge to establish himself here. Wolfgang never said so, and probably did not admit it to him-

self, but from the day he reached Vienna he abandoned
any idea of returning to Salzburg. At the age of twenty-
five, his suppressed independence finally burst its bonds
and for the first time he thought of himself as a free-willed
individual. Papa could still storm, threaten, and command,
but Wolfgang soon learned to know that most intoxicating
of mental retorts: "What can you do about it?" While ever
respectful (from habit) to Papa, he was quite frank in
stating his plans to pursue the openings that followed his
appearances, as a retainer of the Archbishop, before the
nobility. And when he had any time of his own, he had
plenty of use for it. Old friends, and above all his dear
Webers, were always delighted to see him.

Hieronymus had taken a suite of quarters for himself
and his staff in the Deutsches Haus, an ancient yellow
building still standing back of the Stefanskirche, then
occupied by the Deutscher Ritterorden, a religious brother-
hood. "I have a delightful apartment in the same house
with the Archbishop. Brunetti and Ceccarelli lodge elsewhere. *Che distinzione!* . . . We dine about midday,
unfortunately somewhat too early for me. At our table sit
down the two valets, body (and soul) servants, the Con-
troller, Herr Zetti, the confectioner, two cooks, Ceccarelli,
Brunetti, and—my littleness! N.B. The two valets sit at
the head of the table, but I have at least the honor of
sitting above the two cooks! Well, I could fancy myself
in Salzburg. There is much coarse joking at table, but
none with me, for I speak hardly at all, and when necessary with the greatest gravity. When I have finished my
own dinner I go my way. There is no evening meal, but
each person receives three ducats, which will go a long
way! My Lord Archbishop is most gracious, glorifies him-

self through his dependants, robs them of their service and pays them nothing for it!"

The situation was as galling as everything in Salzburg had been. "We had music yesterday at four o'clock, and there were present at least twenty persons of the highest *noblesse.* . . . To-day we are to go to Prince Gallitzin's [the Russian Ambassador]; he was at the party yesterday. I shall now wait to see whether I get anything. If not I shall go to the Archbishop and tell him quite frankly that if he will not allow me to earn anything he must pay me, for I will not continue to live at my own expense."

It was this pretty policy of Hieronymus' that resulted in the ultimate break. For two months Wolfgang lived as a servant on the staff, appearing only at the musicales given by the Archbishop to pay back his social obligations. Meanwhile Vienna was full of people who knew his real ability. He could easily have rounded out an influential circle of patrons. But "it is perfectly true . . . of the Archbishop . . . that his vanity is tickled by possessing my person—but what use is all this to me? One cannot live on it! And I assure you he acts as a screen to keep me from the notice of others!" These phrases were extracted from Wolfgang in answer to the letters that Leopold wrote trying desperately to soothe the youth's outraged feelings and keep him from throwing off the Archbishop's shackles. For Leopold knew very well that if Wolfgang should succeed in breaking from Hieronymus he would thereupon be finished with Salzburg. That would be the end of Leopold's career as manager of a great genius. He would then no longer bask in the reflection of a famous son, or enjoy the fruits of that fame. It would be all over for him and his ambitions.

Mozart

Wolfgang did his best not to hasten the rupture, though he never doubted it would come. He was, quite aside from his genius, utterly different from the coarse louts who made the Archbishop's music, and he soon began to act quite independently of them. He was sought after by the fashionable and powerful people, and he responded to all their advances. He had spent too many years around courts and aristocrats to be troubled by feelings of shyness or inferiority. He spoke fluent Italian and some French, made his way easily, and was charming company. "I have already dined twice with Countess Thun and go there almost every day." This was the dowager countess, head of the great Austro-Bohemian house of Thun, and a brilliant woman famous for her patronage of music. She had found Haydn starving in poverty and had brought him into the popularity that won him his place with Esterhazy. Also, she was one of the few women in Vienna who was a warm personal friend of the Emperor. He came to her house frequently and as her equal. "The Countess is the most charming and amiable lady I have ever met," Wolfgang went on, "and I am in high esteem with her. Her husband is still the same eccentric yet right-minded and upright gentleman." Countess Thun had three delightful daughters, one of them the wife of Prince Karl Lichnowsky, later a good friend to Wolfgang and then Beethoven's great patron.

"I have also dined with Count Cobenzl at the instigation of his aunt, the Countess von Rumbeck. . . . My principal object here is to introduce myself favorably to the Emperor's notice, for I am absolutely determined that he shall get to know me. I should like to run through my opera to him, and then play some good fugues, for that is what he likes. Oh, had I but known that I should be in Vienna before Lent I should have written a little oratorio and performed it at the theatre for my benefit, as that is the custom here. It would have been easy for me to write it beforehand, as I know all the voices. How gladly would I give a public concert as is usually done here, but—I know I should never get permission to do so, for listen to this!" Yes, listen well, Papa, for this is the end.

"You know that there is here a society which gives concerts for the benefit of widows of musicians, at which everyone who has an inkling of music plays *gratis*. The orchestra is 180 strong, and no virtuoso with the least spark of charity refuses to play when asked by the society, for to do so wins him favor with both the Emperor and the public. Starzer was commissioned to invite me, and I agreed at once, saying however that I must first get the consent of my Prince, which I had no doubt of obtaining as it was for a good work, a religious work of a kind, and gratuitous. Yet he refused me permission! All the nobility here took it very ill of him."

They took it so ill, in fact, that a storm was raised round Hieronymus' shaven head. Gallitzin himself took up Wolfgang's cause, and finally the miserably bigoted churchman had to give up. "I played at the Widows' Concert at the *Kärntnerthor* Theatre, and so interminable was the clapping that I had to begin all over again." There followed six weeks of the most mortifying treatment at the Archbishop's hands. Wolfgang later ". . . had no sort of idea that I was supposed to be a valet in attendance, and that proved fatal to me." There were painful scenes with Hieronymus, once when "he called me a scoundrel, a lousy rascal, a vagabond—oh, I cannot write it all down!" For all his insignificant exterior, his sweet disposition, and his tender heart, Wolfgang had spirit, if not a temper. He and Hieronymus had it out in plain words. Wolfgang, always the most sensitive of creatures, suffered keenly. "The Archbishop's many edifying remarks to me during my three audiences, particularly the last, and the subsequent communications from this wonderful man of God have had such an excellent effect upon my health that I was obliged to leave the opera in the middle of the first act and lie down at home. For I was quite feverish, trembled in every limb, and reeled like a drunkard in the street. I also spent the whole of the following day, yesterday, in the house, the morning in bed drinking tamarind water."

He tendered his resignation at each of the interviews and each time it was scornfully refused. He was not even important enough for his resignation to be considered seriously. Finally he hurried to Count Arco, the Archbishop's court chamberlain, who had long given him cause for bitter hatred. The interview that took place was something Wolfgang never forgot, terminating in abandoned temper on both sides, and in Wolfgang's ejection from the chamber on the toe of Arco's boot. The memory of this mortification seared him for years and appeared again and again in his letters to Papa. Always the least vindictive of men, he longed nevertheless to get behind Arco and let him feel *"einen Fuss im Arsch."*

Leopold's rage was indescribable. If he had been furious at Wolfgang three years before for falling in love with Aloysia, he was wild with anger now. For Wolfgang had done something still worse, if possible, than merely to leave the Archbishop. He had, on refusing to return to Salzburg with Hieronymus' staff, thrown ". . . everything into my trunks with all speed, and Madame Weber was good enough to open her doors for me." Poor Leopold! His original hatred for the Webers and fear of their numerous daughters came back upon him in a burning flood. All the tolerance, all the kindness with which he had treated them in Salzburg vanished in his conviction that Caecilia Weber was a designing, slatternly old procuress, that the girls were all no better than they should be—considering Aloysia's career—and that Wolfgang was a miserable weakling who would never be extricated from their clutches. And poor, silly Wolfgang did not want to be. Vienna was full of lodgings and inns where he could have gone, and he had other good friends. But it was straight to the Webers that he went, and in all ingenuousness told Papa that "I have a charming room in their house, and am among helpful people who see that I have ready to hand all the things which one sometimes needs in a hurry (and cannot have when living alone)."

Of all the things he could not have had when living alone, a congenial eighteen-year-old girl was the most to be clung to. Constanze had impressed herself on his consciousness two years before, and now she had developed into a young lady, and had learned enough about life to know when she attracted young men. Her mother had always been a shrew. But now after expectations of a prosperous old age, Caecilia was reduced to poverty again, and she took it with the worst possible grace. She was suspicious, quarrelsome, and even apt to drown her sorrow in the bottle, though Wolfgang "had never seen her drunk." Just what was her attitude toward Wolfgang is not so important as the fact that she had three unmarried daughters, no dowry for any of them, and no position from which to angle for husbands. Whether she deliberately fostered Wolfgang's marriage, either by apparent opposition or by throwing him constantly with Constanze, she certainly was willing for him to marry her third daughter. It was not admiration for him that made her want him for a son-in-law. It was business. He was penniless but his prospects were as good as any other young musician's. And in that point lies the answer to those who sigh that Mozart should never have married Constanze. If not, whom should he have married? In a society that was rigidly caste-marked according to birth and occupation, musicians were a small, inelastic group. They were better than artisans, yet in no way on equal terms with the gentry. Constanze and Wolfgang were on the identical rung of the social ladder. He could not have found very many other girls who were. Also—which was natural—she was the logical and most convenient object for the remains of his passion for Aloysia.

Wolfgang had been obscure when it would have benefited him to be noticed; but now that talk about him was to do him no good, a flood of it began. There were certain malicious Salzburgers in Vienna who could not see him living in Caecilia's house without telling the home town that one of the daughters was his mistress. At first there was little truth in the rumors; later there may have been more, for Wolfgang was not the boy to have free access to the company of a warm-hearted, lively girl without enjoying it to the fullest degree that he dared. Very obviously, the two put some limit of reason on their love-making, otherwise Constanze would have begun sooner than the social law allowed to bear her numerous children.

Mozart

But that there were warm, secret hours in her room or his, safe from the imprecations that Caecilia would have rained on them if she had not had an ulterior motive, there can be no doubt. In his own words, Wolfgang was "too honorably minded to seduce an innocent maiden," and therefore could not have gone so far with Constanze at that time as to feel that he must marry her. For when the gossip reached Papa, who posted off a bitterly abusive letter, Wolfgang realized that the state of affairs could not go on.

He decided to move, ". . . and that solely because people are talking. . . . I should much like to know what pleasure certain folk can find in spreading utterly baseless reports abroad. . . . I live with them, therefore I am to marry the daughter. . . . If ever in my life I have put aside all thoughts of marriage, it is just now! . . . God has not given me my talent that I might dance attendance on a woman, and consequently waste my young life in inactivity. I am just beginning to live, and am I to poison my life for myself? Indeed I have nothing against matrimony but for myself at present it would be an evil." It was a long letter, half in this vein. Then Wolfgang began to consider. How much of it was true? Did he really not want to marry? Or did he want to? Instinct told him that in trying to say what he knew Papa would want him to say, he had overshot the mark. He must not deny Constanze irrevocably. . . . "Moreover, I will not say that I am on bad terms at home with this Mademoiselle to whom they have already married me, or that we never exchange a word—but we are not in love. I play and joke with her when time permits (and that is only in the evening when I sup at home) and that is all. If I had to marry all the ladies with whom I have jested, I should have two hundred wives at least!"

Poor Wolfgang! He was, for the third time in his life, mired into more uncertainty than he could cope with. He tried to make light of it with gasconade that fooled nobody. The truth was that he was in the same position as every other young man who is poor, warm-blooded, and partially possessed of an amiable girl. Of course he does not want to marry, tie himself down, cut off his chances. But it is the only way he can get his girl, the only way he can win free from his elders. It always happens.

Wolfgang did not actually move away from Caecilia's house until September, after living there six months. And once away, he realized that he did, finally, care for Constanze. He took a room in a house on the Graben, from which he went for a daily call to the *Auge Gottes*. Mostly he missed the happy convenience of seeing Constanze as much as he wished, but also it was not so easy for him to work. He had to borrow a clavier. Nobody mended his linen. He could not have meals at any irregular intervals when he happened to feel like eating. He was uncomfortable and, though constantly busy with pupils, writing, and dutiful attentions to his aristocratic patrons, he was lonely. He began to think of a home, of stability, peace, and quiet. Now the idea of marriage appeared in a different light. Suddenly Wolfgang wanted very much indeed to marry. And while he was veering in that direction, Caecilia Weber started a few machinations. She was not going to let her chance slip. She was cleverer than her large coarse face and unholy manners suggested. She went to Johann von Thorwart, the legal guardian of her daughters, and told him that Wolfgang had seduced Constanze and must be made to sign some sort of bond for her protection.

Mozart

The gossips had given Leopold no peace. The first whisperings had been followed by more; now an ill-wisher of Wolfgang's, Peter Winter, was maddening Papa with his talk. Leopold bombarded Wolfgang with a series of letters terrifying in their brutal accusation of everyone concerned. Finally Wolfgang could bear it no longer. He sat down and made to his father an honest confession of all his feelings, an honorable statement of his intentions.

"Dearest father! You challenge me to explain certain words that I wrote at the end of my last letter. . . . I am bent first on making sure of some small regular income—for it is easy to live here with the help of windfalls—and then—on marrying! You are horrified at this idea? I beg you, dearest, best of fathers, give me a hearing. I have been obliged to disclose my wishes to you—now permit me to reveal the reasons for those wishes—my very well-grounded reasons. The voice of nature speaks as loud in me as in others, louder perhaps than in many a strong lout of a fellow. I cannot possibly live as do most young men in these days. In the first place, I have too much religion; in the second place I have too great love of my neighbor, and am too honorably-minded to seduce an innocent maiden; while in the third place, I have too much horror and disgust, too much fear and loathing of disease and too much care for my health to consort with whores. Hence I am able to swear to you that I have never had relations with that sort of female—for if such a thing had occurred, I would not have concealed it from you; for to err is natural enough to man, and to err once were no more than mere weakness—nevertheless I could not trust myself to stop short at one error only if I went astray in this matter. But I would stake my life on the truth of what I have told you. I know very well that this reason (powerful as it is) is not cogent enough. But I can think of nothing more necessary to my disposition, more inclined as I am to quiet domesticity than to revelry (and from my youth up I have never been accustomed to looking after my own effects, clothes, washing, etc.), than a wife! I cannot tell you how much I am often obliged to spend because I do not look after these matters and I am convinced that I should do better with a wife (upon the same income on which I live alone) than I do by myself. And how many useless expenses does one not cut down! True, one incurs others in their stead, but one knows what they are, and can govern oneself accordingly—in a word, one lives a well-ordered life. A bachelor, in my opinion, is only half alive. Those are my views and I cannot help it. I have pondered and considered the matter enough, but I shall not change my mind.

"But who is the object of my love? Again, do not be horrified, I beg of you! Not one of the Webers? Yes, *eine Weberische*—but not Josefa, not Sophie—Constanze, the middle one. In no other family have I ever met with such differences of temperament. The oldest is a gross, worthless, perfidious person, not to be trusted. Madame Lange is insincere and ill-disposed and a coquette. The youngest —is still too young to be anything—an amiable featherheaded little creature. May God protect her from seduction! But the middle one, my dear, my good Constanze, she it is who suffers from all this, and who perhaps for that very reason is the best-hearted, the cleverest, in a word the best of them all. She makes herself responsible for the whole household, and yet she can never do right! Oh dearest father, I could fill whole sheets with descriptions of the scenes between us two in that house! If you ask for them, I will give you them in my next letter. But before I cease to plague you with my chatter, I must make you acquainted with the character of my dearest Constanze! She is not ugly, but one could not call her a beauty. Her whole beauty consists in two little black eyes and a graceful figure. She has no wit, but wholesome common sense enough to fulfil her duties as wife and mother. She is *not* inclined to extravagance—that is an absolute falsehood. On the contrary, she is used to being ill-dressed, for what little her mother has been able to do for her children she did for the two others, and never for her. True, she would like to go neat and clean, but not *fine*. And most things that a woman needs she is able to make for herself. She dresses her own hair every day—understands housekeeping, has the kindest heart in the world, and—I love her and she me with all our hearts! Tell me whether I could wish myself a better wife!

"One thing more I must tell you, which is that I was not in love at the time of my resignation. It was born of her tender care and service when I lodged in their house. Accordingly, I wish for nothing but a small, secure income (of which, thank God, I have well-founded hopes) and then I shall ask your leave to save this poor girl—and myself with her—and I think I may say, make us all happy."

Needless to say, Leopold was very far from happy, and farther still from any idea of giving his permission for the marriage. Then, to his horror, came the rumor of some contract, and in answer to his enraged demand for an explanation, Wolfgang wrote another long letter. He had been forced to sign a "document promising to wed Mademoiselle Constanze Weber within the space of three

Mozart

years; in the unlikely event of my changing my mind she should have a claim on me of 300 florins a year. Indeed, it was the easiest thing in the world for me to sign this, knowing well that I should never have 300 florins to pay, for I shall never forsake her, and even should I be so unfortunate as to be capable of changing my mind, I should be glad enough to be free for 300 florins, while Constanze, if I know her, would be too proud to let herself be bought and sold! But what did that divine girl do as soon as the trustee was gone? She asked her mother for the document and said to me, 'Dear Wolfgang! I need no written assurance from you—I trust your word—thus!'—and she tore up the paper!"

So matters rested for a disturbing period of eight months. Leopold doggedly and brutally refused to give his permission; Wolfgang would not marry without it. Caecilia, impressed with everybody's high code of honor, was nevertheless nervous as to the outcome. She began openly to nag, scold, and make scenes. Constanze, desperate, left the house for a month. But she went to stay with a Baroness Waldstätten, a kind, oldish lady who had a big heart but a doubtful reputation. Caecilia summoned the police to bring her daughter home. Wolfgang, beside himself, bearing the burden of everyone's criticism and ill-will, nevertheless went about the pursuit of his career with the most surprising perseverance. "Every morning at six o'clock my *friseur* arrives and wakes me and by seven I am fully dressed. I then write till ten o'clock. At about ten I have to give a lesson at Frau von Trattner's, and at eleven at the Countess Rumbeck's, each of whom pays me six ducats for twelve lessons. . . . If you are capable of supposing"—(as the malicious Winter had said)—"that

Mozart

I am hated by all the *grande* and *petite noblesse,* do but write to"—a long list of influential names. "In the meantime I merely inform you that the Emperor lately spoke a great eulogy upon me at table, accompanied by the words, *'C'est un talent decidé!',* and that yesterday I played at court!"

But better still was afoot. Wolfgang had met a number of men important in the musical world—Baron van Swieten; Count Rosenberg, the Court chamberlain; and Gottlieb Stephanie the younger, intendant of the National Theatre. During a performance of *Idomeneo* at Countess Thun's house, the subject of a new opera had been tentatively taken up. Stephanie had soon come to Wolfgang with a definite invitation to compose it; a German opera for the German company at the National Theatre. Stephanie had hit upon the idea of using the libretto of an opera by André that had recently been given in Leipzig. This plagiarism was a matter of course everywhere in Europe, but it did not soothe the feelings of Bretzner, the poet who had written the original libretto that Stephanie now stole. The story has a "Turkish" setting. Turkey, in the imperialistic struggles of Russia and the Empire, had come much into the public eye during the past fifty years, and was considered very romantic. A "Turkish" style in music had developed and was used in rondos both by Haydn and Mozart. The new opera *Die Entführung aus dem Serail* (K. 384), was to have this flavor throughout, typified in the delightful overture. Wolfgang threw himself into it with the greatest ardor, spurred on by the knowledge that success would mean his marriage to Constanze.

The title, "The Abduction from the Seraglio," is a

Mozart

sufficient explanation of the plot. The libretto was of course written in German, and the opera, under the imperial patronage, was to be conclusive proof that the spirited quality of the popular Italian *opera buffa* could be successfully transplanted to the truly German stage. Consequently, *Die Entführung* is considered the first German comic opera. Its predecessors in light-opera had all been the usual *Singspiel:* arias interspersed with spoken dialogue. Here, however, Wolfgang used the Italian *opera buffa* style, also with spoken recitative, and transferred it to the German without losing its gay lyric feeling.

It is an open question whether composers are affected by the language of the libretto they are setting, but there seems little doubt that Wolfgang was. When his subject was light and lively he could easily create music that was adaptable to translated texts. As *Il Seraglio, Die Entführung* has made itself a permanent place among Italian *opera buffa* of the period. *Figaro*, by the same token, is immortal in German repertoire and its gay Latin character remains unaltered. But in *opera seria*, or even in any very dramatic passages, the essential racial differences cannot be so easily overcome. In its big scenes *Don Giovanni* is pure Italian "grand" opera and cannot make the same impression when sung in German. On the other hand *Die Zauberflöte*, true German music-drama of philosophic and idealistic character, loses much weight and profundity as *Il Flauto Magico*.

In this new opera, Wolfgang had free play for his dramatic ideas, and was even allowed to influence the libretto to the length of having the heroine named for his own Constanze. Various delays interfered with the première and the opera did not open until July 16, 1782, almost a year after Wolfgang and Stephanie had started work. It was unquestionably a success—but what opera of Wolfgang's could be allowed to enjoy success unmolested by jealousy? After the second performance, Wolfgang asked Papa, "Can you believe it? There was an even stronger cabal yesterday than on the first evening. The whole first act was accompanied by hissing, but they could not prevent the loud cries of '*Bravo!*' during the arias." He sent Papa some of the score, too, accounting for the missing parts— "trumpets, kettledrums, flutes, clarinets and Turkish music . . . as I could not get paper ruled with so many lines."

Wolfgang was sufficiently encouraged by his success— eventually the cabals faded away, turning their treachery in other directions—to consider an immediate marriage. There had been some dreary stretches that tried his patience sorely. Constanze was frivolous and wanted to play, and Wolfgang took his importance as fiancé very seriously. He reproached his black-eyed little mistress, who sulked and pouted at the scolding, for allowing "a young man to measure the calves of your legs." This was a penalty in the popular parlor-game of forfeits, and was of course a very daring thing to do. "No woman who cares for her honor can do such a thing! . . . there are many questions to be considered—'whether there are none but good friends and acquaintances present'; 'whether I am a child or a marriageable girl'; or, more particularly, 'whether I am a promised bride.' But the *chief* thing is 'whether all the company present are my equals' or 'whether my inferiors or even more particularly, my social superiors are among them.' Even though the Baroness [Waldstätten] herself allowed it to be done to her, that is quite a different matter, for she is a woman past her bloom, who could no longer by any possibility excite desire, and in any case, is very promiscuous with her favors. I hope, dearest friend, that you will never wish to lead such a life as hers, even if you refuse to be my wife! If you were obliged to take part in the game . . . you might, in Heaven's name, have taken the ribbon and measured your calves yourself (as self-respecting women have always done in like circumstances in my presence) and not have allowed a man—! Why, I myself would never have done such a thing to you in the presence of others—I would myself have put the ribbon into your hands!"

And so on. Wolfgang was as much upset by his uncertain position as by any suspicion of Constanze's prudence. Caecilia made their lives a hell, disgraced them before the old Baroness, who was a lady in spite of her promiscuity, and determined Wolfgang that, " . . . I must now entreat you, dearest, best of fathers, by all that is sacred, to give me your consent to my marriage with my dear Constanze! Do not suppose that I am thinking only of the marriage—I would willingly wait for that, but I see that for my own honor and that of my girl, for the sake of my health and spirits, it is now indispensable! My heart is restless, my head confused, and how can one think and work to any purpose thus? What is the reason for this? Most people believe we are already married. Her mother is provoked and the poor girl herself is plagued to death." Leopold ignored this plea, like all the previous ones. Wolfgang continued the bombardment until he could no longer believe, though he had had no word, that Papa would withhold his consent. So the marriage contract was signed on the 3d of August, 1782, the ceremony fixed for the 4th. "Having waited in vain for an answer over two post-days . . . I plighted my troth to my dear one before God and in the comforting certainty of your consent. . . . No one was present at the wedding"—which took place in the Stefanskirche—"save her mother and youngest sister, together with Herr von Thorwart as trustee and guardian to both, Herr von Zetto as witness for the bride, and Gilowsky as my witness. When we were joined together both my bride and I shed tears. All present, even the priest, were much moved, and all wept at witnessing these tokens of our deep emotion. The marriage-feast consisted in a supper given us by the Baroness von Waldstätten, and which as a matter of fact was *princely* rather than baronial."

The next day Wolfgang received two letters from Papa. One contained his angry and protesting consent, together with the assurance that he had washed his hands financially of his son and the loathed *"Weberische"* bride. He did not say he would never see them, or that Wolfgang should not write to him any more, but his letter proved him a disappointed, embittered old man, aware that his son had at last cut free from him.

And Wolfgang? "I am just beginning to live," he had said. Little did he know.

PART II

"And some grew weary of the ghastly dance,
And fell, as I have fallen, by the wayside."
—SHELLEY, "The Triumph of Life."

X

WOLFGANG called his marriage *"Die Entführung aus dem Auge Gottes"** and lost no
time in setting up an establishment with his
bride. This was a lodging on the second floor *im Grün-
waldschen Hause zum Roten Säbel*, Hohe Brücke 387.
The present-day address is Wipplingerstrasse 25. He had
lodged at this house with Leopold on their trip to Vienna
fifteen years before, when Affligio had deceived them
about Wolfgang's first opera, *La Finta Semplice*. Leopold's disgusted letter of permission to wed had also contained the sarcastic hope that Wolfgang would not tempt
fortune by continuing to lodge with Caecilia Weber or
allowing her to live with him. Wolfgang relieved his
father on this point and about his finances immediately,
with one of the gentle reproofs which had become a regular feature of his letters. "You are much deceived in your
son if you can suppose him capable of acting dishonestly.
My dear Constanze, now (I thank God) actually my wife,
knew my circumstances, and long since heard from me
what I had to expect from you. But her affection and love
for me were so great that she willingly, most joyfully,
consecrated her whole future life to—sharing my fate; I
kiss your hands and thank you with all the tenderness a
son ever felt for a father, for the consent and paternal
blessing so kindly bestowed upon me."

*"The Abduction from the 'Auge Gottes.'" A word-play on the
names of his opera, *Die Entführung aus dem Serail*, and of the house
called *Am Auge Gottes* where Caecila Weber lived.

Mozart

Persons who undertake an improvident marriage are sure to believe that it is the one cure for all their ills. This was strikingly true of poor Wolfgang. He wanted a home, a permanent position, and stability, and he continued to the end of his life to think that an appointment worthy of his talents was just around the corner. He moved twelve times in the nine years of his marriage. He made several journeys away from Vienna because more recognition was promised elsewhere. There were times when he was by no means a pauper, but his natural and picturesque improvidence made it impossible for him ever to bank any cash. When he had money he spent it in childlike love for pretty things and fun for himself and Constanze. The times when he had no money were usually the occasions selected by fate for delivering a new infant, ordering Constanze to the baths, prescribing expensive doctors and medicine, or sending the sexton to collect for another funeral mass and tiny grave. Then Wolfgang went into debt. Within one year of his marriage he had begun to dig the trench from which he never emerged, and for eight years he wrestled with interest, due-dates, threats, actions, usurers, and, most frequently, with the pawnshop.

Constanze is often blamed for a large share of these misfortunes, and blamed with a certain injustice. She had nothing to do with Wolfgang's ridiculous bringing-up, which left him helpless in the face of every practical exaction of life. That she was a poor and unsystematic housekeeper is true. Her management, however, was no more scatterbrained than Wolfgang's handling of money. One season they would live in lodgings with a kitchen and proper space to dispose the household accoutrements. Then

Mozart

the management as to food and drink would be economical in the highest degree, according to such a grudging witness as Leopold himself. Soon they would move to two rooms with no domestic convenience. They must eat in restaurants, or all the food must be brought in by the servants from cooked-food shops near by. That was rank extravagance. If Constanze had been the daughter of a woman like Mama Mozart a large part of Wolfgang's distress might have been avoided. But *"eine Weberische"* was the child of talent and carelessness. She knew how to sew, but she knew music much better. Though she was but an amateur singer, she sang better than she cooked. She did no housework well enough to dispense with servants, had it occurred to her to economize in that way. Nothing is gained by blaming her for her shortcomings. She and Wolfgang were a pair of children ignorant of all responsibility. She was a bubble of a girl, silly, and swayed by any influence. Naturally flirtatious and coquettish, she made some effort to meet Wolfgang's desire that she behave like a circumspect *Weibchen*. She was confused by his helter-skelter management of money, but later, under her second husband's influence, she developed orderliness and reliability to a surprising degree.

One feature of poor Constanze's life is sufficient extenuation for nearly all her failings; she was pregnant or convalescent from childbirth for six years out of the nine she was married to Wolfgang. The longest interval between pregnancies was seventeen months, the shortest (and that twice) six months. In 1789 she was so ill that she was bedridden for weeks. Her legs swelled, she was lame in one knee, she had fevers and violent upsets. The child she bore that year died at birth after a horrible ordeal.

Mozart

Modern medical skill could not promise to keep a woman with such an obstetrical record in good general condition, while Constanze's doctors and midwives had obviously little if anything to offer in the way of intelligent care. Doubtless she had puerperal infections, and probably miscarriages in the periods between her known pregnancies. No cure suggested for her had much more scientific validity than the one prescribed when she was lame, of footbaths in the water in which tripe had been boiled. In spite of these excessive physical handicaps, she proved repeatedly that her gay disposition, her happy-go-luckiness and her distaste for bickering made her the woman for Wolfgang. If she had been a rigid, efficient, and intolerant *Hausfrau* he would have run away from her in holy horror.

And whatever Constanze's shortcomings, it is peculiarly true that Wolfgang's music took a turn for the immortal about the time he married her. This has nothing to do with any possible inspiration furnished by her. He never considered her as a goddess; she was *"Stanzi-Marini,"* *"Stänerl,"* *"liebstes Herzensweibchen"*—the embodiment of all the delicious diminutives that warmed his heart. He loved her dearly, but he had no romantic fevers on her account. He never finished any of the works he planned to dedicate to her. There was almost nothing of the spiritual in their relationship. They were mates and playmates. Wolfgang had idealistic passion for no man or woman, and idealism itself in its modern sense never touched him until he became a Freemason. After 1785, when he joined the order, he threw himself into its fervid mystic love for mankind, but withheld the same feeling from individuals. This had a profound musical influence. As for Constanze—her breast was consolation, her girlish giggle antidote to the quarrels and turmoils that had jangled around him since childhood. She made him feel important, if only as the head of their little household. She helped him keep open house. She had a valid appreciation of music (though she never grasped the immortal significance of Wolfgang's), typified by her taste for fugues, which delighted him. And while neither he nor Constanze was illumined by an unearthly glow of romance, they were warmed by lasting mutual passion and by a simple German devotion which occasioned comment in a fast and loose community like that over which Joseph II ruled in Vienna.

Wolfgang had married on the crest of one of his ever-recurrent waves of confidence. Of course he could support a wife. *Die Entführung* was going so well that two days after the wedding "my opera was given again—and that at Gluck's request. He complimented me upon it very warmly. I am to dine with him to-morrow." The idea of a permanent appointment stood, as usual, in the forefront of his mind, with Leopold urging him to action. But though Joseph had greeted Wolfgang cordially, and had often joked and chatted with him during the past year, nothing was done in the way of definite recognition. Wolfgang had not yet had time to realize to what limit the Emperor would carry this policy. "These Viennese gentry (by which I mean chiefly the Emperor) must not imagine that I am in the world purely for the sake of Vienna! There is no monarch in the globe I would sooner serve than the Emperor—but I will not be a mendicant for any post. I believe I am capable of bringing honor to any court—and if Germany, my beloved fatherland, of which as you know I am proud, will not take me up—well, let France"—Wolfgang was letting his optimism play tricks with his memory—"or England, in God's name, become richer by another talented German—and that to the disgrace of the German nation. . . . Even Gluck—is it Germany which has made a great man of him?"

Wolfgang was right about Gluck. He had made his reputation in Paris, and had finally come back to Vienna to end his days in glory and comfort, with a salary (ordered by Maria Theresa in 1774) of 2,000 florins as Imperial *Kammerkompositor*. Evidently a man must have made himself a matter of rivalry between courts before Joseph would do anything more than make friends with him. "Countess Thun, Count Zichy, Baron van Swieten, even Prince Kaunitz [Joseph's Prime Minister] himself, are all very displeased with the Emperor because he does not value persons of talent more, and lets them leave his realms. The latter recently said to the Archduke Maximilian, when the talk turned on me, that such people came into the world only about once in a century. . . . You cannot imagine with what kindness and courtesy Prince Kaunitz treated me when I went to visit him."

As Wolfgang had no public position it is doubtful if he had had the honor of dining with Prince Kaunitz, who entertained in a manner that confirmed his reputation as "a most eccentric personage, but reckoned nevertheless a great statesman. He was said to be very proud of having made up the match between Louis XVI and the unfortunate Marie Antoinette. For several months in the year he kept open house for all strangers, provided they had been presented to him by their respective ambassadors; he kept a splendid table, and those who were by their introduction entitled to dine with him had only to send their names to his porter before ten o'clock in the morning.

Mozart

For my own"—(Michael Kelly's)—"part I have wondered how he could get any persons to be his guests, so extraordinary was his mode of receiving them. He rose very late in the day, and made a point before dinner of taking a ride in his riding-house, which he never commenced until the whole of his company were assembled for dinner; after having deliberately ridden as long as he thought fit, he proceeded, without making any excuse, to make his toilette. . . . Another of his eccentricities was that at all times when he had at his table ambassadors, foreigners, and ladies of the first distinction, he would, immediately after dinner, have all the apparatus for cleaning his teeth put down upon the table; literally, tooth brushes, basins, etc., and without the least excuse to his company would go through the whole process of cleaning his teeth; a ceremony which lasted many minutes." Such was Wolfgang spared.

His next idea was to get himself appointed music-master to the Archduchess Elizabeth. This brought him to grips with the chief court composer, Antonio Salieri, whose jealousy was to lead every cabal that kept Mozart from recognition in Vienna. Salieri—no pianist himself—was as ready now to take the bread of teaching from Wolfgang's mouth as to take the meat of opera-composing later. "Salieri is certainly not equal to instructing her in the clavier—all he can do is try to injure me with Someone Else [the Emperor] in this matter! Very likely. But the Emperor knows me, and the Princess liked my lessons on a former occasion." Whether the fault was Salieri's or not, Wolfgang did not obtain the Princess for a pupil, but he continued to give lessons to pupils sent him through his powerful friends. Before his marriage his charge for les-

sons amounted to five English shillings apiece and he
never raised his prices much. Few of his aristocratic pupils
made names for themselves in music; they chose to study
with him to bask in the reflection of his virtuosity. But
Johannes Hummel, the son of a poor man, was one of his
famous pupils. Wolfgang heard him play as a nine-year-
old boy in 1785, took him into his house, and gave him
spasmodic, if priceless lessons. He fell into the habit of
making little Hummel play the new music he wanted to
hear, being too lazy or too busy to play it himself. Often
enough, on returning at night from a late party, he and
Constanze would find the boy asleep on two chairs. Wolfgang would take off his coat, eyeing the new music left
by someone during his absence.

'Stanzi, wake him up and give him a glass of wine,'
Wolfgang would say, yawning, and when the boy had
finally come to, 'Here, Hans, somebody left this to-night.
Sit down and play it for me. And properly, mind you!'

A musician could not support himself by giving lessons, nor did Wolfgang want to. While awaiting a good
appointment, he plunged into concert playing, which kept
him busy, and into composing. His periods of pianoforte-
performing were thus always marked by voluminous
clavier composition, since he wrote new sonatas and concertos for each performance. He had no way of protecting himself against piracy; anyone who got possession of
a score was sure to have it published and sell it, not as his
own work, but without any payment to the composer.
Under these conditions Wolfgang took great pains to
keep his work from being stolen. When he went on tour,
playing with orchestras, he had to take the full scores
for the players, but for himself he used a skeleton of

the clavier score, so flimsy that nobody else could understand it. Between these few outlined notes in the bass and
treble, he could play the entire concerto from memory,
though ". . . when I play I always put in what occurs
to me." His difficulties with the publishers and pirates did
not reconcile him to giving up his work too cheaply.
Baroness Waldstätten communicated an offer to him, to
which he replied that, "as regards the concerto I played in
the theatre, I really should not like to surrender it under
six ducats." That he needed all the money he could get
is plain from his going on to say, ". . . that beautiful red
coat which took my fancy so vastly, pray, *pray* let me
know where it is to be had, and at what price—for *that* I
have quite forgotten, having been unable to take in anything at the time but its splendor! Indeed such a coat I
must have—one which will really do justice to certain
buttons with which my fancy has long gone pregnant! I
saw them once, when I was choosing buttons for a suit, in
the Kohlmarkt at Brandau's button-shop, opposite the
Milano. They are made of mother-of-pearl, with some
sort of white stones around the edge and a fine yellow
stone set in the centre of each. I should like to have all
my things of good quality, workmanship, and appearance!
How is it, I wonder, that those who have not the means
would be prepared to spend any amount on such articles,
while those who *have* the means—do not do so! Well, I
believe it is high time I made an end of my scrawl."
Wolfgang concluded the letter in his own English, of
which he was very proud: "J kiss your hands, and hoping
to see you in good health the Tuesday, J am, Your most
humble servant, M."

He felt very deeply his many obligations to the Baroness, and tried to discharge them by appealing to Papa in Salzburg to send him some delicacies for her—the famous Salzburg tongues, and some *Schwarzreuter*. She was planning to leave Vienna, and expressed a desire for a small clavier that she could easily take with her; Wolfgang ordered one, through Papa, from the clavier-maker in Zweibrücken. The weight of obligation, however, remained on his side. With childlike naïveté, he wrote her notes asking for anything he seemed to want, and sending her in return "the rondo in question, together with the two volumes of Comedies and the little book of stories." He then writes a piece of doggerel about *Ein Frauenzimmer und ein Bier* (a woman and a pint of beer), complimenting himself on bringing it very neatly into the letter, ". . . but now *senza burle*. If your Ladyship could send me a pint this evening you would be doing me a great favor. For my wife is—is—is—and she has longings—but only for beer prepared in the English manner. Now bravo, little wife, I see that you are at last good for *something!* . . . ever your faithful vassals, *Mozart Magnus, corpore parvus et Constantia omnium uxorem pulcherrima et prudentissima.*"

Soon after this the harebrained newlyweds moved from their first home to lodgings a few doors away—*im Kleinen Herbersteinchen Hause*, Hohe Brücke 412 (Wipplingerstrasse 17). The house belonged to Baron von Wetzlar, a rich Jewish patron of music who kept open house for artists and constantly befriended them. Almost immediately upon settling in the house the Mozarts gave a ball, ". . . in our own rooms. But of course the men each had to pay two gulden. We began at six o'clock and ended at seven. What! Only one hour? Oh, no—seven o'clock next morning! But you will wonder, I expect, how we could make room? . . . Well, I have a room here (1,000 paces long and one wide!) a bedroom, an antechamber, and a fine big kitchen. Then there are two more fine big rooms next to ours which still stand empty, so I used these too for the dance. Baron von Wetzlar and his wife were there, the Waldstättens, Herr von Edelbach, Gilowsky der Windmacher (i.e. The Windbag), young Stephanie *et uxor*, Adamberger and his wife, M. and Madame Lange, etc." It was Carnival time, ". . . and there is just as much dancing here as in Salzburg and Munich. I should like very much to go as Harlequin (but unknown to everyone) as there are so many—indeed nothing but!—asses at the masquerades. So may I ask you to send me your Harlequin dress? But it must be very soon. . . ."

The Carnival balls were public, and few distinctions of rank were made; when the whole town was—as Kelly saw it—"dancing mad; as the Carnival approached, gaiety began to display itself on all sides, and when it really came nothing could exceed its brilliancy. The Ridotto Rooms [the famous *Redoutensaal*], where the masquerades took place, were in the palace, and spacious and commodious as they were, they were actually crammed with masqueraders. I never saw, or indeed heard of, any suite of rooms where elegance and convenience were more considered; for the propensity of the Vienna ladies for dancing and going to carnival masquerades was so determined that nothing was permitted to interfere with their enjoyment of their favorite amusement—nay, so notorious was it, that, for the ladies in the family way, who could not be persuaded to stay at home, there were apartments prepared, with every convenience for their accouchement, should they be unfortunately required. And I have been gravely told, and almost believe, that there have actually been instances of the utility of the arrangement. The ladies of Vienna are particularly celebrated for their grace and movements in waltzing, of which they never tire. For my own part, I thought waltzing from ten at night until seven in the morning a continual whirligig, most tiresome to the eyes, and ear—to say nothing of any worse consequences."

Vienna already waltzing in 1783? It was indeed. The waltz was the ultimate development of the minuet and was first danced to music in minuet time. Most of the court composers were expected to provide new orchestra dances for the *Redoutensaal* balls; Wolfgang turned out prodigious numbers of them, as well as sets of country dances for the simpler parties of his *bürgerliche* friends. He wrote dance music in three forms, all forerunners of modern dances: minuets and *Deutsche Tänze*, whose 3-4 and, of the latter, occasionally 3-8 time, in the stately beat of the formal square dances, finally became the famous *Wiener-Walzer. Kontretänze*, the third form Mozart used, were in 2-4 time, variants of the gavotte and polka, and so ancestors of the two-step and finally of the fox-trot. They and the *Deutsche* were not danced at court balls. When the waltz first appeared, in a gradual transition from the figures of the formal minuet, it was far from the "disgusting" spectacle recorded by sour commentators of the early nineteenth century in England. As Kelly says, the postures of the women were charmingly graceful, and the men comported themselves both gaily and gallantly. There was no encircling of arms such as appeared after the French Revolution; the dance started as a minuet, and halfway through, when the partners came face to face in a curtsey and bow, they would put the tips of their fingers very lightly on each other's waists, and continue the stately tread of the minuet so united. Gradually the dance became more waltz and less minuet. This early waltz was the rage about 1802 at the Tivoli Gardens in Paris where its spectators thought it most exquisite; by 1813, its poses had reached such excess in England as to call forth from Byron—of all Puritans!—his famous invective.

Baroness Waldstätten had procured for Wolfgang the beautiful red coat about which he had written her so longingly, and in it, with its wonderful fancy buttons, he became a familiar figure in the streets and drawing-rooms of Vienna. But he was already showing some bad effects of long sitting at his writing-table. He was pale, thin, and beginning to stoop slightly, which made him seem even smaller than he really was. His physician, Dr. Sigmund Barisani of the General Hospital, prescribed fresh air, walks, and exercise. The doctor's prescriptions were exceedingly well received, since they involved the purchase of a billiard-table with five balls and twelve cues, which immediately became the social magnet for half the composers and musicians in town. Wolfgang took the greatest delight in his billiards and also in bowls, at both of which games he usually won. He was always ready for a match —partly because he never took his working hours very seriously, partly because he always felt justified—"doctor's orders." If no one else was about, he made Constanze play with him, or would even play alone. He also formed the habit of writing at a standing-desk, and soon began to rise at five every morning and go to the Augarten to ride. He was no great sight on a horse, never having been properly taught to handle one, but he stuck on and enjoyed it. He loved pets so intensely that his home was never without one—a dog, a cat, or even more certainly a bird.

Vienna was then, as it has been in our time, a dual city, a great centre of education, science, and art, as well as a magnet for bon-vivants and pleasure-seekers. Side by side with dazzling court society there flourished fine intellectual families of bourgeois stock whose daughters did not think the term "bas-bleu" a stigma, and whose sons were as devoted to learning and the arts as to taverns and stage-doors. Such was the Martinetz family, where Metastasio made his home for fifty years, and such were the Greiner and Jacquin households, in all of which great musicians were welcome on terms of intimacy that were unthinkable in connection with the nobility. Wolfgang was a familiar of these houses, but was particularly devoted to the Jacquins, whose son Gottfried was his closest friend. They criticized each other's music (for Gottfried played and composed like the children of all such people), and were also comrades of the billiard-table and the punch-bowl. The Jacquin house was in the Botanical Gardens in the Landstrasse suburb. Wolfgang preferred it, with its setting of flowers and birds, to any other place he visited.

Quartet-parties were the favorite form of entertainment among these groups, and so became the source of much of the great chamber-music of the time. Wolfgang himself established open house on Sunday mornings, where he and his friends and colleagues played for their own pleasure, but for which he had to charge admission, as at his ball, to provide for the punch that made the party go. Every one in like circumstances did the same. At gatherings like these Wolfgang often saw "Papa" Haydn, who came to town with Esterhazy for the winter season. The acquaintance ripened into a noble friendship unique in Wolfgang's life, which soon inspired him to begin the famous set of six quartets dedicated to Haydn. At this time he was working on the first, in G (K. 387).

These quartets are not only the best-known of his chamber-music, but they are the pure, personal medium in which Mozart speaks to those who understand him best. Though he was master (and perhaps the only master in all music) of every known form of composition; though there was nothing, from opera to symphony, from masses to concerti, to which he did not make an immortal contribution, his chamber-music reveals the side he showed to his intimates in his hours of relaxation. That his most serious and most spiritual emotions are found in his trios, quartets, and quintets is therefore a foregone conclusion. His intimacy with the Jacquin family has been commemorated by some of his most inspired chamber-music, as well as by delicious nonsense like *Das Bandel* (K. 441), a three-part song with words in Vienna argot, which he wrote one day when Constanze lost her girdle and Gottfried ransacked the disorderly room until he found it for her. The parts are, of course, for soprano (Constanze), tenor (Wolfgang), and bass (Gottfried).

As Lent approached, when the theatres and the opera would be closed, he began to make plans for giving private subscription concerts which were the only form of musical entertainment permitted. Countess Thun helped to provide him with a list of "my one hundred and seventy-four subscribers. I alone have thirty subscribers more than Richter and Fischer together. I commence with three subscription-concerts in Trattner's Hall, on the last three

Mozart

Wednesdays in Lent, beginning on the 17th of March; the price of the three is six florins. . . . The entire forenoon is taken up with pupils, and in the evening I have nearly every day engaged to play. Here is a list of the concerts at which I am engaged." There follows a list of twenty-one engagements between the 26th of February and the 3rd of April, all, except his own private concerts, at the palaces of Prince Esterhazy and Prince Gallitzin. These concerts were no mere matter of playing a concerto, a sonata, and a group of short pieces. Everything played was of Wolfgang's composition. A typical programme (this one a benefit for Aloysia Lange, when every box was taken) follows:

1. The new "Haffner" Symphony, in D, conducted by Wolfgang.
2. Air from *Idomeno*, *Se il padre perdei*, sung by Aloysia.
3. The third subscription concerto, in C major, played by Wolfgang.
4. Countess Baumgarten's scena, sung by Adamberger (a famous German tenor).
5. The short Sinfonia-Concertante, conducted by Wolfgang.
6. The favorite concerto in D, played by Wolfgang.
7. Scena from *Lucio Silla*, sung by Mlle. Täuber.
8. Impromptu Fantasia by Mozart, beginning with a short fugue "because the Emperor was there," followed by variations on an air of Paisiello, *Salve tu Domine*. When the thunderous applause obliged him to play again, he chose as a theme for variations *Unser dummer Pöbel meint*, from Gluck's opera, *The Pilgrims of Mecca*, as a delicate compliment to its composer, who was sitting in a box next to the Langes.

9. A new rondo composed for Aloysia and played by her.

10. The last movement of the first symphony.

This concert, with its prodigiously long and beautiful programme, was one of Wolfgang's typical gestures of generosity to Aloysia. Her marriage to Josef Lange was already proving to be such a barnyard squabble that the gossip-sheets of Vienna had taken it up. Lange made public scenes and disgraced her repeatedly with filthy and jealous accusations. Nothing remained of Wolfgang's passion for Aloysia but a good-hearted affection. For her singing he had a tremendous regard. She had by now fulfilled all her promise and was the only soprano in the ranks of German singers worthy of his important scenas and arias. Her voice was amazingly high and her execution famous for its power and perfection. Stephen Storace compared her singing to that of Bastardella, who had so impressed Wolfgang in his childhood. Wolfgang wrote and gave to Aloysia numbers of magnificent dramatic arias, and was always ready to lend his hand or his pen to any form of benefit for her or Lange. He did the same for anyone he cared for. Leutgeb, the famous horn-player, a buffoon whom he had known since his childhood, was the recipient about this time of three horn concertos. In writing one of these, Wolfgang used inks of all colors and wrote the most difficult passages in bright blue, putting running comments in the margin, "What do you say to that, Master Leutgeb?" He dedicated the second concerto in delicate phrasing: "Wolfgang Amade Mozart takes pity on that Ass, Ox, and Fool Leutgeb, here in Vienna, the 27th of May, 1783."

Mozart

The balmiest, most delicious of all seasons—spring in
Vienna—held him and Constanze in thrall. They spent
whole days in the Prater, lying on the soft new grass,
plucking pink and yellow wild primroses to twine in each
other's hair, making garlands and love-knots. In their own
unintelligible jargon they murmured amorous idiocies,
Wolfgang setting them to music and singing softly while
Constanze blinked at the blue sky and thought about the
unfinished little socks in her work-basket. Lazy pecks of
kisses would travel over her face and down her neck, and
naughty white fingers pinch her gently, here and there,
sure of feeble reproof. "I cannot possibly make up my
mind to go back into the town so early. The weather is
far too lovely, and it is far too pleasant here in the Prater.
We have taken our meal out of doors, and shall stay on
until eight or nine o'clock this evening. My company consists solely of my pregnant wife and her—not pregnant—
but fat and flourishing husband. I must ask you to wait
patiently for a longer letter and the aria variations—for of
course I cannot accomplish them in the Prater, and I cannot miss this beautiful weather for my dear little wife's
sake. Change and exercise are good for her health."

This sort of change and exercise, surely. But there had
been other change and exercise in the past few weeks;
they had been moving again. Their comfortable establishment with the room "a thousand" paces long had been
broken up because "Baron Wetzlar has taken a woman
into his house and therefore to please her we are turned
out into a dirty lodging on the Kohlmarkt. However, he
has not charged anything for the three months we did
lodge with him, and he has taken on himself the cost of
the moving. Under these conditions we sought really good

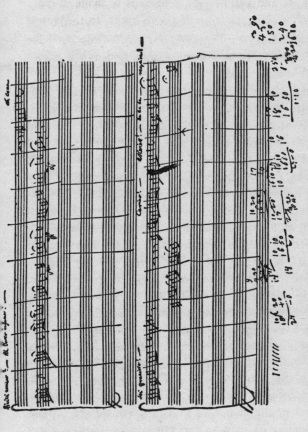

A page from one of the horn concertos for Leutgeb, where Mozart calls him *porco infamo* and *asino*, and scribbles accounts in the margin. Courtesy of the *Preussische Staatsbibliothek*, Berlin.

quarters and found them on the Judenplatz where we accordingly are. He also paid all the expenses on the Kohlmarkt. Our address is therefore *am* Judenplatz, 244, *im Burgischen Hause,* first floor. Now we wish for nothing better than to embrace you—both of us—very soon." If Wolfgang could have kept Wetzlar for his landlord for the next eight years how many scrapes and mortifications he would have escaped!

These domestic preoccupations were such that he produced only five short works in the first five months of 1783, one of the horn concertos for Leutgeb, three arias for Aloysia, and one aria for the tenor Adamberger. But in June he began work on the second of the six quartets for Haydn, the D minor (K. 421). Its overwhelmingly tender and moving emotion is best understood when Wolfgang is seen being waked from a sound sleep at half-past one in the morning of June 17th. Constanze's first childbirth pains had begun. For two and a half hours he did what he could for her, but at four o'clock sent for Caecilia Weber who came bustling and took complete charge. Wolfgang was told to send for the midwife. After she came there was nothing for him to do. Caecilia refused to have him hovering by the bedside. He tried staying in the anteroom but could not endure Constanze's cries. Finally he got his work and sat down by Constanze's bed, as much as possible out of the way of the busy women. There, in the last stretch of her agony, he wrote the heartrending Andante, whose piercing, up-sweeping Crescendos no woman could fail to understand. When her last moan had died away and Constanze lay white and flat, with her eyes closed, and he had looked at the red thing squirming in Caecilia's arms, he turned away and wrote the Menuette

Mozart

and Trio. The spontaneously tragic feeling of the D minor quartet is in one of Wolfgang's weirdly premonitory moods. It suggests the cumulative heartache of all his domestic tragedies.

Constanze was no better prepared for motherhood than she had been for marriage. "I hope to God that by taking care of herself she will come well through her child-bed. From the condition of her breasts I have some fear of milk-fever! And now against, and yet by my will, they have got a wet-nurse for the child! I was always quite determined that, whether she were able to do so or not, my wife should never suckle her child—and yet I was equally determined that my child should take no stranger's milk. I intended to bring it up on water like my sister and myself, only the midwife, my mother-in-law and the majority of people here have begged me not to think of it, simply because it is the water which causes most of the children's deaths here, as the people do not know how to use it. That moved me to give in, for I should not like to have anything to reproach myself with." There speaks the eighteenth century, whose children were born and died like the haphazard accidents they were. Constanze could not nurse her children like a peasant (probably a hearty relief to her) so they must be starved on water or given out to nurse, under conditions which were always precarious, and often fatal.

The infant was christened Raimund Leopold, though Wolfgang had told his father some weeks before that, boy or girl, the baby should be named for him—Leopold or Leopoldine. But "Baron Wetzlar [the late landlord] (who is my good and true friend) . . . came at once himself and offered to stand godfather. I could not refuse him . . . he said joyfully, 'Now you have a little Raimund' and kissed the child. . . . After all, Leopold is one of his names!" Early in August the child succumbed to one of the usual levellers—malnutrition, ignorance, insanitation, disease, perhaps all; he was the first of a mournful little procession that traversed the background of Wolfgang's life. Soon afterwards, the young couple made preparations to go to Salzburg for a long-promised visit to Leopold. They had given up their lodging, arranged to have their belongings cared for, packed their bandboxes, and were entering the travelling-coach when an ominously burly figure appeared and Wolfgang found himself arrested on the step of the carriage, for a forgotten debt of thirty florins. Followed a distracting scene; Wolfgang blanching and biting his lip, then squaring his shoulders and protesting for his honor. He explained desperately that this trip was vital, and that he had not a kreutzer more than enough for travelling expenses—here, look into my purse and see—finally a flurried exchange of papers, a rush into the house for pen and ink, a grudgingly convinced ruffian, a brief postponement of the debt—and Wolfgang flung himself back against the cushions, his pale lips moving in a series of sotto-voce curses.

Leopold received them with no particular cordiality. He really detested Constanze. Nannerl, on whom Wolfgang depended, took her cue from Papa and was polite, but not sisterly. Constanze was not a winning person. She could not discover how to propitiate the family, and perhaps she did not care. The three months passed unpleasantly. Wolfgang was supersensitive, and exaggerated each apparent slight. Leopold had resorted to teaching and had several pupils living in his house—an added irritation which he managed to blame on Wolfgang. For if his son had obtained a fine appointment instead of a scatterbrained wife, would not Leopold be ending his days in comfort and religious meditation? Assuredly!

Salzburg seemed more disagreeable than ever. None of his childhood friends were congenial, and the houses he visited were crude and provincial after the amusing salons of Vienna. With time heavy on his hands, he looked up the dramatic poet Abbé Varesco, who had written the book of *Idomeneo*, and started a comic opera, *L'Oca del Cairo*, but became bored with it and set it aside. He also undertook a thanksgiving mass which he had vowed to compose and produce if he should finally marry Constanze. This was the great C minor mass (K. 427), begun last January in Vienna and planned on a tremendous scale, but like every other work dedicated to Constanze, it was never finished. At the rehearsals at Salzburg he found it necessary to substitute the missing parts from one of his earlier masses. Constanze herself sang the soprano solo— how, it is not profitable to conjecture, but as it is very difficult, she probably demonstrated the same natural ability as all her sisters. She never sang at any other time in public. The mass was produced in the Peterskirche of Salzburg, because Hieronymus, ever acidulous toward Wolfgang, had refused the use of the Cathedral. Nothing, in short, took place that might sweeten Wolfgang's bitter opinion of Salzburg and everybody in it. He made an exception of Michael Haydn, elder brother of "Papa," whom he had always loved, and wrote two duos for violin and viola (K. 423 and 424) for him. Then he prepared to pack up and leave. There was an unpleasant scene when Leopold refused to give Constanze any of the multifarious baubles that Wolfgang had collected in his childhood journeys. With this rankling in their minds, but with formal protestations of loyalty, and gracious acknowledgment of the paternal hospitality, they heaved a great sigh of relief and rolled out of Salzburg, forever, on the 27th of October.

The journey home was more of a honeymoon than they had ever had. When they reached Linz, with its memories of Wolfgang's childhood, they were delightedly received by the local member of the Thun family, the old Count, who had heard from Bohemia that *Die Entführung* had been produced with great success in Prague. Wolfgang was urged to give a concert, which he was not loath to do since he had practically no money; but he had brought no symphony scores with him. He retired into solitude, and the Linz symphony in C major (K. 425) came into existence. He wrote it in four days, and conducted it on the third of November to the great enthusiasm of Count Thun and all his townspeople. Immediately afterward the Mozarts left for the remainder of their journey home (how emphatically was Vienna home now!) and before Christmas were once more settled with their beloved *Billard* and all their possessions. This time they found quarters on the Graben, *im Trattnerschen Hause*, on the third floor. Wolfgang's first composition after settling at home was one of the most beautiful of all his noble piano works —the fugue in C minor for two pianos (K. 426). So compelling is the theme that he himself never lost sight of it, and four years later rewrote it as a string quartet. Beethoven copied it from the score. This fugue and the C minor mass marked a tremendous increase in the power and beauty of Wolfgang's compositions; he was about to step into the brief, miraculous years when his genius would bear its loveliest flowers. Meanwhile he busied himself with lessons and with plans for the concerts of the forthcoming Lenten season. Constanze became pregnant once more. Destiny, having looked over Europe, picked the shining lights of the musical and dramatic world, brought them all together in Vienna, smiled, and waited.

XI

1783-1784

IN 1779 a slight blond youth of sixteen sailed away
from his Irish home with a gold watch, ten guineas,
and a forte-piano, to learn to be an opera singer in
Italy. This was the tenor Michael Kelly, who became one
of the famous lights of the British stage, and used his
astonishing career as material for his *Reminiscences*, written in his old age. Michael was the son of a Dublin eti-
quette-teacher, and had learned enough of his father's art
to make a good impression on Sir William Hamilton when
he arrived in Naples.

After studying with the great Aprile he set out to carve
himself a career in the Italian opera-houses, and one evening disembarked on the Mole at Leghorn, wrapped in a
Sicilian capote, with his long fair hair hanging over his
shoulders. Nearby stood a young man and a girl, and
Michael pricked up his ears when he overheard them
speaking English.

"Look at that girl dressed in boy's clothes!" the girl
said. Her companion snickered, but Michael walked up to
the pair, and with a handsome bow, answered in English,
"You are mistaken, Miss; I am a very proper *he* animal,
and quite at your service." All three laughed, and the
dénouement was a happy lifelong friendship. The English
girl and boy were Nancy Storace and her brother Stephen,
brilliantly talented; he was studying composition, and she,
though only fourteen, had already made a reputation with
her beautiful soprano voice. She had been taught by Rauz-

The pastel, of unknown origin, once owned by the sculptor Tilgner.
The date, 1786, was inserted during a retouching; it is thus impossible
to know whether the likeness was done from life. Courtesy of Frau
Rosa Chavanne, Vienna.

Leopold Mozart, at about the time his son Wolfgang was born.
Courtesy of the *Mozartmuseum*, Salzburg.

Mozart at the age of six, in the court costume given him by the Empress Maria Theresa. Courtesy of the *Mozartmuseum*, Salzburg.

The family—Nannerl, Wolfgang, and Leopold—in 1780. As the mother had died in Paris, a portrait of her was copied into this group. Courtesy of the *Mozartmuseum*, Salzburg.

Constanze Mozart

Constanze, shortly after her marriage. Painted by her brother-in-law, Josef Lange. Courtesy of the *Mozartmuseum*, Salzburg.

Mozart in 1782—83. Unfinished portrait by his brother-in-law, Josef Lange, husband of Aloysia Weber. Courtesy of the *Mozart-museum*, Salzburg.

Prague: Mozart's lodging, the *Three Golden Lions*, right, and Da
Ponte's, *zum Platteis*, left, where they stopped when writing *Don
Giovanni*. The second-floor windows, second and third from the
right, were Mozart's, from which he shouted across to Da
Ponte at the balcony window on the left.

The last portrait of Mozart. Silver-point drawing by Dora Stock, done when he visited Leipzig in 1789. Courtesy of the *Bibliothek Peters*, Leipzig.

zini, the great *castrato* for whom Wolfgang had written the *Alleluia* aria six years before. Michael and Nancy and Stephen spent a few days together at Leghorn, gave a benefit concert for themselves, and parted with assurances of a reunion at the first opportunity.

But they were brought together even more fortunately than they had dreamed, for one day early in 1783, when Michael was singing at the opera-house in Venice, he was requested to present himself to the Austrian Ambassador, Durazzo. The diplomat told him that the Emperor Joseph had wearied—after one year's trial—of his native German opera company (for which Mozart had written *Die Entführung*) and had sent his ambassador orders to recruit for him the best permanent opera company in Italy. It was to replace the German company in the *Hofburg* (the court) theatre in Vienna, and no expense was to be spared to engage artists of the first rank. Joseph never stinted foreign talents. Kelly was offered an engagement at a large salary, with free lodging, fuel, and four wax candles a day. Of course he accepted instantly, and was then told that Nancy and Stephen had already been engaged. Among the other singers were the great Mandini, and Benucci, who was considered the best *buffo* in Europe. Shortly afterward Kelly arrived in Vienna and put up at the popular White Ox where the Mozart family had stayed on their first visit. He had letters to all the influential diplomats and politicians, to Sir Robert Keith, the British Ambassador, and of course to Salieri, the czar of the musical world, who soon had him settled in fine lodgings, with a carriage at his disposal to take him to rehearsals and performances. Michael, like Nancy and Stephen Storace, was taken up with gusto and spent all his spare time in a whirl of balls, horse-races, gambling-parties, carnival masques, and drinking-bouts.

At this time Vienna was unquestionably the most brilliant court in Europe. It was, as well, the home of the light-hearted, delightful people who had fascinated sober-minded outsiders for centuries. Everything in the beautiful city—the opera, the plays, the climate, the parks, the delicious *Backhuhn* and *Schnitzel*, above all, the *joie-de-vivre* shining from the lowliest faces—made it a pleasure-ground. In addition, it was at that time the political centre of Europe, filled with brilliant statesmen and soldiers, and with nobility who came to pay their respects to the emperor. There were plenty of those gay blades—at this time nearly all British—who have always followed wit and beauty to their capitals. In a house on the Graben a group of visiting British heirs and titles had set up a dining club, where Kelly and Storace were often the guests of young Lord Barnard (great-grandson of Charles II and Barbara Villiers), or of the Earls of Wycombe, Crawford, and Granard, or of Lords Dungarvon, Strathaven, Carbery, deClifford, and others. It was also on the Graben, in a private room behind a grocer's shop, not far from Wolfgang's lodgings, that the young dandies gathered to carouse on "the finest champagne and hock in the country. There we always found excellent Parmesan cheese, anchovies, olives, and oysters. No tablecloth was allowed, but each person had a large piece of brown paper presented to him by way of a napkin. I wish I had in my cellar now the excellent wine I have seen drunk in that room. Everything was good except the oysters, which were somewhat of the stalest; none could be procured nearer than Trieste, which was so far from Vienna that they never arrived sweet; but the Germans liked them just as well stale."

In the fashionable season—from Easter until Joseph left town for Schönbrunn at midsummer—the princes of all the imperial tributaries came to the capital and opened their town palaces. These included counts and barons from Hungary and Bohemia, and other nobles from the small principalities of Germany and Italy. Entertaining was lavish, beautiful, and civilized, music being one of its most important features. The town palaces were vast square piles of grey granite or white stone, with ornate baroque façades, and great courtyard gates that always stood closed until the visitor's lackey jumped down from the box and knocked. Then they swung open to admit the gilded, plumed, and crested carriage to the courtyard, which would be closed on all four sides, though one side might be a garden wall, hiding flowers, statuary, and a fountain. These palaces were built on a tremendous scale. The formal staircase was usually of polished marble, and terminated in great corridors on which the drawing-rooms opened.

The rooms, with high ceilings and long double casement windows, were decorated in the most lavish baroque, the woodwork carved and painted white with gilt ornament, the walls covered with damasks and brocades of red, blue, green, gold-color, or rose. Sconces on the walls, and ornate hanging chandeliers glittered with thousands of crystal prisms and were lighted at night by hundreds of yellow wax candles. The grate fireplace was unusual in Austria; each room had a towering stove built into a wall from the other side of which the *Ofenheizer* tended the fire. The stoves, of common tile in ordinary rooms, were works of art in fine white and gold porcelain when designed for salons. The furniture was all French or adapted from the Louis XV and Louis XVI pieces that fashionable people brought from Paris. Rows of white-wigged flunkeys lined the halls, brilliant in the liveries of the great families, and a cup of coffee was the occasion for solemn service by a small squadron.

Kelly was by no means the only Irishman among the brilliant foreigners in Vienna. Joseph took advantage of the Gaelic temperament and perennial poverty to offer posts in his army to half a dozen Irish generals, all with good old Erin names. He supposed that the "O" prefix was part of every Irish patronymic, and used it for all Irishmen regardless. Kelly he called O'Kelly, and the puzzled typesetters who made up the programmes for the Italian opera finally decided that "Ochelli" was the best they could do with such peculiar nomenclature. "Ochelli" made friends everywhere, in society and in Salieri's musical circle which was just as brilliant in its way as the court. The flower of Italian and German composers were all in conclave and in bitter rivalry assembled. In addition to Salieri himself, who was head *Kapellmeister* in charge of opera, court positions were held by Ditters von Dittersdorf, by Martini, Joseph's favorite (really a Spaniard named Vicenzo Martín y Solar, and not connected with old Padre Martini of Bologna), and by Righini, of no great merit even then. The German contingent, none of whom succeeded in impressing Joseph in proportion to their worth, included Hoffmeister, Albrechtsberger, and Wanhal. Gluck, the great "French" composer, was on the verge of retirement, and Haydn lived in rural seclusion at Eisenstadt with Prince Esterhazy, making occasional short trips to the capital. Lastly, working hard for a place in the sun—Wolfgang. His rivals, however, considered him dangerous. He had too much genius, his music was too full of daring and novel harmony. They thought it intensely melancholy, and could not understand it. What they did not understand they disliked and feared. His musical mood was the most serious that had yet been heard, his mastery of counterpoint appalling. He had too much assurance. He had not got it from success—what, then, but his own opinion of himself could make him so confident? When the Emperor had said to him of an aria in *Die Entführung*, "It has too many notes in it," Wolfgang had answered, "Sire, there are just as many notes in it as there ought to be."

He appeared constantly at the important palaces and had learned very early not to be overawed by their grandeur, but his position was like that of any other artist invited into society. He knew perfectly well that he was only sought for his piano virtuosity, and unlike Beethoven never made blunders revealing ridiculous social ambition. That was one reason for his happiness in marriage. Where Beethoven was always agonizing over a hopeless passion for some titled and inaccessible woman, Wolfgang knew that he and Constanze had their own place in the social scale, and would be much happier if they kept it. He had pride in an assurance of established, if humble birth, and he met all people on grounds of mental equality.

One evening Kelly "went to a concert at the celebrated Kozeluch's [a Bohemian composer]. I saw there the composers Wanhal and Dittersdorf, and what was to me one of the greatest gratifications of my musical life, was there introduced to that prodigy of genius, Mozart. He favored the company by performing fantasias and capriccios on the pianoforte. His feeling, the rapidity of his fingers, the great execution and strength of his left hand particularly, and the apparent inspiration of his modulations astounded me. After this splendid performance we sat down to supper, and I had the pleasure to be placed at table between him and his wife. . . ."

Wolfgang took to his Irish neighbor at once. The two slight, blond men had much in common; mostly Wolfgang's love of good singing and Kelly's love of good music to sing; but also a genuineness of character that was not usual in the circles where they moved. Kelly sensed then the true immortality of Wolfgang, though he could not have recognized the full extent of his genius before *Figaro* was written. He saw Wolfgang first simply as "a remarkably small man, very thin and pale, with a profusion of fine fair hair of which he was rather vain. He gave me a cordial invitation to his house, of which I availed myself, and passed a great part of my time there. He always received me with kindness and hospitality. He was remarkably fond of punch, of which beverage I have seen him take copious draughts. He was also fond of billiards, and had an excellent billiard-table in his house. Many and many a game have I played with him, but always came off second best. He gave Sunday concerts at which I was never missing. He was kind-hearted and always ready to oblige, but so very particular when he played that if the slightest noise were made he instantly left off. He one day made me sit down to the piano and gave credit to my first master, who had taught me to place my hand well on the instrument. He conferred on me what I considered a high compliment. I had composed a little melody to Metastasio's canzonetta, '*Grazie agl' inganni tuoi*,' which was a great favorite wherever I sang it. It was very simple, but had the good fortune to please Mozart. He took it and composed variations upon it which were truly beautiful; and had even the further kindness and condescension to play them wherever he had an opportunity."

Wolfgang's time was now crowded with concerts and the composition of a wonderful succession of brilliant piano works. He was expected to write a new concerto or set of variations for each of his appearances and was becoming so pressed for time that his habit of putting off the actual writing until the last possible moment was growing more and more firmly fixed. Long usage had trained his memory to the accomplishment of anything he expected of it. In April, 1784, "we have here the famous Madame Regina Strinasacchi from Mantua, a very good violinist. I am just engaged upon the composition of a sonata which we are to play together on Thursday at her concert in the theatre." Just what happened to Wolfgang—whether too many guests or some more pressing piece of work—he did not get around to *writing down* the B flat violin and piano sonata (K. 454) until Wednesday evening, by which time poor Strinasacchi was frantic. He sent her part out in time for her to study it during the day, Thursday. In the evening he turned up at the theatre with a calm, cheerful grin. The Emperor was in his box, and the sonata, played without any rehearsal, was warmly received. But Joseph had been eyeing the music-rack through his lorgnette. When the sonata was finished he beckoned to Wolfgang to bring him the score. . . . As he had expected, the music-paper was blank but for the ruled staffs. "What!" exclaimed his

Mozart

Majesty, "are you up to *that* again?" Wolfgang bowed respectfully. "May it please your Majesty," he said, "there was not a single note lost." To which, certainly, no reply could be made.

He always managed, however, to find time for parties. One evening, early in 1783, he went to one at Baron Wetzlar's, where the fun was running high. The rooms were crowded. Wolfgang was making his way across to the punch bowl, smoothing his ruffles and waving to groups of friends, when Wetzlar approached him, leading by the arm a tall dark-skinned man of most singular appearance. He might have been of any age, though really not above thirty-five, for his remarkably long, bony jaw jutted out below a pair of thin lips sunken deep into that part of his skull where his teeth should have been. Above this intaglio a great beak of a nose divided two glowing, coal-black eyes, deeply recessed under a fine, intelligent brow. The twinkle and play of the eyes offset heavy lines caused by the collapse—for want of inner support—of the originally ample cheeks, whose high bones made two additional accents. The whole impression was of a face of startling length and narrowness, redeemed by the strength of the jaw and brow. The man advanced with a remarkably awkward gait, swinging a cane from hands clasped behind his back, throwing the lower part of his body forward, and carrying his shoulders in an exaggerated arc. He was dressed in the height of dandified excess, his gangling figure enveloped in embroidery, batiste, laces, cut-velvet, and fancy buttons; and draped with a profusion of glittering trinkets which put Wolfgang, in his best frock-coat and satin waistcoat crossed by two watch-chains, quite out of the sartorial running.

Mozart

Speaking Italian, Wetzlar said, 'Wolfgang, I want to present to you the Abbé Da Ponte—Lorenzo Da Ponte—the new court opera-poet.'

Wolfgang bowed and murmured his pleasure. The Abbé—(Abbé, in such a turnout?)—also bowed, very elaborately, and in a broad Venetian accent with a strong lisp occasioned by the escape of air through his gums, protested his extreme delight.

If Wolfgang had not already known who this eccentricity was, and if he had not been aware that the man was considered an able poet, he might well have allowed his lips to twitch. He had already heard, however, of Da Ponte's recent arrival from Dresden, about the same time that Durazzo, under orders from the court chamberlain, Count Rosenberg, was rounding up Kelly and the new Italian opera company in Venice. Nothing was known of Da Ponte in Vienna except that he bore a note to Salieri from the poet Mazzolà, a note so glowing in its eulogy of "my beloved Da Ponte" that Salieri had no trouble in putting its bearer into immediate favor with the Emperor. It soon leaked out that Da Ponte had left Dresden at the urgent advice of those who saw probable dire consequences in his having had illicit relations simultaneously with his landlady and her two young daughters. He had been expelled or had absconded from a succession of previous stopping-places under similar, if not identical circumstances. He had managed to eat and to acquire his gorgeous raiment by a series of escapades not much different from those of Signor Giacomo Casanova, whose acquaintance he had made some time since. He had also enhanced his reputation by the composition of numerous poems of all kinds, both in Italian and in the Venetian dialect, and at the time of his abrupt departure from Dresden had been engaged in the pious work of translating some of the Psalms.

He was born in 1749, in the Ghetto of Ceneda, in the Venetian State. His parents were orthodox Jews, surnamed Conegliano, which his father prefixed for him with the honest Hebrew, Emanuel. But when little Emanuel Conegliano was twelve, his mother died. Shortly afterward his father married a Catholic woman for whose sake he and all his children were baptized, Da Ponte adopted for the family name, and proper Christian names distributed as needed. Lorenzo was educated by the Church, and had started a career as an Abbé, when youth, the devil, or his own inclinations coupled with the atmosphere of Venice caused him to plunge into a whirlpool of sin which swept him all over Central Europe. He showed no desire to extricate himself until in 1792—still an Abbé—he married. The concomitant settling-down did not come until much later. He crossed to London with his bride, where he hoped to turn his comradeship of Vienna days with Kelly, the Storaces and Wolfgang's pupil Thomas Attwood, to account. He was not only unsuccessful, but the jaws of the sponging-house yawned so wide that Mister Da Ponte thought it well to move on again. Having closed to himself the doors of every Continental capital, he had small choice of destination; he must go west. He arrived, accordingly, at the Philadelphia Custom House on the morning of June 4, 1805, and eventually appeared in New York, where in Riley's bookstore on Broadway he struck up an acquaintance with Clement Moore, the future author of "The Night Before Christmas." Da Ponte's extraordinary education and complete mastery of classic literature, as well as his charm and exquisite manners, made him the lion of the social season of 1807. His wife, the former Anne Celeste Grahl, was a perfect complement, and they prospered, though life never became uneventful for them. He gave private lessons in Italian to the fashionable New York youth and through Mr. Moore, one of the Trustees, became the first Professor of Italian at Columbia College. He also supported himself by, among other ventures, farming, brandy-distilling, and a grocery-store. As a citizen of the new world, he lived in various remote parts of Pennsylvania and New Jersey, and left a long and talented progeny which—half adhering to the Holy Catholic Church and half to various Protestant denominations—continues to flourish to the present day.

Lorenzo was a crony of Casanova's, and his admirer to the point of imitation. At their last meeting, at Dux, he had found Casanova writing his Memoirs, which put ideas into Lorenzo's head. The fruit of those ideas appeared in New York in 1826, and it is in them that he describes his thoughts as he was introduced to Wolfgang that night in Vienna "at the house of Baron Wetzlar, his great admirer and friend. Though gifted with talents superior perhaps to those of any other composer in the world, past, present, or future, Mozart had, thanks to the intrigues of his rivals, never been able to exercise his divine genius in Vienna, and was living there unknown and obscure, like a priceless jewel buried in the bowels of the earth and hiding the refulgent excellence of its splendors. I can never remember, without exultation and complacency, that it was to my perseverance and firmness alone that Europe and the world in great part owe the exquisite vocal compositions of

Mozart

that admirable genius. The unfairness and envy of journalists, gazeteers, and especially of biographers of Mozart have never permitted them to concede such glory to an Italian; but all Vienna, all those who knew him and me in Germany, Bohemia, and Saxony, all his family and more than anyone else, Baron Wetzlar, under whose roof the first scintillation of that noble flame was allowed to glow, must bear me witness to the truth which I now reveal."

Lorenzo had been but a short time in Vienna when he received his appointment as court theatre-poet, for "Salieri managed the affair so deftly that I went to Caesar for my first audience, not to ask a grace, but to give thanks for one. Before this occasion I had never spoken to any monarch. Everyone had told me that Joseph was the most humane and affable of princes. Yet I could not appear before him without the greatest awe and perturbation. But the cheery expression of his face, his suaveness of intonation, and above all the utter simplicity of his manner and his dress, nothing of which I had dreamed of in a king, not only restored my self-possession, but left me scarcely aware that I was standing before an Emperor. I had heard said that he often judged men by their faces: mine could not have displeased him, such the grace with which he received me and the benignness with which he accorded me that first audience.

"Of great curiosity on all subjects, he put to me many questions relating to my country, my studies, the reasons that had brought me to Vienna. I replied to everything briefly and to the point, whereat he seemed to be favorably impressed. Finally he asked me how many plays I had written, to which I responded frankly:

" 'None, Sire!'

Mozart

" 'Fine! Fine!' he rejoined smiling, 'We shall have a virgin muse!' "

Yet this was the prince who could leave Wolfgang the only composer in Vienna without recognition or position. Joseph was without doubt a big man, the finest of the enlightened eighteenth-century rulers, a truly great patron of the arts. But in many ways he was ignorant because of a miserable education, and his early training had made him dangerously insincere. Surprisingly, he lacked the arrogance and despotism of the Habsburgs, and his disarming personal charm endeared him to all the artists who knew him. Yet he treated them and most other dependants so meanly that Horace Walpole called him "His Imperial Rapacity."

At this time he was only forty-two years old, but he lived his private life like an old and saddened man. He had no queen—his adored first wife, Isabella of Parma, had been twenty years dead, and his loathed second consort, Josefa of Bavaria whom he married for political reasons, died in 1767 after having made him completely wretched. After that, aside from the usual shrugging *petits amours*, he took no pleasure in any women except a few of the older great ladies of Court society, to whose houses he liked to go as a private guest. Countess Thun was honored by this friendship, as well as Countesses Liechtenstein, Schwarzenberg, and Lobkowicz. Joseph's real pleasure was attending concerts and the opera, usually in his own theatre, but often outside. Hardly a musical event of importance took place that the Emperor was not in his box from the beginning until the end. He did not need book-learning to adore music.

He held his court most of the year in the Hofburg, the

town residence whose jumble of four centuries' architecture had settled into a thing of remarkable beauty. Within its walls were thirteenth-century courtyards, Renaissance galleries, baroque banquet-halls, sweeping corridors and grand staircases in marble magnificence to the taste of *Le Grand Monarque*; the bewitchingly beautiful court theatre in the style of Joseph's own time; the festive *Redoutensaal* with its frosty white walls, glittering crystal chandeliers, huge mirrors, satiny *parquet* and graceful musicians' gallery. There was a fine court for *Jeu de Paume* (tennis), the Emperor's favorite game, and salons given over to the amusement of visitors from the noble and artistic worlds of Europe. Every afternoon at five, after his solitary, invariable dinner of "one dish, boiled bacon, which the people, from his partiality to it, called *caizer fleisch*," Joseph might be seen walking in the corridor adjoining his dining-room, dressed in a green or a white uniform with red facings, and "whilst there, was accessible to the complaints of the meanest of his subjects; he heard them with complaisance and was ever ready to redress their grievances." As he listened, whether to a woodman from the *Wienerwald* protesting his landlord's rapacity, or to the widow of a court artist seeking a pension, he was "continually putting chocolate drops, which he took from his waistcoat pocket," into his mouth. He was a tall, handsome man with a kind, intelligent face. He wore his own hair, simply curled and plaited behind, not powdering it except for formal dress. The white dress wig had gone out entirely by now, and powdering for everyday costume was already on the wane, except with such sticklers as Prince Kaunitz who, at his daily toilette, "had four valets with powder puffs puffing away at him until his head was powdered to

Mozart

his satisfaction, while he walked about his dressing-room in a mask." Kaunitz was a legacy, with all his ideas, from the reign of Maria Theresa, but Joseph, with the greatest determination, applied himself to changing the *ancien régime*. Whether it was a radical public move like the suppression of monasteries, or a radical private one like allowing only one servant in his dining-room, his institutions always occasioned remark.

Rising at five in the morning was one of the Emperor's austerities, and his example was followed, certainly with no great joy, but very generally. Even Wolfgang had his domestic troubles in connection with the fashionable rising-hour. He had "out of pure pity to help her when she was a stranger in Vienna" taken a low-born girl from Salzburg into his house as parlor-maid. She had addressed a letter to her mother in such fantastic spelling that it could not be posted, so ". . . I said I would address it afresh for her. Being inquisitive, but rather to read more of this beautiful composition than to penetrate any secrets, I opened the letter. In it she complained that she had to go to bed too late and get up too early—but I should have thought one could get enough sleep between eleven o'clock and six— that is seven hours, after all. We ourselves do not go to bed till twelve, and get up at half-past five or even five, as we go to the Augarten almost every morning early. She further complained about the food, with the impertinent remark that we should starve, all four of us, as my wife, I, the cook, and she had less to eat here than she and her mother had between them at home!"

How Wolfgang could afford two or sometimes even three servants is plain when one discovers he had "promised her 12 gulden a year and she was quite content with

Mozart

it, though she now complains about it in her letter. And what is it she has to do? To clear the table, hand the dishes round and take them to the kitchen, and help my wife to dress and undress! Moreover, apart from her sewing, she is the clumsiest and stupidest creature in the world." Wolfgang was now becoming so wrought up over his household she-devil that he was thoroughly enjoying his own letter. "She cannot even light a fire, let alone make coffee,—things which a girl who pretends to be a parlor-maid should be able to do. We gave her a gulden and the very next day she asked for more money. I made her"—says the sober, systematic householder!—"give me an account of her expenses, and found that beer made up the greater part of them! A certain Herr Johannes travelled here with her, but he dare not show his face at my house any longer. Twice, when we were from home he came here and ordered in wine, and the girl, who is not used to drinking wine, filled herself so full that she could not walk without support, and the last time was sick all over her bed! Who in the world would keep such a person under such conditions? . . . P. S. Pray do contrive to send me the buckles by the next diligence. I am burning with eagerness to see them."

In August, Nannerl was married to Baron Berchtold zu Sonnenberg, and went to his home at St. Gilgen, close to Salzburg, where she spent the rest of a long life with her memories. Wolfgang and Constanze did not go to the wedding, but Wolfgang wrote Nannerl a long letter of congratulation and advice. He was greatly concerned for Leopold " . . . who will now be left so utterly alone!" Wolfgang wanted to see his father retired on a pension from the Archbishop, to spend the rest of his life in peace and quiet. Certain twinges of conscience may have had something to do with this empty hope. "And now I send a thousand good wishes from Vienna to Salzburg, more especially that you two may live together as happily as—we two! So accept a little piece of good advice from the poetic treasure-house of my brains. Listen:

> In marriage you will learn to fathom
> Much that before was half a riddle;
> Experience soon will teach to you
> What Eve herself had once to do
> 'Ere she gave birth to Cain and Abel.
> Yet, sister, those same marriage-dues
> Are what your heart will gladly choose,
> For trust my word, they are not heavy!
> Yet every object has two faces,
> And wedlock, bringing many graces,
> Brings also troubles in a bevy.
> So when your man an angry brow,
> Which, as deserved, you'll now allow,
> Discloses to your sight,
> Think, ''Tis but menfolks' freakish way.'
> Say, 'Lord, thy will be done by day
> But mine be done by night!'
>   Your faithful brother, W. A. Mozart."

Wolfgang had good reason to wish for Nannerl a marriage as happy as his own. His had turned out well, from the personal point of view, and if he could have stabilized his life economically he would have been a happy man. He was beginning by now to adjust himself to minor responsibilities, and knew that his own great failing lay in his handling of money. In the early spring of 1784 he came home one day waving a little quarto blank-book.

'What is that, Wolfgang?'

Mozart

'My account-book!' he exclaimed proudly. 'See—it has lines in it to put down what you receive, and what you spend—*undsoweiter*. Isn't that fine?'

Constanze smiled. 'What are you going to do with it?'

'Do with it? Why, keep my accounts in it, of course! It will show me how much I earn and how much we spend and where all those *verdammte Gulden und Kreutzer* go when they take wings and fly away!'

He sat down at his table, tucked up his ruffles, dipped his quill in the ink and pulled a long sheet of paper toward him. Constanze looked over his shoulder from time to time. On this paper he entered all items of income since the first of the year; so much for lessons to Attwood, so much from Barbara Ployer (for whom he had just written the brilliant G major piano concerto, K. 453); so much from Artaria, the music publisher, for the C minor piano sonata (K. 457), so much from Prince Kaunitz for concerts, so much from Count Zichy. With every item neatly entered, it made a respectable total. Then he began entering expenditures in his new account-book, and every day went to his table and carefully noted every copper he had spent. On May-day, 1784, he came home with flowers for Constanze, then wrote in his book, "Two lilies of the valley . . . 1 Kreutzer." One day he was carried away by a miracle. He was passing a pet shop and would have gone by when he stopped dead in his tracks, transfixed by the singing of a bird. Wolfgang blinked, cocked his head toward the shop door, stared blankly. *It wasn't possible!* But the bird was singing the Allegretto theme from his G major concerto, written just five weeks before. Wolfgang drew a long breath and dashed into the shop.

'*Wo ist dieser Vogel?*' he cried. 'Am I crazy?'

Mozart

The proprietor took down a cage, its occupant a starling.
Wolfgang peered inside.

'How much?' he said.

'Vier-und-Dreissig Kreutzer.'

Wolfgang pulled out his purse, counted the money, laid
it on the counter and seized the cage. He rushed home.
'Stanzi!' he cried. 'Stanzi-Marini, look what I have here!'

The *Vogel-Stahrl* having survived the reception, Wolfgang entered it in the book. Under its price he wrote its
song, identical, but for the G sharp and the grace-notes,
with the first five measures of his Allegretto. Then he
wrote, *"Das war schön."* If the chronology of this coin-
cidence were reversed, it would be much easier to believe,
for Wolfgang might easily have borrowed his theme from
the bird. But this was not the case. He had gone so far in
his new passion for order as to begin, along with his accounts, a complete catalogue of his works, which he kept
nearly the rest of his life, though the accounts soon died of
neglect. He had entered the concerto in the catalogue with
its pink flowered cover on April 12, and the starling in the
account-book on May 27, 1784.

XII

1784-1785

IN the fall of that year Wolfgang was distractedly busy with domestic affairs. He had expected Constanze's confinement in the first days of October, but on the twenty-first of September she gave birth to their second son, Karl. Once again they had to have Caecilia Weber, most officious of mothers-in-law, come in to take charge, to wear the keys and give the orders and cause the cook to rebel. Her daughter Sophie came along too. Clasping his spinning head in his hands, Wolfgang ran downstairs and asked his landlord, Johann von Trattner, to stand godfather to the infant. Then he rushed out to find a wet-nurse and get a housemaid to replace Loiserl from Salzburg. Each time the baby fell asleep under the ministrations of scowling, tiptoeing women with pursed lips, Kelly or Stephen Storace or Jacquin would come bounding upstairs clamoring for a game of billiards. Caecilia would stick her large face through a door and hiss—'Chut!'—but not soon enough to prevent howls from the cradle. The midwife demanded her money, the apothecary pressed for his. Wolfgang thought the butcher's and baker's bills big enough for a regiment. Having spent a lazy summer he must scramble now to pay for everything. But how? He scratched his head. Hah! Dances always brought quick cash. Immediately he sat down in the corner and began turning out sheet after sheet of manuscript; *Fünf Menuette, Sechs Kontretänze, Zwei Menuette mit einge-*

fügten Kontretänze (K. 461 to 463). He sold them readily for cash and then hastened home in a mood to settle all the bills. But entering the crowded rooms again, he stopped; women dashing this way and that (where had all these women come from, anyway?), clashing pans in the kitchen, a soup-plate on his clavier, baby-linen on the best armchair. He sighed and thrust his hand in his pocket, where it encountered his newly filled purse. Wonderful idea! Why not move, right now, to a really good lodging, some place with room enough to escape all the women and dishes! He ran into the bedroom.

'Stänzerl,' he said, sitting down on the bed and putting his arms around his pale wife, 'tell me, darling, do you feel well enough to move?'

'To *what? Ach*, Wolfi!' She closed her eyes and sighed.

'But, Stanzi, to a lovely clean place with big rooms and a——'

'Again, Wolfi?' She pulled her shawl across her breast. 'Oh, no!'

He leaned down and began to kiss her face and neck. He tickled her under the chin, gently bit her ear.

'Nah, Stanzi, don't be a tease. Don't scold your Wolfi.' One by one he kissed the tips of all her fingers. She opened her black eyes and began to giggle.

'Do you feel well enough, darling? Shall I go out and find a *wunderschönes Häuschen* for my little wife and big son? Say yes, *Liebling*. There, that's a good girl. I knew you would.'

Again he seized his tricorne and hurried out. He househunted expertly, and soon found what he wanted, across the Stefansplatz in the Schulerstrasse, 846, *am Carmi-naschen Hause* (to-day Schulerstrasse 8). As much room

Mozart

as he needed, on the first floor, which would be easy for Constanze, and the rental four hundred sixty gulden a year. Marvellous!

'We will be here next week,' he told his new landlord as he paid the first rent. 'See that the rooms are ready for us.'

They moved in with a flourish and Wolfgang felt so pleased with himself that he wrote a piano concerto, in B flat (K. 456), as breezy as his own spirits. Then he sobered down a little, and five days later, in serious vein as became such a responsible paterfamilias, he wrote the famous C minor piano sonata (K. 457). He dedicated it to his pupil, Frau Therese von Trattner, perhaps as consolation for his moving away from her husband's house on the Graben. The following year he wrote the C minor (K. 475), the noblest and greatest of his fantasias, and sent it to her to be played with the sonata, as it has been ever since. The Trattners remained intimate friends, so much so that they had the rôle of godparents to all of Wolfgang's children, Johann standing up at the font for the boys and Therese for the girls.

Evidently Wolfgang had chosen his new home more wisely than any previous one, for they stayed there longest. As soon as Constanze felt stronger she took over the household management with more determination than she had ever shown or indeed would ever show again. They recommenced their Sunday morning quartet parties which had died in the confusion of Karl's birth and the moving, and Wolfgang made serious plans for a winter of hard work—clavier concerts on a big scale, and the corresponding mass of new music to be played at them. He was also very eager to finish the set of six quartets for "Papa"

Mozart

Haydn. On the 9th of November he finished and entered in his catalogue the fourth of the series, the beloved "hunting quartet" in B flat (K. 458). Toward the close of the year Leopold responded to Wolfgang's repeated invitations and promised to come to Vienna for a visit early in February. Wolfgang reacted like a small boy. He rushed to finish all the work he had planned, that he might have plenty of new compositions to prove to Papa that he was industrious and in earnest. His subscription list for the forthcoming Lenten concerts was larger than ever, and his engagement-book filled with concert appointments at noble houses. But ready money was, as always, lacking. The midwife, the tradesmen, and the dray-driver were still clamoring and threatening. On November 20, Wolfgang borrowed money, light-heartedly, sure of making enough during the winter to pay this debt and keep ahead of future ones.

But he was not altogether satisfied. It was hard to sit by and watch the public receive and applaud the mediocre operas that Salieri and Martini wrote for the court theatre. His *Entführung* was still given from time to time, but Wolfgang knew how much slighter it was than any opera he might write now, if only he could get the chance. Paisiello turned up in Vienna on his way back from a long tenure as court composer to Catherine of Russia—who had rewarded him in her usual manner—and, with the poet Casti, was making a strong bid for the operatic crown. The whole pack of Italians wrangled and intrigued among themselves, yet let the slightest whisper of favor toward a German composer reach their ears, and they formed a solid phalanx of underhanded opposition formidable enough to discourage any man, certainly one like Wolfgang. At Baron Wetzlar's, where he went very frequently, he got all the current reports of the dirty dealings in the operatic world. No one tried to belittle Wolfgang as a pianist, but Salieri and the others had succeeded in convincing Joseph that Mozart could not write an opera. And Wolfgang, spending half his time with Kelly and the Storaces and Da Ponte, could hardly concentrate on his parade of brilliant concertos and sonatas, so eager was he to have an opera to write.

Wolfgang was inclined to think more of Paisiello than of the other Italians; ". . . nobody better can be recommended for those who seek light music." One of Paisiello's operas, *Il Barbiere di Seviglia*, had been set to a libretto adapted from a comedy that Beaumarchais had written for the court theatre in Paris. At Wetzlar's, one evening, Wolfgang heard that Beaumarchais had written a sequel to the *Barbiere*. It had been produced in Paris the previous April.

'And wonderful,' his informant assured him. 'Dirty, oh yes, but you know—the real thing. A touch here, a smack there, a little *tendresse*——'

Wolfgang licked his lips.

'And then it has ideas—something you can put your teeth into.'

The Emperor, it seemed, on the grounds of indecency, had refused permission for *Le Mariage de Figaro ou La Folle Journée* to be played at the court in Vienna. Wolfgang bought the book at once. He took it home and read it, jumping up from his chair every little while to wave it over his head and cry, 'Stanzi, come and listen to this. *"C'est mon époux! grands dieux! Vous sans manteau, le cou et les bras nus, seul avec moi, cet air de désordre, un*

Mozart

billet reçu, sa jalousie . . ." Stanzi, can't you see that scene? *Du lieber Gott,* I must have this for an opera!'

'What can you do about it? The Emperor won't have it on the stage.'

For the moment there was nothing to do. Meanwhile he hurried to finish his quartets. Haydn would be in town for the midwinter, and he wanted to have them ready. On the 10th of January he completed the fifth, in A (K. 464), and four days later the sixth and last in C (K. 465). The brief Adagio opening of the latter, in A minor, is stranger and more daring in harmony than anything Wolfgang had written, and caused a storm of protest everywhere. The music-sellers in Italy to whom Wolfgang's publisher Artaria sent scores returned them as being full of mistakes, and one Hungarian prince, after scolding his *Kapelle* for not knowing their music, tore up the sheets when he read them. As a matter of fact, there is more in those twenty-two bars to suggest the musical departures of the past ten years than in much of the radical music of the nineteenth century. When Wolfgang was finishing up the quartets a friend asked him why he was so determined to dedicate them to Haydn.

"Because," Wolfgang answered, "I consider it my duty. It was from Haydn that I learned to write quartets."

Leopold arrived from Salzburg on the 10th of February. Constanze made him comfortable in a pleasant room with a good writing-table, where he wrote Nannerl detailed accounts of everything he heard and saw. Constanze made the supreme effort of her career as a housekeeper, prompting the one commendatory remark Leopold ever made about her—and that indirectly. Toward the end of his visit he was moved to conjecture that "if my son has no debts to pay"—happy Papa in his ignorance!—"he will now be able to place 2,000 florins in the bank. The money is certainly there, and the household management, as far as food and drink are concerned, is economical in the highest degree." Leopold could not have been able to stay in his son's house for a day without making every detail of the routine his own business. It is easy to imagine him poking into cupboards, questioning Constanze about the servants' habits, telling her how she should care for Karl, reminding her how Nannerl kept house at St. Gilgen, and how she practiced several hours every day and looked after five stepchildren as well. Constanze bore his didactics with surprising grace. She did only one thing in the entire nine years of her marriage that was a helpless surrender to a wave of rancor. She burned every letter that Leopold wrote Wolfgang from the day of their marriage until Papa's death.

On Friday, the day after Leopold's arrival, Wolfgang gave the first of his six season subscription concerts in a hall on the Mehlgrube. The admission price for the series was three ducats. He played ". . . a new and admirable concerto, on which the copyist was at work yesterday when I arrived, and your brother had not time to play the rondo once through, because he was obliged to superintend the copying. The concerto is in D minor (K. 466)." Wolfgang played half at sight, and half by memory, with an improvised cadenza that brought down the house. Next day he played at the opera house at a benefit for the singer Signora Laschi; this time it was the new B flat, of the moving-day. ". . . I was well placed in a good box, and had the pleasure to hear all the changes in the instruments so admirably that the tears came into my eyes. On your

Mozart

brother's departure the Emperor took off his hat, complimented him, and cried, *'Bravo*, Mozart!' As he went out after playing, the clapping and applause were without end."

After the concert they hurried back to the Schulerstrasse. Wolfgang had invited all his close friends to a party, one he had been planning for months. It was partly in honor of Leopold, but mainly the occasion for presenting Haydn with the finished quartets. Poor old Leopold, now sixty-six, was dressed in his best velvet and satin, his gouty old knees encased in silk stockings, his lame, knobby feet in buckled shoes, an old-fashioned white dress wig above his lined, sunken face. His cold gray eyes warmed with pleasure as Wolfgang came across the room arm in arm with "Papa" Haydn. The two Papas discussed Wolfgang affectionately, Leopold with a touch of arrogance, Haydn with genuine tenderness.

'It is good of you to be so kind,' Leopold said.

Haydn's handsome brown face beamed, his graceful lips curved in a warm smile. His large, dark eyes sparkled. "I tell you," he said, "calling God to witness and speaking as a man of honor, that your son is the greatest composer I know, either personally or by repute. He has taste, and in addition, the most complete understanding of composition."

Leopold's eyes clouded and he made his way across to a seat where he could listen to the three last quartets, which Wolfgang, Haydn, and the two Tindi brothers were now preparing to play. Wolfgang had never cared for the violin, but at these quartet parties, both at his own house and elswhere, would always play if there were no one else available, or if he were asked particularly. Stephen

Mozart

Storace gave a party during the season at which quartets were played, the ensemble consisting of Haydn, first violin, Dittersdorf, second, Wanhal, 'cello, and Wolfgang, tenor. "Truly," says Kelly, "there were giants on the earth in those days."

Giants, perhaps, but not all visible to Joseph's imperial eye. Leopold plainly showed his nervousness at Wolfgang's lack of a fixed appointment, even though he masked it in glowing accounts of the concert triumphs. Every two or three days he had some new success to report to Nannerl. "Since I have been here, your brother's pianoforte has been carried at least twelve times to the theatre, or to Prince Kaunitz', or Count Zichy's. He has had a great *forte piano* pedal made, which stands under the instrument, is about three spans long, and amazingly heavy." Wolfgang had earned himself the reputation of the greatest pianist in Vienna; some said, in all Europe. His hands were small and white, and surprisingly plump for all the exercise he gave them. He often had cramps in his fingers from holding his pen for hours on end, and frequently had to rush from his writing-table to the concert hall without time to limber up his fingers or rest. He was so unused to any other manual effort that it annoyed him to handle a sharp knife at table, and usually he had Constanze cut up his meat for him.

He had inherited nothing of Leopold's pedantry and dictatorial pedagogy, but he revealed enough strength of opinion about piano technique to mark him as his father's son. He was uncompromisingly impatient of careless, hasty, or affected playing. When he played the piano, his head, body, arms and hands were as quiet as he could hold them. The pianist's hands, he thought, should be so light and supple as to turn difficult passages into "flowing oil." To him the worst fault of all was hurrying and disregarding the tempo. Repeatedly he damned players who made brilliant, flashing, and inaccurate effects. The most pointed of all these remarks were directed at the great pianist Clementi, of the perennial *Gradus ad Parnassum*, whom Wolfgang had encountered the year before his marriage, when he was first trying to establish himself in Vienna. Joseph brought the two together at court in a piano-playing contest in which he bet on Mozart, and won. Clementi's account of the affair began with an impression of "an individual whose elegant attire led me to mistake him for an imperial valet-de-chambre. But we had no sooner entered into conversation than it turned on musical topics, and we soon recognized in each other with sincere pleasure brother artists." His account of the contest itself could not possibly be more polite, more gracious, or more fair; Wolfgang's is shockingly rude. After each had preluded and played a sonata of his own (Clementi's, in D, being the theme which Wolfgang later took for the overture to *Die Zauberflöte*), "the Grand Duchess produced some sonatas by Paisiello (in his own miserable manuscript), of which I was to play the allegro and Clementi the andante and rondo. Then we each took a subject and carried it out on two pianofortes. . . . Clementi is a good player, and that is all one can say. He plays well as far as the execution of his right hand is concerned. His forte lies in passages in thirds. But he has not an atom of taste or feeling, in fact he is a mere mechanist." Later, "Clementi is a charlatan, like all the Italians! Every one who plays them [Clementi's sonatas] must be aware that as compositions they are valueless. . . . I should strongly advise you not to be too taken with these, for they are the ruin of a firm and quiet hand, and would soon take away its lightness, flexibility, and flowing rapidity." And as he grew older Wolfgang became even more outspoken in criticism of pianists as well as of composers and singers, until he finally found himself in the midst of cacti whose seeds had been his own biting words.

One of his victims was Leopold Kozeluch, just such a brilliant and slipshod pianist and composer as Wolfgang always piqued with his rapier. Kozeluch was the small sort of man who made conspicuous criticisms of all the artists who were obviously greater than he. Once when he and Wolfgang were listening together to a Haydn quartet, Kozeluch found fault with each successive phrase, finally saying, "I should never have done it that way."

Wolfgang's eyes blazed. "Nor should I," he said quietly, "but do you know why? Because neither you nor I would have had so good an idea."

On the other hand, age had softened several of Leopold Mozart's bigotries. Though he still liked to dictate, both in spiritual as well as in practical matters, he was readier to allow Wolfgang the right to think for himself. More surprising still, he was willing to be influenced by his son, so actively that during his visit to Vienna he went with him to several meetings of the Freemasons, and finally joined the order under Wolfgang's sponsorship. Submitting to a credo of brotherly love, gentleness, and mutual confidence was a marked change from lifelong adherence to the uncompromising dictation of the Church. Just how much consolation he got out of it is questionable; Leopold's disappointments were sunk much too deep to be eradicable by any process of thought. Yet, in spite of his excessive

Mozart

worry about Wolfgang's unsettled condition, and his ever active dislike of Constanze, he came nearer to Wolfgang's heart as a Masonic brother than he had since the days of the bedside chair and "*oragna figata fà*." As the time drew near for him to return home, he increased in tenderness to Wolfgang and his family. On the 25th of April, having embraced and blessed his too-beloved son for the last time, he feebly hoisted himself into the coach, and was carried back to loneliness in Salzburg.

Wolfgang had just completed his most successful concert season, with a wonderful list of piano music and the six quartets to add to his catalogue. But bill-collectors still came regularly. Nuisance though they were, Wolfgang was much more troubled by the apparent hopelessness of getting an opera to write. The more he composed for instruments, the more desperately he longed to write for the voice. As if to console himself, certainly because he needed the expression, he wrote five of his loveliest German songs, among them *Das Veilchen*, set to Goethe's enchanting lyric. The privy-councillor Anton Klein of Mannheim had sent Wolfgang a tentative opera libretto in German, inviting him to compose it, but Wolfgang did not jump at that. He wanted to compose for Joseph, in the first place, and he wanted even more to have a chance at an Italian opera to show the local plotters what he—a German— could do on their ground. He grew more and more bitter over the plight of German opera in Vienna, where his own *Entführung* could hardly hold the stage single-handed. Wolfgang was intensely patriotic, and unable to reconcile himself to the fact that his emperor, whom he loved, could so completely lend himself to intrigues that spelled the death of German art. Wolfgang had not only German loyalty, but a German artistic conscience, and when he excused himself to Klein for his long delay in deciding about the proposed score, he told the simple story of his hopes, ideals, and loyalties:

"A man of so much insight and experience as yourself will know even better than I that these things [possible libretti], however carefully and attentively read, need reading through not only once, but many times. Hitherto I have not had time to read it through even once without interruption! All that I can say for the present is that I should not like to part with it yet. Will you therefore pray entrust the piece to my keeping a little longer? In case I should be inclined to compose upon it, I should like to know beforehand whether its production has been arranged for anywhere, for a work like this, as regards both poetry and music, deserves better than to be completed and yet come to nothing!"

Wolfgang had paused there to look back over his own years of hard labor brought to nothing by intrigue and deception. At twenty-nine he was finally beginning to reap the bitter benefit of his experiences. He was becoming cautious, if never very wise. With utter cynicism he sat by and watched the aimless gyrations of those who were attempting to found an independent German opera in Vienna.

"It is to be opened early in October. I for my part have no great hopes of its success. According to present plans it looks more as if they were attempting to bring final ruin upon German opera, which at present is suffering only a temporary eclipse, than to raise it up and preserve it. My sister-in-law, Madame Lange, is the only one who is to join the German opera company. Madame Cavallieri, Adamberger, Madame Täuber, all Germans of whom

Germany may well be proud, are to stay at the Italian opera—to compete against their own fellow-countrymen! . . . The tale of German singers, male and female, is soon told. . . . I cannot but feel that the directors of our theatre will prove too parsimonious and too little patriotic to pay large sums to get strangers to come here when they could get better singers on the spot, or at least as good, for nothing. . . . Most unfortunately, both orchestral and theatrical directors have been retained who by a combination of ignorance and inactivity have done much to ruin their own enterprise. If there were but *one* patriot on the board—the affair would take on quite another aspect! Then perhaps the vigorously sprouting German national theatre would actually begin to flower—and what an everlasting shame it would be for Germany if we Germans were seriously to begin to think German, to act as Germans, to talk German, and even—to sing German!

"Pray do not take it amiss, my dear *Herr Geheimrath*, if in my zeal I have perhaps gone too far. Secure that I was speaking to a true German, I gave my feelings rein, a thing unhappily so seldom possible in these days that one might boldly follow each such heart-outpouring with a drinking-bout without danger of doing any injury to one's health!"

Without waiting for "heart-outpourings," however, Wolfgang attended many a drinking-bout among the taverns with Kelly, Storace, and Da Ponte. These were his most warm, most colorful friends. To them he added his Masonic Lodge, where he joined in the rites with unreserved fervor, more German, more serious, more idealistic there than anywhere, and felt that he was understood by his simple Masonic brothers. About this time two of the important brothers died, a Mecklenburg, and an Esterhazy, and Wolfgang was asked by the lodge to write the memorial music. His *Maurerische Trauermusik* (K. 477)

Mozart

is rich with deep Teutonic feeling, utterly sincere, like all his Masonic compositions, and beautiful in a serene, intellectual way. Shortly before he wrote it, the Society of Widows and Orphans of Musicians was preparing to hold a festival and asked Wolfgang to write a cantata. They wanted it very soon. Wolfgang pursed his lips and whistled.

'It cannot be done,' he said, shaking his head. 'I need more time.'

'Oh, surely you can do it, *Herr Kapellmeister*. You can do anything you wish!'

Wolfgang thought a moment, then said, 'Very well. Perhaps I can. Give me the text.'

He rummaged through his manuscripts until he found the unfinished C minor mass that he had written for Constanze. He took the *Kyrie* and the *Gloria* and set the Italian words of *Davidde Penitente* (K. 469) to them. Then he added several parts from other unfinished works, and a few themes which were sketched in his notebook. Finished, the cantata had ten parts and astonishing unity, ending in a tremendous choral fugue. Wolfgang was satisfied and so were the widows and orphans.

Then he went back to German songs. He loved his small library and often came across a poem that he could not resist setting to music. He was not like Schubert, of whom Robert Schumann said that if no other text had offered itself, he would have set a handbill to music. Wolfgang was inclined to see more in the scope of a song than an opportunity for beautiful melody. After passing through the musical formalities of his early Italian training, and the conventional operatic forms as he used them in *Idomeneo*, he was now groping for a keyhole into which

Mozart

he might fit the key that would open the door to a new conception of opera. That was, if it could be summed up in a word, characterization. More and more surely Wolfgang felt his way; and now he knew that he needed but a libretto worthy of his idea, and a production worthy of his music, to offer the world something more than a series of beautiful arias in stereotyped form. He did not dare give himself up to hope. Desultorily, because he had to, he wrote some concert music—a piano quartet (K. 478), a concerto (K. 482), a sonata (K. 481), one or two choral songs (K. 483 and 484). He fiddled with his sketch-book. Frequently he took down Beaumarchais' *Figaro* from the shelf and sat at his table turning the pages, sometimes chuckling, sometimes biting his lip, frowning, burying his blond head on his arm.

But one day he had a surprise visit from Da Ponte.

'Well, see who the devil has brought! How goes it, Lorenzo?'

'Ah, *bene, bene*. And you, are you hard at work?'

Wolfgang shook his head. 'I should be. But I haven't much heart for it. What have you been doing?'

'Finishing *Burbero* for Martini. I have had the devil's own time.'

'With Martini?'

'No, he is really very decent, Wolfgang. I like him. But with that damned Rosenberg.'

Rosenberg was the court chamberlain who arranged for the writing, composing and producing of all operas at the Hofburg. He was Salieri's man and always up to his eyebrows in intrigue.

'What has Rosenberg done?'

Lorenzo sucked in his flabby cheeks and turned up his

Mozart

long beak in disgust. 'The filthy dog tried to wreck *Burbero* because Casti wanted to have somebody else write another libretto. They mixed up little Storace in it and you never smelled such a mess.'

Wolfgang got up and called the parlor-maid. 'Here,' he said, flinging a coin into her apron, 'run out to the tavern and bring us in a pitcher of punch. And boiling hot, mind you.' He opened the stove door, stirred the fire, and dragged an armchair forward. 'Sit here, Lorenzo. It's cold out. Well, does the Emperor know about Casti and his beloved Rosenberg?'

'Certainly, he knows.' Lorenzo leaned forward and poked Wolfgang in the ribs. 'And not only that, little one, but I will tell you what he said.'

Between gulps of hot punch the Italian wiped his mouth with a fine lawn kerchief and told his story. Joseph had not only supported him against the cabal but treated him with such pronounced favor that Lorenzo felt ready to dare anything at the opera, sure now of the royal support. Wolfgang listened, squirming about in his chair, now jumping up and trotting around the room, now flinging himself back, crossing his knees, making faces. He leaned forward suddenly when Lorenzo said:

'Now, Wolfgang, what about you?'

'Well, what about me?'

Lorenzo smiled. 'Don't be a child. Why,' he said, pushing his long face into Wolfgang's, 'why shouldn't you and I do an opera?'

Wolfgang jumped as a cold chill of excitement shot down his spine. Then he bowed his head and sighed.

"I would do so most willingly," he said, "but—oh, I am certain I could never get permission."

Mozart

Lorenzo stood up and threw out his chest with a gesture. "That," he announced, "will be my affair."

Wolfgang looked up at him doubtfully. 'You don't really think so? Are you going to get permission for me?'

'I am not. We will write the opera first and worry about permission afterward.'

Wolfgang shook his head. It was dangerous, it might be a criminal waste of time. But an opera, a chance to write a real opera . . . *Figaro!* 'All right,' he said suddenly. 'I'll do it. Have you any ideas?'

'Oh, I don't know,' Lorenzo said, 'I could find some.'

Wolfgang stared at him for a moment. 'I have one,' he said breathlessly. 'Look!'—he ran for his book and thrust it at Lorenzo. 'Couldn't you make an opera out of that? Did you ever see such a comedy? *Basta!* do you know the plot?'

Lorenzo rubbed his chin. 'Yes,' he said, 'I do. But the German theatre has just been forbidden to give it.'

'I know all that. But you could fix it for an opera? You could take out the *Dreck*, couldn't you? Slide away from it a little? In the music——'

Lorenzo suddenly slapped the book on his thigh. 'In the music, eh? A bit of irony?'

The two men stared at each other in excited silence.

'Well,' Lorenzo said at last, 'when do we start?'

'Right away,' Wolfgang cried. 'Oh, right away, to-night . . . this afternoon!'

Lorenzo roared with pleasure and clapped Wolfgang's little shoulder so hard that he winced. 'Settled, then!' he cried, getting up to go. '*Evviva il delitto!* Just leave everything to me. Good-by, little one, and remember— we'll show them!'

Mozart

He stowed the book in his pocket and clattered down the stairs. At the bottom he turned around and shouted up, 'Come over to Wetzlar's to-night and meet me there. We'll talk to him about it.'

'*Gewiss*,' Wolfgang cried over the banister. 'With all my heart!'

That night Wetzlar's kind eyes glowed when they took him off in a corner and told him the plan.

'I may be ruined by this,' Wolfgang said, 'but I am going to write a good opera.'

'You most certainly shall not be ruined,' Wetzlar answered, 'and don't worry about it. Look here,' he said, drawing Lorenzo and Wolfgang together, 'if there is any trouble about this, I will pay Lorenzo for the text and I will positively get the piece staged for you, Wolfgang, in Paris or London. What do you say to that?'

'You are too generous and noble,' Lorenzo said. 'Don't commit yourself so far. First we will write this secretly here and I will offer it to the Emperor when the time is ripe. If we fail—then we may have to throw ourselves on your mercy.'

'Well,' Wetzlar said, filling three brandy glasses, 'in any case, I wish you luck! To you, Wolfgang—to you, Lorenzo—and—to *Figaro!*'

Viva. They drank bottoms up.

XIII

1786

WOLFGANG began making sketches at once. Lorenzo had *Burbero* still to finish, and after that had planned to start another opera for Martini. The Spaniard, who has remained alive in one lovely song, *Plaisir d'Amour*, gathered that Lorenzo had some other composer on his mind. "With laudable high-mindedness, and because of his esteem for Mozart, he agreed that I should delay working for him until I should have finished the libretto for *Figaro*." Unless Lorenzo exaggerated Martini's generosity, it is a rare instance of its kind in Wolfgang's life.

The winter was now beginning. Wolfgang wanted to finish *Figaro* (K. 492) before Lent, when he knew he would be pressed for time, with his usual round of concerts, lessons, and composing. Early in January he was surprised to receive a commission from the Emperor. The Governor-General of the Netherlands had come to Vienna on a visit, and Joseph was entertaining him at Schönbrunn. He planned to give several short operas in the Orangerie, and quite unexpectedly, to include the despised German opera company in the festivities. It was probably a question of policy—the Emperor of the Germans saw political, if not artistic reasons, for acknowledging their existence. Wolfgang's commission was a short musical farce for which his friend Stephanie wrote the libretto—*Der Schauspieldirektor* (the Impresario) (K. 486). It depicted the trials of a rural theatre manager—in Salzburg—assembling a company for a new opera house. The piece was unimportant and did nothing to raise Wolfgang in Joseph's eyes as an opera-composer. But the overture is brilliant and delightful, and is still played to-day.

Other minor obstacles to his work on *Figaro* kept presenting themselves: two dramatic *scenas*, and two piano concertos (K. 488 and 491) which Wolfgang wrote for himself, the second of them in C minor with a hard, strange, almost a brutal note of excitement. Moreover, after a year and a half of comparative quiescence, Constanze had begun to wear a greenish look of mornings, and presently whispered in her husband's small ear that he could expect another infant next October. Wolfgang turned pale. But he quickly reproved himself—that was no way for a good husband to act—and went to mass at the Stefanskirche with Constanze. They prayed for themselves and Karl, for the coming child, and for the blessing of God on *Figaro*. For it was by now apparent that Wolfgang must make money out of it.

Lorenzo had seen *Burbero* into production and was attacking *Figaro* vigorously; and it was no longer possible to keep Wolfgang's venture a secret. In one way or another it leaked out—Wolfgang's own enthusiasm was irrepressible—and all his intimate friends gloated as song after song of ravishing beauty appeared on his desk. . . . Lorenzo was mightily pleased with his own work. "To be sure, it was only a translation from Beaumarchais; but it had some fine verses, yes, sir, and some splendid songs. There were, for example, two most charming lines:

> *Non più andrai, farfallone amoroso,*
> *Notte e giorno d'intorno girando. . . ."*

This seems like great modesty on Lorenzo's part, for in reality he achieved a masterful libretto construction. The requirements of a comic opera, with its constant succession of solos, duos, terzets and other concerted numbers, the necessity for shortening as much as possible the stretches of recitative by which the action is carried, the radical changes to be made in timing and business, were all grasped by him with wonderful clarity. *Figaro* as an opera does not, of course, cut as reasonable a path through the mazes of parents, *fiancés*, spouses, *amoureux*, and the law as does *Figaro* the play; but the very tightening necessary to the opera increases its pace and accent. The deleted trial scene could have been no addition to *Figaro* as Lorenzo reshaped it. Indeed, Da Ponte was a first-rate theatre poet, how only his own protecting God could tell, for he had had little enough experience. His lines had both brilliance and flare, which struck themes from Wolfgang's imagination like hammers upon flint. Thus the characters of *Figaro*—and later, of *Don Giovanni*—came alive in music, and were perhaps the first characters ever to spring forth from this medium. This composer and this librettist were a combination whose equal has never since been produced.

"As fast as I wrote the words, Mozart set them to music." This meant that every day or two Lorenzo would come stamping up the stairs shouting 'Wolfgang! Come and see what I have for you. Hurry up, this is wonderful. *Ah, buon giorno, Signora Constanza, come sta?*' Wolfgang could not have kept his friends away if he had wanted to. Before long his house was like a club, where Kelly came nearly every day, bringing Stephen or Nancy or Attwood or some other admirer eager to hear the latest song. Jacquin was so fascinated he could hardly be pried out of his chair beside the clavier. Someone was forever running out for a bottle of wine or a litre of rum for punch. Someone was always singing or playing, and if nobody else, poor little Hans Hummel, whom they dragged out of corners. Constanze was placid and easygoing. One evening Kelly dropped in and found Wolfgang in his characteristic pose, draped over the standing-desk with his thin legs crossed and his elbows propped on either side of his manuscript, his hair escaping from its black ribbon.

"Ah, Kelly!" he cried, looking up and beaming with pleasure. "I have just finished a little duet for my opera; you shall hear it."

He sat down at the clavier. Kelly stood beside him, ". . . and we sang it. I was delighted with it, and the musical world will give me credit for being so, when I mention the duet, '*Crudel! perchè.*' A more delicious *morceau* was never penned by man." Kelly was so charmed with the opera that he threw all his influence, which was considerable, onto the side of *Figaro*, when the struggle for preference began. Salieri and Righini each had an opera ready, and Wolfgang knew it would be a bitter battle for the decision. "There was much jealousy, and each sought the *pas* in production. Cabals were formed by members of the Opera Company, and all manner of Court influences and intrigues were at work. Mozart was as touchy as gunpowder, and swore he would put the score of his opera on the fire if it were not produced first."

'I mean it,' Wolfgang said to Lorenzo. 'My heart is so wrapped up in this thing that I would rather destroy it myself than have those damned snakes strangle it at birth.'

But Lorenzo was doing his share. He went, "without saying a word, to offer *Figaro* to the Emperor."

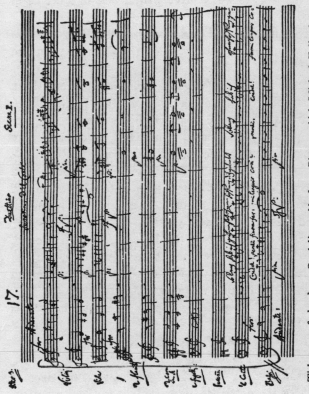

Title-page of the duet, *Crudel! perchè*, from *Figaro*, which Michael Kelly first sang, with Mozart, on the evening when he composed it. Courtesy of the *Preussische Staatsbibliothek*, Berlin.

Mozart

" 'What?' Joseph said, 'don't you know that Mozart, though a wonder at instrumental music, has written only one opera and nothing remarkable at that?'

" 'Yes, Sire,' I replied quietly, 'but without Your Majesty's clemency I would have written but one drama in Vienna!'

" 'That may be true,' he answered, 'but this *Mariage de Figaro*—I have just forbidden the German troupe to use it!' "

Lorenzo explained how he had cut and omitted all the objectionable scenes, and everything "that might offend taste at a performance over which his Serene Majesty might preside. 'The music, I may add, as far as I may judge of it, seems to me marvellously beautiful.'

" 'Good! If that be the case, I will rely on your good taste as to the music and your wisdom as to the morality.' " Lorenzo smirked and bridled. Joseph waved his hand. " 'Send the score to the copyist!' "

Lorenzo backed out of the Presence, turned around, jammed on his hat, tore down the state staircase, and into the street. He ran all the way to the Schulerstrasse and burst in on Wolfgang, who was working quietly.

'Wolfgang!' he gasped, mopping his scarlet face. 'It is done! I have *done* it!'

'Wha—what?' Wolfgang asked over a hanging jaw.

'The opera! *Figaro!* He has commanded—it is——'

At that moment there was a loud bang on the door.

'Who is there?' Wolfgang called.

'Open, in the name of his Imperial Majesty!'

Wolfgang exchanged glances with Lorenzo and went to the door. A court page, very much out of breath, handed him a note with the royal seal. He waited while Wolfgang broke it and read.

Mozart

'You may say,' Wolfgang said to the flunkey, 'that I am coming at once.'

He shut the door and turned to Lorenzo. They stood and stared at each other. Suddenly Lorenzo rushed forward and threw his long arms around Wolfgang. They began to dance round and round the room, faster and faster. In one voice they broke into chorus, *fortissimo*. *Non più andrai, farfallone*— Crash! They banged into the door as Constanze opened it. Her hand flew to her throat.

'*Wolfi!* What has happened! Are you crazy?'

Wolfgang let go of Lorenzo and flung his arms around Constanze.

'Stanzi, Stanzi, go and get out my court suit and the new silver buckles and my pointed lace and——'

'What for? Where are you going?'

'To court!' Wolfgang shouted, peeling off his clothes. 'To take *Figaro* to the Emperor!'

Though Joseph ordered *Figaro* to be copied and put into rehearsal at once, the intrigues were by no means ended. Most of the singers, brought from Italy, were naturally in league with Salieri. Casti the poet would gladly have cut out Lorenzo's heart, and Rosenberg stopped at nothing in his attempts to wreck the opera. A certain Bussani, an insignificant hanger-on, heard that there was a ballet in *Figaro*. He ran to Count Rosenberg and told him that "the *Signor Poeta* has put a ballet in his opera!" Rosenberg sent for Lorenzo and verified the scandal.

" 'The *Signor Poeta* does perhaps not know that the Emperor has forbidden dancing in his theatre?'

" 'No, Excellency.'

" 'In that case, I tell you so now.'

" 'Yes, Excellency.'

" 'And I will tell you further, *Signor Poeta*, that you must take it out!'

" 'Yes, Excellency!'

"His *signor poeta* had a significant tone of its own which gave the phrase the meaning of *signor jackass*. . . . But my 'Yes, Excellency' and 'No, Excellency' had their innuendo, too."

The upshot of the interview was that Rosenberg burned the two sheets of manuscript containing directions for the ballet. Lorenzo was furious. He ran straight to Wolfgang.

'The black-hearted dog!' Wolfgang cried. 'What in the devil shall we do? I won't have it,' he cried, waving his arms and tramping around the room. 'I'll thrash that damned Bussani! No, I won't, I'll go to the Emperor myself. No, I won't, *Gott verdammt*, I'll burn the score,' he cried, brandishing it.

Lorenzo took it away from him.

'No, you won't, little one. Leave it to me!'

That was the day of the dress rehearsal. Lorenzo was a match for the other Italians, and succeeded in one stroke in replacing his ballet, exposing Casti and Rosenberg, and intrenching himself still further in Joseph's favor. Wolfgang had certain partisans of his own in the cast—Kelly, who sang the double rôles of Don Curzio, the stuttering judge, and Don Basilio; and Nancy Storace, who sang Susanna. Of course Wolfgang had her in mind when he created the part, with all its delicacy, its teasing sweetness, and its tenderness. He takes her through every variation of coquetry and intrigue, makes her a little cat in her passes with Marcellina, and finally gives her *Deh*

Mozart

vieni non tardar, which has been universally called the
loveliest bridal song ever written. For the Contessa Ro-
sina, still young and in love, but embittered and mortified by Almaviva's shameless behavior, he wrote two of
the most heart-stirring arias in his whole treasury of song
—*Porgi amor,* and *Dove sono,* which has a similar theme
to the *Agnus Dei* of his *Krönungsmesse* of seven years
before. And though every would-be soprano of the past
century and a half has outraged them, nobody has been
able to make banalities of Cherubino's two immortal arias,
Non so più cosa son and *Voi, che sapete,* the latter probably the most familiar of all Wolfgang's hundreds of
songs. Figaro himself was one of Wolfgang's particular
loves. The great *buffo* Benucci created the part, so gloriously that Mozart was overcome. Kelly remembered
that "at the first rehearsal of the band, Mozart was on
the stage with his crimson pelisse and gold-laced cocked
hat, giving the time of the music to the orchestra. Figaro's
song, *Non più andrai,* Benucci gave with the greatest animation and power of voice. I was standing close to Mozart, who, *sotto voce,* was repeating, 'Bravo, bravo Benucci!'; and when Benucci came to the fine passage,
'Cherubino alla vittoria, alla gloria militar,' which he
gave out with stentorian lungs, the effect was electricity
itself, for the whole of the performers on the stage, and
those in the orchestra, as if actuated by one feeling of delight, vociferated, *'Bravo! Bravo! Maestro! Viva, viva
grande Mozart!'* Those in the orchestra I thought would
never have ceased applauding by beating the bows of their
violins against the music-desks. The little man acknowledged, by repeated obeisances, his thanks for the distinguished marks of enthusiastic applause bestowed on him."

Such a demonstration at a rehearsal was a revelation to Wolfgang, and he went home trembling with excitement. Then came the première on the 1st of May. Before the first act was well launched, it was plain that the snakes had been at work in the grass. Half the cast purposely bungled their parts, forgot their lines, sang flat. Wolfgang's blood ran cold. Sweat moistened the palms of his hands, and Constanze, watching from her seat, turned pale with pain for him. As soon as the first-act curtain fell, Wolfgang rushed round to the Imperial box. His agitation was so plain, his face working so pitifully, that Joseph, as he held out his hand to be kissed, pressed Wolfgang's fingers and turned to Count Rosenberg, who had been at the bottom of the trouble, trying to revenge himself on Lorenzo. One glance at the chamberlain's face was enough.

'Go and tell those singers,' Joseph commanded in a terrible tone, 'that they stop their treachery instantly and sing that opera as they should, or they all leave my service to-night!'

Rosenberg backed out of the box and slunk away. The curtain rose on an excellent second act; Wolfgang and Lorenzo had finally won. The concerted numbers received uproarious applause. Wolfgang's own favorite was the second-act sextet, where one melody overtakes another in a breath-taking pattern of loveliness. The individual characterizations are so clear, so perfectly sustained, that any six singers can do the piece and make a true and perfect impression. The famous letter-duet of the Contessa and Susanna received its own ovation. *Crudel! perchè* delighted as Kelly had predicted. Wolfgang had the joy of seeing his dearest artistic dream realized, his conviction that he could make of the players not parts, but *characters*. He did it, of course, by pure inspiration and genius, but if the matter is reduced to technicality, the secret is his freeing the voice of the burden of incidental action and situation, and putting that expression into the accompaniment, usually string quartet or occasionally woodwind. The characteristics of the situation, real and emotional, are expressed by the instruments; the pure personal feeling by the singer. So, in the marvellous recitative that precedes *Dove sono*, the unsatisfied yearning of the woman for her faithless husband, the plaintive sighs of desire, are expressed by the violins. She herself would be too dignified to put such feelings into words. In *Via resti servita*, the duet where Susanna and Marcellina, two spitting cats, are ready to gouge out each other's eyes, the real violence of their feelings is heard in the strings. The two women confine themselves to suavely nasty dialogue. In *Sull' aria*, the letter-duet, the continuous movement of writing is carried by the fiddles; the lady and her maid discuss what the letter should say. And in the passage where Benucci so distinguished himself, derisively urging poor little Cherubino on to *gloria militar*, the military note is supplied by the orchestra with a stirring, warlike, yet mirth-provoking march. Perhaps in his delineation of irony, Wolfgang went further into the possibilities of song than anyone had ever done. Whether the gentle teasing of Susanna and Zerlina, or the broad, raucous satire of Figaro, Leporello, and the Don, human nature in its devious ways did not conceal much of itself from him. So entirely are his characterizations his, and not what the singer puts into them, that, given a reasonable voice and technique, a man may sing Figaro one night and Almaviva the next, and seem two different persons.

Mozart

After the cast had begun to sing properly, they won themselves glory. Whatever their characters, they were an extraordinarily fine company. Kelly, who lived long enough to be a good judge, had never seen an opera stronger cast. "At the end of the opera I thought the audience would never have done applauding and calling for Mozart; almost every piece was encored, which prolonged it nearly to the length of two operas, and induced the Emperor to issue an order on the second representation that no piece of music should be encored. Never was anything more complete than the triumph of Mozart and his *Nozze di Figaro*, to which numerous overflowing audiences bore witness. . . . I shall never forget his little animated countenance when lighted up with the glowing rays of genius; it is as impossible to describe as it would be to paint sunbeams."

The "complete triumph" was far from what it seemed. Wolfgang received 450 gulden for his score, and never another penny. The opera did play a few times during the spring to "overflowing audiences." But no one—save Haydn, Lorenzo, Michael Kelly, one or two obscure players, and Wolfgang himself—had the remotest idea that *Figaro* was an immortal classic. It was shelved after a few performances. Other composers had operas ready. Joseph, who was a sound connoisseur of music, had applauded and yelled *"Bravo, Mozart!"* at the performances, but if he suspected the worth of *Figaro* and its composer, he never showed his suspicions. No appointment came Wolfgang's way. He was no better off after *Figaro* than before. He was better known, and that was all. In the excitement of writing the opera, he had allowed many other things to slip—some of his pupils and some of his concert patrons.

Mozart

The net result was freedom of intercourse with the Emperor, a few nods from smart society, and exhaustion from the effort of writing a masterpiece with his heart's blood. This resulted in serious illness a year later.

XIV

1786–1787

WHEN the truth penetrated to Wolfgang—that he had written his beloved *Figaro* only to have it treated as a passing fancy and receive no permanent recognition—his point of view began definitely to change. From the time he had first settled in Vienna he had been willing to concede that a composer must stand in well with Society, and play and write to its taste if he were to be a success. So long as Wolfgang thought there was ultimate benefit to be derived from such tactics he threw himself into them and tried to become a fashionable music-master. But as soon as he saw that he had gained nothing, the empty routine began to pall. "You lucky man," he said to Gyrowetz who was leaving for Italy, "How I envy you! And I am off to give another lesson to earn my daily bread." Wolfgang had no certainty of a living if he were to abandon his pupils and patrons, but he always had plenty of hope, and on it he relied when nothing more tangible was in sight.

Summer found him enjoying himself with his friends, often spending days at a time at the Jacquins' in the Botanical Gardens, where Constanze, now growing large and awkward, could have fresh air and company while he and Gottfried amused themselves with games and with criticising each other's music. Sometimes he would slip away and fling himself down on a chair on the nearest café terrace, to order a pint of white wine and lose himself over it in heavy abstraction. It was very hot, unbearably hot, he thought, as he loosened his high white stock and pushed his club of hair away from his sweating neck.

From time to time he would wander past the closed Hofburg and wearily shake his head. The court was out at the Laxemburg summer palace at Schönbrunn where one Italian opera followed another in quick succession, keeping Lorenzo and Kelly and Nancy busy and well paid. Wolfgang was busy too, but not so well paid. He turned out a steady succession of chamber music and short piano pieces, most of which were played at musical parties and then sold to the publisher Artaria. Among them was the trio in E flat (K. 498) which he wrote for Gottfried Jacquin's sister, Franciska, to play on the clavier with two friends, a clarinettist and a viola-player. Its Rondo Allegretto is one of the most perfect lyrics in all his work. Wolfgang knew he would use these compositions at his concerts the following winter, but he was beginning now to write more for himself than for the popular taste. If the public was not pleased, he did not care. The mood crystallized in the C major piano concerto (K. 503), as utterly different from the brilliant series of the previous year as night from day. It is grave and thoughtful, a complete repudiation of glittering concert salons and their shallow patrons. In August Wolfgang received a letter from a childhood friend, Sebastian Winter, *Kammerdiener* to a noble of the Empire, Prince Josef von Fürstenberg. The letter contained a sum of money, at which Wolfgang nearly fainted with surprise. It was an unsolicited advance payment for which he was to select one of his most recent compositions and send it to the prince. Wolfgang scarcely thought it possible that a good opening had come his way; that he, who was already growing resigned to oblivion, should be sought by

Mozart

anyone. He allowed his imagination to run away with him. Perhaps this meant a permanent appointment at the Fürstenberg court! Haydn's happy existence with Esterhazy danced across his mind. Perhaps he, too, would have a wonderful orchestra, all his own, to conduct and compose for!

" . . . I place at the end of my letter a list of the latest-born children of my fancy"—four symphonies, five piano concertos, a piano and violin sonata, a trio, and two piano quartets—"amongst which his Highness has only to choose that I may hasten to serve him. If his Highness pleases, I could in future pay him my respects with each of my pieces as it is completed. Moreover, I venture to make his Highness a little proposal in the matter of music which I would ask you, my friend, to lay before your Prince."

Wolfgang stopped and bit the end of his quill. Then he rubbed his forehead and thought a moment. No, it would not do to be too eager. He could not ask for an appointment. But he could hint at it; "Since his Highness possesses an orchestra, his Highness might like to possess certain orchestrated pieces of mine for use solely at his Court —in my poor opinion a possible gratification to him. If his Highness would be so gracious as to commission me, year by year, with a certain number of symphonies, quartets, concertos for different instruments or other pieces . . . and if he would be pleased to endow me with a fixed yearly salary therefor, his Highness should be well and punctually served, and I"—Wolfgang paused and stared at the wall a moment, then set his lips tight and finished— "should be able to work with a more collected mind, being sure of having that work to do! I hope his Highness will not take my proposition amiss, even should he be disin-

Mozart

clined to accept it, for indeed it arises from an impulse of genuine zeal to serve his Highness diligently, which in such a situation as mine is only possible if one be secure of at least a certain support and can consequently afford to reject work of the meaner sort."

Wolfgang never received the offer from Fürstenberg. He wasted no time conjecturing; he simply took this as another indication that he need not put his faith in princes. But where should he put it? There were more unpaid accounts in the house than two *Figaros* could have settled. Constanze's approaching confinement would be another of those horrible ordeals for him as well as for her, with her mother and sisters running wild all over the place. Why was it so hard for him to live? He did not think his own demands excessive—all he wanted was enough to pay his debts, and freedom from the necessity of composing trash. Sometimes Wolfgang doubted whether Vienna, for all his love of it, was the place for him. He heard from time to time of composers doing brilliantly in England, in Paris, even in Russia, which was supposed to be a land of barbarians.

In the fall Joseph and the Court returned to town and the Italian opera company followed. Wolfgang was delighted to see Kelly and immediately got out his best red coat and silk stockings, for Kelly's company meant gaiety at any hour of the day or night. One evening after the opera he came around for Wolfgang and they went to the *Milano* coffee-house. Kelly looked troubled.

'Is anything wrong?' Wolfgang asked solicitously.

'Yes,' Kelly answered. 'I had some bad news from Ireland to-day. My mother is very ill. She is not expected to live and I must start home soon.'

Mozart

'Oh, I am so sorry!' Wolfgang said quickly. 'We shall be sad here, and Nancy and Stephen will be lost without you.'

'No,' Kelly said, 'that they won't. They are going back with me.'

Wolfgang blinked.

'Leaving? Going to England? But why?'

'Nancy has received an appointment as prima donna at Drury Lane. And Stephen wants to go home. He has learned a great deal here and in Italy, and he can have a fine career in London. Tom Attwood is going back with us too.'

Wolfgang looked wistful. He twisted a lock of hair thoughtfully.

'Is it so easy to have a fine career in London?'

Kelly took a draught of wine.

'It is not easy anywhere, Wolfgang, unless you have great talent. And if you have,' he said meaningly, 'it should be easy.'

Wolfgang nodded. 'It should be. But look at me. Oh, Michael,' he said suddenly, in a sort of sob, 'why do they treat me so miserably? I have talent! I know I have!' He stretched out his hands pleadingly.

Kelly turned aside, coughed loudly and blew his nose. Then he leaned across the table, batting his eyelids.

'Wolfgang,' he said earnestly, 'I don't know what is the matter here, unless it is intrigue. Your Emperor is kind, even lavish with me. Only to-day he gave me twelve months' leave with full salary, and promised my appointment whenever I choose to return.'

Wolfgang drew in his breath and stared. 'I—never heard of such a thing,' he said slowly.

Mozart

'But you should have heard such things!' Kelly exclaimed. 'You, with your glorious talent, your genius for every known form of music, your kindness, your . . .' He broke off and suddenly banged the table with his hand.

'Wolfgang!' he said. 'Why do you stay here anyway? What in the world is there for you in Vienna—with all these Italians waiting to gouge out your heart!'

Wolfgang sighed. 'I don't know. I love it—it is my home——'

'But you can't starve just to be at home! Think, Wolfgang—why don't you come to England? Come with us! You know how your people are honored there. Think of Händel, and Christian Bach!'

Wolfgang looked at him eagerly. He leaned across and took Kelly's hand. 'Do you really mean it? Do you think I could get an appointment in England?'

'I know you could. Stephen will help. And they have powerful friends, the Storaces.'

'But why should Stephen help me?' Wolfgang asked slowly. 'He is a composer himself.'

'Because he is English,' Kelly said crisply, 'and that is the way Englishmen treat their friends. Now look here, do you think you could be ready at midwinter?'

Wolfgang scratched his head and puckered his brows. 'You have swept me off my feet, Michael,' he said. 'I must think about it. I should love to go! The queen was very kind to me,' he said eagerly, 'when I was a little boy! But then,' he remembered, 'there is Constanze. She is——'

'I know,' Michael said. 'But that is soon, isn't it? She will be well in time.'

'But—*two* children——' Wolfgang gasped.

'Oh, you couldn't take them. You'd have to leave them

[257]

here until you got settled. You could leave them with her mother, couldn't you?'

'Never!' Wolfgang declared with a glare. 'But—I could—at least, I could ask my father. . . .'

'Well, try,' Kelly said. 'See what you can do.'

Constanze chose to have another son just then, and while she was convalescing Wolfgang told her the plan. She agreed that it might be the solution for all their troubles. She did not mind being separated from the children, no indeed! So Wolfgang wrote to Papa. Would he take Karl and the new baby, Johann, with their nurse, just until Wolfgang found a position in England and established himself there? It might mean the most wonderful happiness and good fortune for them all! Wolfgang ran to the post with the letter, his heart pounding with excitement and hope. While they waited for Papa's answer they built golden castles in the air. Wolfgang could not believe it was not already settled.

'You had better start packing, Stanzi,' he would say anxiously. 'We can't make ready in two days, you know!'

So, for want of better occupation, they wore themselves out dragging bandboxes about, sorting the furniture, folding and shaking and tying and strapping. Then Leopold's answer came. As Constanze burned it, his subsequent account to Nannerl is the best reflection of his last gesture toward his son.

"I have had to answer to-day a letter of your brother's which has cost me a great deal of writing, so my letter to you must be short. You will realize that I had to write him very emphatically when I tell you that he made me no less a proposition than that *I* should take charge of his two children as he wished to make a tour through Germany

Mozart

and England, etc., at mid-Lent. I have, however, written very explicitly and have promised him a continuation of my letter by the next post. A pretty suggestion indeed! They are to set out light-heartedly on their travels, die perhaps, perhaps stay in England—in which case I could come running after them with the children and so on!—or else, with the payment he offers me for the children and their nurse— *Basta!* My refusal is a forcible one—and instructive, too, if he will but profit by the lesson!'"

Wolfgang trembled as if he had been struck. He looked silently at Constanze, his face white, his lips shaking. He stumbled across the littered room, barked his shin on a heavy packing-case, fell into a chair. Suddenly he put his head down on his arm and burst into loud sobs. Constanze ran over and took him in her arms.

'Wolfi, darling, *Liebchen*,' she murmured, 'don't cry! There, there, my dear, don't think about that letter. Forget him, Wolfi!'

She turned away, and bit her lips to keep back the blazing words that burned them. She dug her nails into her palms. Wolfgang's shoulders shook. She knelt down by him and clasped his head to her breast.

'Don't mind, darling,' she said in a shaking voice. 'Don't think about it any more. Surely something will turn up here. Surely *this* year the Emperor will reward you!' They clung together and dried each other's eyes.

Within a month the baby had died.

In the reaction from his bitter disappointment, Wolfgang expressed himself, for the first time in three years, in a symphony. Into it he poured that intensely serious and vital force which permeated his three subsequent symphonies and culminated in the Olympian Jupiter, his last.

Mozart

After the cruel blow from Leopold, he withdrew into himself, temporarily, but definitely enough to learn how lonely the soul becomes before it comes to create the immortal. This December symphony (K. 504), which he wrote in one of his favorite keys, D major, has not the tragic passion of the later G minor, the pure serenity of the E flat, nor the intellectual majesty of the Jupiter. But it departs from the insouciant and ravishing flow of melody that marks his earlier work into a new field of spiritual power and thought. It is Mozartean; he could not write music that was not perfect melody perfectly treated. But it goes beyond that. It is premonitory. For a reason that will presently be seen, it is called the "Prague" symphony to distinguish it from the earlier and much-loved "Haffner" in the same key.

A short time later he prepared to say good-bye to the friends he loved and through whom he had grown so interested in their country that ". . . I am an arch-Englishman, you know!" When they were all together he presented a score to Nancy, a *scena* and *rondo* for soprano with solo-piano obbligato (K. 505). Over his autograph he had written, *"für Mlle. Storace und mich."* Nancy clasped it to her heart, then turned, and throwing both arms around Wolfgang's neck, kissed him tenderly. They went to the clavier, and with Kelly, Stephen, Tom Attwood, Gottfried, and Constanze forming a circle around them, Nancy sang the *scena*. Then Kelly, with a furtive glance at several pairs of moist eyes, seized a glass, waved it high.

'To Nancy!' he cried, 'and to Wolfgang! *Viva, viva!*'

The pain of actual parting was lessened for Wolfgang by several letters he received just then from Prague.

Canone à 4 Voci.

Vienna. the 24 april. 1787.

Don't never forgit your true and faithfull friend

Wolfgang Amadé Mozart

Memento sent by Mozart to an English friend, probably Stephen Storace or Attwood.
Courtesy of the *Mozartmuseum*, Salzburg.

Mozart

Figaro, it seemed, was a riotous success there. It had been given at the National Theatre almost every day for the past six months, and showed no signs of exhausting its unprecedented favor. Wolfgang was dumbfounded. Could such a thing happen to him, or to anything of his? But he went on to read—the letter was from Count John Joseph Thun, son-in-law of his friend the Vienna countess—that the whole town was Mozart-mad, that every day someone inquired if there were no way of getting the composer to visit there. If Wolfgang would come they would promise him a great triumphal reception. An old acquaintance of Salzburg days, Franz Duschek the pianist, wrote a few days later in the same vein, and enclosed a petition from the whole orchestra. Wolfgang rubbed his eyes and wondered if he were crazy. But on thinking it over there seemed no sensible reason for not going to Prague and enjoying whatever the demonstrative citizens were so eager to offer.

The day after Nancy and Stephen, with their mother, Kelly, Attwood, and a lapdog left for England, Wolfgang set out for Prague with Constanze. It was January, cold, and the roads buried in drifted snow. But Wolfgang, who had travel in his blood, and had not been out of Vienna for over three years, was a transformed character. He was suddenly filled with irrepressible good spirits. He bounced about on his side of the coach, pointing out to Constanze the cold black hills with their white peaks, or sinking into contented reverie, when half-audible little tunes would escape from his pursed lips. Sometimes he sat up very straight and stared into space, and his pale face would redden. Then Constanze knew he was composing. He would suddenly paw at the side-pocket on the door,

Mozart

pull out a scrap of music-paper and scribble some minute hieroglyphic on it. "He used to keep scraps of music-paper at hand for such fragmentary notes . . . these scraps, carefully preserved in a case, were a sort of journal of his travels to him, and the whole proceeding had a sort of sacredness to his mind which made him very averse to any interference with it."

When Wolfgang tired of concentration, he turned to Constanze and began to chatter in the unintelligible jargon that they alone could use.

'*Nun, Schabla Pumfa,*' he cried, 'it's pretty fine to be on the way somewhere, *net wahr?*'

'What did you call me, Wolfi?'

'*Schabla Pumfa.* A good name, or as good as any other!'

'How Gottfried would shout at that,' Constanze said.

'Gottfried? Hah! *Hikkiti Horky!* There, that's a name that will settle Gottfried.'

'Oh, we'll have to have a name for everybody if you go on that way.'

'Very well. There's my good servant Joseph out on the box. His name is Joseph no longer. He is—let me see— *Sagaradata!*'

'And you yourself?'

'That's a hard one. I must think. Ah—*Punkititi*—will that do?'

By now Constance was laughing. 'Hofer will love this,' she said. Hofer was their brother-in-law, married to her oldest sister Josefa.

'Hofer is a good clown,' Wolfgang agreed. 'Well, let's call him *Rozka Pumpa.* That has a Hungarian flavor, what?'

'And that fool windbag Stadler,' Wolfgang continued,

Mozart

'I'll call him—*Notschibikitschibi. Wunderbar!* And while I'm disposing of musicians, I'll give Madame Quallenberg *Runzifunzi* for a name, and Ramlo, *Schurimuri*. Now have we finished for to-day?'

'No,' Constanze said. 'Not yet. You've forgotten Soukerl!'

Soukerl was their dog.

'*Potz sapperment!*' Wolfgang cried, 'so I have! Well —his name is now *Schomanntsky!* There, now I'm through, and I want a reward for my labor,' he added, moving over to squeeze her tight against the cushions.

Count Thun received them joyfully. They were to stay at his house, where he had had comfortable rooms set aside for them, Wolfgang's with a fine pianoforte. Wolfgang asked him anxiously if it were true that *Figaro* was so well liked.

'Wait until you go out,' the Count said, smiling, 'and you will see.'

"Immediately upon our arrival (on Thursday the eleventh, at noon) we had all we could do, what with ruffles and *coiffure*, to be ready for dinner at one. After dinner old Count Thun regaled us, for an hour and a half with music played by his own people."

This was a traditional custom in the noble houses of Bohemia, where no servant, not even a stable-boy, could get a job unless he were master of some instrument. Every great house had its own orchestra, usually composed of all the servants, who played wearing the family livery. "I will enjoy this great entertainment daily," Wolfgang continued to Gottfried. It was now the height of the social season, when all the nobles of the Empire of Bohemian descent were in residence in their town palaces in Prague.

Mozart

"At six o'clock I drove with Count Canal to the so-called Breitfeld Ball, where the cream of Prague's beauties are wont to assemble. That would have been the very thing for you, my friend! I can just see you chasing all the lovely girls and women—no, not running, *hobbling* after them! I did not dance, and I did not make love, the first because I was too tired, the second because of my native bashfulness. But with the greatest delight, I watched all these people hopping round in the joy of their hearts to the music of my *Figaro* turned into *Kontretänze* and *Deutsche*. For here they talk of nothing else but—*Figaro!* They play, they sing, they whistle nothing but—*Figaro!* No other opera draws except *Figaro*, always *Figaro!*— truly a great honor for me!"

The truth about Wolfgang's abstinence in dancing and flirting was his own joyful preoccupation with the overwhelming success of his opera. In his red dress-coat with his beloved jewelled buttons, point-lace ruffles, silver buckles, and freshly powdered hair, he stood aside, slight and elegant, but pale, a bit heavy-eyed, and already so thin that his little face deserved its recent epithet— *"enormbenast"* (enormous-nosed). But when the jolly Prague dandies took him up to be presented to gay beauties who deserted their beaux to gush over him and twitter with pleasure about *Figaro*, his features lighted up, he blushed and smiled shyly, bowed his thanks over and over again, kissed their hands with charming ease, and won their hearts. At first Wolfgang had difficulty realizing to what extent the popular passion for *Figaro* had gone. He soon found that the music had been transcribed into every form that could be played: piano solos and duets, wind serenades, string quartets and quintets, and dances. The gamins whistled the tunes in the streets, and beggars played them on the steps of pot-houses. There being as usual no royalty laws in that gay century, for all this success Wolfgang received not a penny.

The man who owed the most to Mozart was Bondini, the manager of the Prague opera-house, who had been on the point of bankruptcy just before staging *Figaro* with his Italian company. But ever since then his theatre had been packed, he was looked upon as a town benefactor, and he in turn considered Wolfgang his lucky angel. While Counts Thun and Canal and their macaroni friends took Wolfgang to the fashionable palaces, Bondini commandeered him at every chance and whisked him away to the arms of the musical community. Strobach the orchestra conductor was so extreme in his praise for *Figaro* that Wolfgang protested. "No, I tell you the truth," Strobach said, "my men are so enchanted with that score that every one of them would gladly play it straight through again as soon as they have finished a performance!" Wolfgang grinned and buried his nose in a beaker of Pilzner. It soon became evident that he could hardly stay in Prague without appearing publicly, so great was the clamor about him. He had anticipated concerts and brought some new scores.

The first concert, given in the opera-house, was the première of the "Prague" symphony. This was rapturously received. Then there were some concertos, and finally Wolfgang was left alone at the clavier. He played a fantasia with improvisations, which lasted half an hour. This was so vehemently received that he was forced to encore with another improvisation, after which the audience settled down to a tornado of noise that did not abate until he appeared a third time. After he had taken his seat and the whole house was waiting breathlessly for the first note, a voice suddenly cried "From *Figaro!*" The audience answered with a unanimous shout. Wolfgang bowed and began to play *Non più andrai,* which he used as the theme for twelve brilliant and very difficult extempore variations. The evening ended in a furore of indescribable enthusiasm. The following Wednesday *Figaro* was given for the first time since Wolfgang's arrival. He had told Gottfried that "I shall hear it—if I am not deaf and blind by that time!" Of course he had to conduct, and the enthusiasm was so wild that when, panting and mopping his forehead, trembling with excitement and emotion, he found himself in Bondini's arms after the final curtain, he said, "Your Bohemians understand me so well that I shall have to write them an opera of their very own."

Bondini answered with a shout. 'You will? Three thousand cheers! God bless you, Mozart! *Evviva il Maestro!*' Then and there they drew up the contract; Wolfgang to select the subject, arrange for the libretto, compose the score, have it ready for the next season. Price, one hundred ducats. Bondini was foolish for joy.

'This will make me,' he gloated. 'You have saved my life, now you will make my fortune!'

Wolfgang supposed he would. He wasted no thought on his own fortune; he was beginning to admit it a chimæric idea. But he did love Prague! He spent a month in utterly irresponsible gaiety. One ball followed another, Wolfgang composing all the dance music he was asked for. And now, neither too tired nor too shy, he danced to his heart's content—and did make love.

Constanze? It was then that she vindicated herself as the wife for Wolfgang. She was even younger in her child-

ish enthusiams and her love of pleasure than he. She was
a coquette at heart. She loved to flirt. Prague was full of
willing partners in trifling crime. There was invitation in
her twinkling black eyes, and amusement in her ready
chuckle. Constanze's life at home was anything but a continuous *festa;* the round of pregnancy, childbearing,
housekeeping, and debt was exactly opposite to her giddy
tastes. Here she was in a strange, gay city, feeling well and
looking her best, receiving much attention as the wife of
the town lion, eating food and drinking wine that she had
neither to purvey nor to worry about paying for. All her
cares were left behind, and she was free to enjoy herself.
Why nag Wolfgang? She was not possessive, and she
never pursued him with a chain in one hand and a prayer-
book in the other. She accepted his immensely demonstrative lovemaking, giving him a measure of nearly equal
warmth in return. There were times when she protested
his free-and-easy manners, a part of his Salzburg heritage
that accounted for his saying the most shocking things to
any woman who took his fancy. But on this particular holiday, Constanze proved herself a paragon of tact and good
humor. If Wolfgang had treated her carelessly, neglected
her, left her behind to mend his shirts while he pranced off
to pirouette and whisper into rosy ears in orangeries, she
might have turned into a virago. But Wolfgang was too
kind, too affectionate, and too clever to do any such stupid
thing. He made sure that Constanze was enjoying herself
(though he also preached gently about wifely dignity and
virtue) and then he reaped the profits of being the town
sensation. Whether it was a great lady who condescended
to reward the little composer in her own gracious way, or
whether it was an opera singer who looked up to the great

man and handed out her admiration with her favors, we shall never know. We do know that Wolfgang would come back to Thun's palace when the dawn was picking out the sharp spires of Prague from the winter night, and slip upstairs into Constanze's bedroom. There he took off his party clothes, folded them carefully and put them all away. Then, as he eased his little body carefully into bed beside her, hoping she would not wake up, she opened one black eye and cocked it at him.

'Wolfi!'

'Stanzi!'

'Wolfi, *Du schrecklicher Kerl,* where have you been?'

'*Ach,* Stanzi . . ."" he blushed and flapped one little white hand across his eyes. Then he turned over slowly and burrowed into the pillow beside her ear.

'Wolfi!' she said slowly, wagging one finger, 'you have a very, very guilty conscience!'

He flung one arm across her and hitched himself closer. He pressed his lip to her ear.

'I'm sorry, Stänerl. I have been very bad. I am a wicked, shameful man. Scold me, Stanzi-Marini. Please scold Wolfi and make him thoroughly ashamed!'

Constanze held him off at arm's length and looked long at his thin little face, his big, dim eyes, his trembling mouth.

'*Bitte,*' his lips formed. '*Bitte,* Stänzchen!'

Suddenly she clasped him tight in her arms and pulled his head down on her breast.

"He was so good," she told her sister Sophie. "It was impossible to be angry with him."

XV

1787

WOLFGANG had no sooner settled at home in Vienna than he experienced a profound reaction from the headlong gaiety of Prague. He had had a month of adulation and honors, a first taste of being the idol of a city. Now he had only to consider the musical ineptitude of Vienna, the blind stinginess of the Emperor, and the success of his inferiors, to be plunged into an abyss of indifference and gloom. He had made a thousand florins in Prague; it was gone before he knew whether he had bought a coat or paid some usurer's interest with it. Left to himself, he began to brood over his ignominious position and then to convince himself of the fallacy of mundane well-being. He lost weight and appetite, grew moody, and gave himself over to contemplation of the mystic. He spent much time in his Masonic lodge. When he heard from Nannerl that their father was far from well—Leopold was now sixty-eight, crippled with arthritis and tired from a life of hard work—he wrote him, "I am sure I need not tell you how greatly I long for reassuring news from yourself. Indeed I expect it, even though I have accustomed myself to expect the worst on all occasions. Since death, when we come to consider it, is seen to be the true goal of our life, I have made acquaintance during these last few years with this best and truest friend of mankind, so that his image not only no longer has any terrors for me, but suggests, on the contrary, much

Mozart

that is reassuring and consoling! And I thank my God for blessing me with the opportunity (you understand me) of coming to recognize Him as the key to our true blessedness." Wolfgang was referring, of course, to the Masonic teachings that had replaced so many of his earlier unquestioning allegiances to church dogmas.

"I never lie down upon my bed without reflecting that —young as I am—I may perhaps never see another day— and yet not one of those who know me can say that I am morose and sad among my fellows! For this blessing I daily thank my Creator and wish with all my heart that my fellow-men may share it. I had already declared my mind to you on this point on the occasion of the death of my dearest, best of friends, Count von Hatzfeld. He was just thirty-one years old, my own age. I do not grieve for him—but I do from my heart pity myself and all who knew him as well as I. I hope, I wish that while I write this you are getting better. But should you, against all expectation, be no better, I beg you will not . . . will not conceal it from me, but tell me, or have me told, the whole truth, so that I can come with all human speed to your arms!"

This was Wolfgang's frame of mind, this preoccupation with death and the remote and spiritual, when a young traveller was brought in to see him. The visitor was a pianist, already of reputation, and had come from Bonn to Vienna, a meeting with Mozart being one of his objectives. The youth's name was Ludwig van Beethoven. He was seventeen, though his broad, scowling face topped by a shock of wild brown hair looked much older. He was unhappy and nervous. Wolfgang asked him to play. Ludwig chose one of his host's concertos, and played well but with so little spirit that Wolfgang could not force himself to pay attention. He was even more restless than usual to-day, unable to sit in one place or keep his hands and feet still. He had been quietly visiting with Jacquin and several other friends when Beethoven's visit had interrupted them, and he had left them in the next room while he went to hear the young man play. Beethoven noticed his distraction, and unwilling to leave without some better reaction, asked Wolfgang for a theme on which to improvise. Wolfgang rose and went to the clavier, listless and bored; Beethoven, even in the presence of an admired master, was sullen. How different each would have felt had Beethoven known that Mozart was grieving for his dying father, or Wolfgang known that his guest was wracked with despair for his mother, then lying on her deathbed! Beethoven took Wolfgang's theme and began to improvise. Then the abstracted little man sat up and listened. A torrent of astounding music filled the room, and the ugly pockmarked face above the keyboard was transformed. Wolfgang arose and went to the doorway where Jacquin and the others were grouped in silent astonishment.

"Keep an eye on that young man," Wolfgang said. "He will make a noise in the world some day."

Beethoven came back before leaving Vienna to ask Mozart to give him lessons. But Wolfgang was tired and worried, and unwilling to make the effort, and young Ludwig soon left for Bonn, reaching there in time to see his adored mother die. Wolfgang's anxieties were then increased by Constanze's again becoming pregnant. There was no good news of Leopold, and Wolfgang became so unsettled in mood that Gottfried Jacquin urged him to come out to the Landstrasse and take a tiny cottage with a

Mozart

garden near the Jacquin house. He did so, but they were no sooner settled in it than Wolfgang received a sad blow; the *Vogel-Stahrl* died. This was the same starling he had bought three years ago, when he heard it singing his melody as he walked up the street. He buried it in the garden with touching ceremony, and wrote this epitaph for its miniature tombstone:

> "A little fool lies here
> Whom I held dear—
> A starling in the prime
> Of his brief time,
> Whose doom it was to drain
> Death's bitter pain.
> Thinking of this, my heart
> Is riven apart.
> Oh reader! Shed a tear,
> You also, here.
> He was not naughty, quite,
> But gay and bright,
> And under all his brag
> A foolish wag.
> This no one can gainsay
> And I will lay
> That he is now on high,
> And from the sky,
> Praises me without pay
> In his friendly way.
> Yet unaware that death
> Has choked his breath,
> And thoughtless of the one
> Whose rime is thus well done."

MOZART.

June the 4th, 1787.

Wolfgang could not easily account to himself for his elusively troubled feeling; for really he was no worse off than he had ever been. The memory of Prague was still a delight, and he had lost no time telling Lorenzo of *Figaro's* success and the commission for the new opera. He had not seen anything of Lorenzo for several months, as the quick succession of operatic mediocrities at court was taking all the poet's time; but when a new libretto was needed Wolfgang wasted no consideration on anyone else. Lorenzo was ideal.

'Let me think it over,' Lorenzo had said, 'and I'll let you know when I have a good idea.'

He soon had a good idea. "For Mozart I chose the *Don Giovanni*, a subject that pleased him mightily." Lorenzo had run through some recent librettos, and having neither literary conscience nor modern copyright laws to reckon with, calmly decided that the legend of the roué who killed a man and invited his statue to supper was a fine idea for Wolfgang. That Giuseppe Gazzaniga, the Venetian composer, had just done the opera, or that Righini, one of Wolfgang's bitterest enemies, had used it in Prague ten years before, did not cause Lorenzo to turn a hair. Beginning with the story as told by the Madrid monk Gabriel Tellez, a contemporary of Lope de Vega, and considering all the subsequent versions as given at the most famous theatres in Europe, Lorenzo did one of his splendid jobs of tightening, speeding up, and coloring, and he threw in his usual excellent operatic poetry for good measure.

Just at the same time, Salieri and Martini both came to Lorenzo for new librettos; and as theatrical politics and the imperial favor all depended on his not disappointing either of them, he added their necessities to his desire to write a book for Wolfgang, and " . . . went to the Emperor and explained that my idea was to write the three operas contemporaneously.

"'You will not succeed,' he replied.

"'Perhaps not,' said I, 'but I am going to try. I shall write evenings for Mozart, imagining I am reading the *Inferno*; mornings I shall work for Martini and pretend I am studying Petrarch; and my afternoons will be for Salieri. He is my Tasso!'

"I returned home and went to work. I sat down at my table and did not leave it for twelve hours continuous—a bottle of Tokay to my right, a box of Seville [snuff] to my left, and in the middle an inkwell. A beautiful girl of sixteen—I should have preferred to love her only as a daughter, but alas! . . . was living in the house with her mother, who took care of the family, and came to my room at the sound of the bell. To tell the truth the bell rang rather frequently, especially at moments when I found my inspiration waning. She would bring me now a little cake, now a cup of coffee, now nothing but her pretty face, a face always gay, always smiling, just the thing to inspire poetical emotion and witty thoughts. I worked twelve hours every day, with a few interruptions, for two months on end; and through all that time she sat in an adjoining room, now with a book, now with embroidery, but ever ready to come to my aid at the first touch of the bell. . . . The first day between the Tokay, the snuff, the coffee, the bell, and my young muse, I wrote the two first scenes of Don Giovanni, two more for the *Arbore di Diana*"—for Martini—"and more than half of the first act of *Tarar*"—for Salieri.

Wolfgang had seized Lorenzo's idea enthusiastically and started a few sketches as he caught glimpses of the scenes written under such typically Venetian conditions. But as several months would go by before he had to have his score ready, he fell into his usual procrastination and laid it aside, knowing perfectly well that he would write it all in a burst of fire when the time came. Meanwhile he received word that Leopold had died on the 28th of May. He was "neither astonished nor shocked." His loyalty to Papa had been tremendous, but it had been dealt a very grave blow by Leopold's cruelty in making it impossible for him to go to England. After that Wolfgang could write to him calmly and resignedly about life and even more convincingly about death; but Leopold's last hold on an obedient son had been broken. He died all alone, a hard, bitter, prejudice-ridden old man. With his extraordinary combination of love, conscience and knowledge, Leopold had been instrumental in the development of a great creative genius. Yet his false ambition, his bigotry, and his material greed did their most to wreck it.

With Wolfgang it was a point of honor, as he had told his father, that if he chose to occupy his mind with death and its promises, he should not impose any gloomy thoughts on his intimates. He strove to throw himself into their games and parties at times when he felt anything but festive, and he had such control over his mind that he was able to do it wholeheartedly. The world has seen fit to call Mozart frivolous and childish because he acted so. But those who understand his real duality of mind see beyond the obvious, beyond the gay little man dancing minuets while creditors thundered outside. His lightness and love of play were, in relation to his true gravity of mind, as his writing down of music to his real composing. The composing was done in his head, in silence and solitude. The writing down from memory was mechanical and a burden. To be surrounded by chattering friends relieved the tedium. Just at this time, therefore, when his permanent burden of care was augmented by grief for Leopold and worry about Constanze, who had to be bled from time to time, he forged along with the work for which he had orders, turning out six ravishing songs, among them the charming *An Chlöe* (K. 524) and *Abendempfindung* (K. 523). Then there were his promised pieces for the summer parties of his various friends and *Ein musikalischer Spass* (K. 522) (A Musical Joke) which—purposely full of mistakes—he wrote ostensibly to satirize a country band playing on the village green, but really to ridicule the counterpoint of his successful rivals. For all his philosophy, however, Wolfgang was not strong enough to fight indefinitely against financial, emotional, and professional odds. Since *Figaro*, over a year before, he had been growing thinner and more nervous. Now, in July, he caught a fever. Insanitary living conditions accustomed most people of that time to resist minor infections, and Wolfgang too might have remained immune. But in his run-down condition the infection, probably similar to typhoid, took a fierce grip on his slight body. His kidneys were also affected. Sigmund Barisani made daily trips from the general hospital to the Landstrasse for almost a month. He was a rare individual, a medical man far in advance of his time, but not so far advanced for instance as to devote his talent to relieving the troubles of women. Therefore Constanze was left to the mercies of midwives and barber-surgeons, while Wolfgang received care that was, within the limitations of the age, remarkably intelligent. If Barisani, who died soon after, had lived longer,

Mozart

Wolfgang's life might also have been *l*engthened. This time he recovered quickly, and by early August was allowed to sit up and push his pen a little every day. He promptly extracted from his mind, where he had composed and stored it away during his illness, *Eine Kleine Nachtmusik* (K. 525), a string serenade of exquisite beauty, scored for two violins, viola, 'cello and bass.

By the time Wolfgang was able to move about as much as he pleased, Constanze had begun to recover from the early violent disturbances of her fourth pregnancy. Together they wandered about the Botanical Gardens with Gottfried and his father, Wolfgang raising a pale, pointed face and heavily circled eyes to look at the trees and birds that the old professor pointed out. He was shaky still, but recuperating quickly, for he had something to look forward to. Bondini had written from Prague that they wanted to open *Don Giovanni* (K. 527) in October. Wolfgang had sent word to Lorenzo, who had promised to have the libretto finished in a month—it was now late in August—and also to come to Prague himself to help drill the singers. With this delightful prospect before him, Wolfgang regained his normal but always deficient strength, and now in the mornings, when he was washing his hands, Constanze lying in bed would hear him humming and knocking his heels together as he splashed water about. If she spoke to him, he did not hear her. She smiled. Wolfgang was beginning to compose in earnest, and she knew that the bigger the task the more he loved it. Plainly he was in love with *Don Giovanni*, and when he was talking to Gottfried about it said, "I am writing this opera for Bondini, surely, and for the people of Prague too—but mostly for myself and my friends." Gottfried knew they

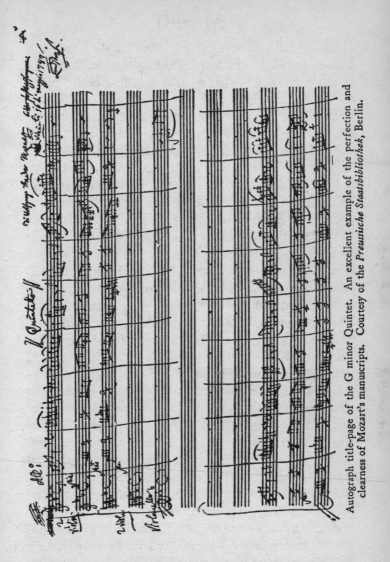

Autograph title-page of the G minor Quintet. An excellent example of the perfection and clearness of Mozart's manuscripts. Courtesy of the *Preussische Staatsbibliothek*, Berlin.

Mozart

could expect something rare. He helped Wolfgang arrange for Karl to be boarded out again while they were away. As the weather grew cooler and their health better the Mozarts bubbled over with good spirits. Wolfgang acted as if he had entirely overcome the recurrent depressions of the past year. Temporarily he had; but he had not really dammed or changed the swift course of his short life. No year that had produced what this one had could be lived and forgotten. It had been epitomized and immortalized by a treasury of work; and chiefly by a masterpiece, the G minor quintet (K. 516) with two violas.

This quintet is a glimpse into Wolfgang's soul; an epic statement; a summing-up; a prophecy. The man who has been called superficial gathered all the hidden pain and passion of nine troubled years and gave them an expression that lives and will live forever in its sheer elemental truth. The piece sets and holds a keynote of intense, passionate excitement which more than accounts for the apparent absence of this in Wolfgang's visible life. It is possible to interpret the work in terms of his own misfortunes, expounded and then protested in vivid poignancy. But it is better to know that he, true artist, rose above autobiographical emotion and turned his personal passion into universal force. The tragic mood of the first four movements, culminating in the black sorrow of the last Adagio, is swept away in the supreme bliss of the final Allegro. This is no conventional happy ending, but a moment when Wolfgang opens the door to his spirit, which is clear and radiant and beautiful, and not to be extinguished by any mortal hardship. That he knew always. No biographer, no commentator, critic, or interpreter can ever reveal Wolfgang Mozart entirely. Every attempt to

Mozart

know him truly, to relive his life, is incomplete without his own musical revelations.

Such are this quintet and his Requiem. To know them deeply is to know him.

XVI

1787

THE best of ham, beer, and music have always delighted visitors to Prague; Wolfgang was never an exception. How he had loved it last January when he was there as Count Thun's guest! Now, in September, he and Constanze started off in the highest spirits. The coach clattered along between golden harvest fields and steep reddening hills, stopping to change horses in little villages where women with gay skirts tucked up over their ample hips pounded linen at the town pump. Round rye loaves, with slices of rosy ham oozing sweet juice, and tall beakers of cold, well-crested Pilzner beer were handed through the open windows at every stop where they changed horses. Wolfgang sat back in his corner, staring at the rich blue sky and the floating horizon, smiling when a bird's trill caught his ear. He was enchanted with the difference in the landscape since he had last seen it buried in snow. Constanze was comparatively well—pregnant, of course, but not violently sick—and so pleasing company. Everything combined to raise his spirits to the point where his ideas would flow "best and most abundantly." Under the oddly large, sandy poll, and behind the round, near-sighted grey eyes, *Don Giovanni* took further shape in one of the most perfect of "pleasing, lively dreams." A little of it was already finished, but most of it still to be worked out. Saving the presence of Constanze, a very usual exception, the condi-

Mozart

tions were ideal for Wolfgang's unique way of composing, of which:

"I really can say no more on this subject than the following; for I myself know no more about it, and cannot account for it. When I am, as it were, completely myself, entirely alone, and of good cheer—say, travelling in a carriage, or walking after a good meal, or during the night when I cannot sleep; it is on such occasions that my ideas flow best and most abundantly. *Whence* and *how* they come, I know not; nor can I force them. Those ideas that please me I retain in memory, and am accustomed, as I have been told, to hum them to myself. If I continue in this way, it soon occurs to me how I may turn this or that morsel to account, so as to make a good dish of it, that is to say, agreeably to the rules of counterpoint, to the peculiarities of the various instruments, etc.

"All this fires my soul, and provided I am not disturbed, my subject enlarges itself, becomes methodized and defined, and the whole, though it be long, stands almost complete and finished in my mind, so that I can survey it, like a fine picture, or a beautiful statue, at a glance. Nor do I hear in my imagination the parts *successively*, but I hear them, as it were, *gleich alles zusammen*, all at once. What a delight this is, I cannot tell! All this inventing, this producing, takes place in a pleasing, lively dream. Still the actual hearing of the *tout ensemble* is after all the best. What has thus been produced, I do not easily forget, and this is perhaps the best gift I have my Divine Maker to thank for."

All this inventing, then, all this producing, absorbed Wolfgang in the coach. Sometimes he reached absently for the door-pocket, took out his case of illegible scrap-papers and jotted down a theme or phrase. Mostly he sat back turning this or that morsel to account, and storing the whole in his memory after it satisfied him, to be drawn out upon demand. His eyes vacant, he leaned against the cushions, drumming his nervous little fingers, crossing and uncrossing his legs, making grimaces with his sharp, long-nosed features. Constanze sat quietly in her corner, saying nothing unless he spoke to her.

Soon they saw once more in the distance the soft haze that has ever embraced Prague; then they recognized the needle-spires of St. Vitus; then the yellow-grey masses of old houses clustered on the Moldau, and the steepled towers of the Karlsbrücke. Presently they rumbled through scattered outskirts, and into the heart of the old town, pulled up with a great clatter, and jumped out to greet the excited Bondini, who rushed about chattering in Italian to Wolfgang, and in German to the porters struggling with the luggage. According to his contract as manager, he had found them good rooms, he said, in the Three Golden Lions on the Kohlmarkt; a nice, comfortable inn, right in the centre of town, near the opera house, and close to all the good *Bierstuben* and *Weinkellern*—with a wink at Wolfgang.

'Come along now, come up and see the pleasant apartments I have for you, get settled quickly, we have much to do, everyone is wild to see *Kapellmeister* Mozart again, everybody wants to drink your health—*Evviva il grande Maestro!*'

They swarmed up the dark stairs after Bondini jabbering and waving his arms. The rooms were pleasing, a good-sized drawing-room and a smaller bedroom with windows on the curve of the street. Until recently these same rooms were, appropriately enough, the offices of the Prague Philharmonic Orchestra. Everyone bustled around,

Mozart

Wolfgang grinning and rubbing his hands, Constanze exclaiming, Bondini throwing coppers to the gasping porters. Finally the boxes were unstrapped and opened, some of the travel-dust hurriedly washed off, powder dabbed on Wolfgang's head—'Come on,' Bondini cried, 'hurry, we have much to do. You, *Signora*,' with a low bow, 'will surely be glad of a short rest and an opportunity to unpack the many baggages—' and throwing an arm across Wolfgang's thin shoulders, he dragged him, shouting, out of the room and down the stairs, and onto the street and into the arms of Prague, waiting in the coffee-houses to cheer the little wizard from Vienna and drink his health to three times three.

Meanwhile, northward in the dark mountains near Teplitz, there sat, in the library of the ancient Bohemian castle of Dux, seat of the Counts Waldstein of Wallenstein, a tall old man with flabby yellow skin—once the warm olive of the Venetian—a few stumps of bad teeth, and two black eyes like half-live coals. The librarian had a big writing-table in the window-embrasure of the immense room. All around him, reaching to the vaulted, whitewashed ceiling, were ranks of bookshelves, painted white, and filled with the coffee-cream vellum and golden leather of beautifully bound tomes. These the old man was obliged to arrange and catalogue. But those mountains of mussed papers on his table, the reams strewn about the floor, are not the orderly notations of a cataloguist; they are the memoirs of Giacomo Casanova de Seingalt, now in his sixty-third year.

He had been Count Waldstein's librarian for three years, a position he held because he was penniless and pathetic, and because Waldstein had a kind heart and a sense of humor. He was willing to subject his household to the rages of the impotent old diavolo for the privilege of having his still brilliant conversation at table and in the library. Casanova's memories were lurid, if his actions could no longer be, and his tastes unchastened: "I like highly spiced dishes, macaroni made by a Neapolitan cook, the *olla podrida* of Spain, fine, white salt cod from Newfoundland, high game, and strong cheese; the latter I consider perfect when the little creatures which form in it become visible." So whenever things were not as he liked them, he heaped brutal invectives on Faulkircher, the castle steward, not in fact, but on paper. Faulkircher earned them for his filthy ridicule of Casanova, and the knavish servants under him delighted in tormenting the explosive, easily irritated old man.

Small wonder that in October as soon as he had ready his manuscript of *Icosameron*, which followed the famous *Escape from the Leads*, he should vent his excitement on Faulkircher in a profane tantrum, command a place in the post-chaise, and, spluttering and wheezing, showering Venetian curses, hoist himself into it and hasten the grouchy coachman on to Prague. In Prague was the printer who had brought out *I Piombi*; in Prague there were loose and witty women (though he could only gaze), and music, and fast society, and gaming tables (for which he had no money); and in Prague, when he reached there, was his old crony, Lorenzo Da Ponte—just arrived from Vienna with an unfinished libretto. He had come to wind it up, and "superintend rehearsals" with Mozart. Just how and where the two Venetian lights of history had first connected is a tale better told elsewhere than here. But that they were well acquainted, that both were scamps, though within sight of reform, that one rose from the gutter-level of strolling actors, and the other from the Ghetto, that both had lived by their wits and both turned their share of shady deals, and both ruined more than their share of pretty women, bound them together in tacit and thoroughly mischievous confederacy.

Lorenzo had arrived a few days after Wolfgang and had found rooms, not without suggestions from him and Bondini, in the Platteis, a big lodging-house on the Ferdinandstrasse. Its rear rooms opened on the little curving street which runs from the Kohlmarkt to the Martinskirche, and on which the Three Golden Lions faces. Thus Lorenzo, who had two fine French windows, could go out onto his balcony, cup his hands, and shout to Wolfgang, whose windows were directly opposite; they could almost clasp hands across the street. They used this convenience joyously. Passersby beneath saw the long, dark face and black hair leaning over the railing to shout bawdy jokes, or indulge in raucous but good-natured disagreement about the *Don* with the thin fair face and sandy hair hanging out of the Golden Lions casement.

Then this childish amusement would succumb to man-sized thirst, and Lorenzo roar that they should stop acting like nincompoops: 'Come downstairs *subito*, Wolfgang, we will go and have a glass of punch, or two or three, and ho! for the great Da Ponte and great Mozart, and ho! for the brave Prague players, and *bravo! Il Don Giovanni*, that would make them both famous, *per Dio*, you see if it wouldn't!'

So they would meet at their street doors, and cock their tricornes on the sides of their pigtailed heads, and throw up their chins, and slap each other on the shoulders, and link arms, and swagger off to the coffee-house, where the whole room would stand and cheer when Mozart hove into the doorway, and the blind harpist on the step instantly strike up *Non più andrai*, everybody singing in chorus, and coppers clinking at the old beggar's feet.

Then—was it possible? Could the old man sitting stiffly alone at a corner table be whom he looked? Could that thin face, that sloping forehead, and those blazing eyes belong to anyone else? Never, impossible! Of course, it cannot be—but it is—è Giacomo! è Casanova! Oho, my old friend Da Ponte—*benvenuto, saluti*—ah, a happy day for all, a happy day indeed. Embraces, salutes, exclamations.

'Here is Mozart, Casanova. Mozart, the composer who wrote *Figaro* with me, you know, the great Mozart. *Cavaliere* Casanova de Seingalt—*Kapellmeister* Mozart. Boy, a bottle of your best Orvieto!' 'And cheese, Lorenzo!' '*Si, si, si, formaggio*, here boy, bring cheese, and bread, and ham. Ha, ha, ha, ha'—slapping their thighs, offering snuff, black eyes snapping and broad throats warming with wine.

'But what are you doing here?' 'And what are *you* doing here?' both questions at once, and Casanova's interest rose when Lorenzo said:

'An opera. A new opera, Giacomo, better even than *Figaro*. We are writing it for Prague, for Bondini at the opera here. The première is soon. Wolfgang here has done fine work, and I—I am not so clumsy. The plot? *Basta*, we have a fine plot—*il Don Giovanni*, the Spanish legend. A mighty stallion that, a fellow worthy of yourself. In fact, Giacomo, now that I think of it'—Lorenzo's eyes dilated and he brought his palms together with a triumphant smack—'but Casanova, he *is* yourself! Wolfgang!', swinging about in his chair, 'Wolfgang, *pizolo mio*, here is Don Giovanni! Ah, you will help us, Giacomo! And we have no problems, no troubles, all is merry as the marriage bell!'

Nor was anyone better qualified to give Da Ponte any such pointers on the fine art of seduction as he himself lacked. Eagerly Lorenzo dragged a sheaf of papers from his pocket, shoved them across the table at Casanova, while Wolfgang stared over the rim of his glass at the wreck of the world's greatest lover. The two Italians were soon lost in the fine points of Don Giovanni's behavior. 'Just what shade of insinuation should there be in the words of *La ci darem*, and how would you say that filly would react, Giacomo? Would she succumb quickly? How much does she know? Plenty?—Ah, you sly dog,' with a dig in the ribs. Wolfgang took it all in. To his already extraordinary facility for ironic delineation, he added, in those bouts with Da Ponte and Casanova, a canny grasp of rascally motives; Don Giovanni should sing them to the world.

Prague saw the three roisterers parading the tiny cobbled streets—huge, toothless Lorenzo, with his booming laugh, senile Casanova with sparks of old fire in his eyes; between them, Wolfgang, trotting along in a vacuum of bliss and ideas, a quiet little man, looking up at each in turn to catch the last outrageous remark and cap it with some *Salzburger dreckiger Witz* that made them pound his slight back and bellow with joy. They drank rivers of wine and punch and beer, widening the circle to include Bondini, Strobach, the orchestra conductor, Franz Duschek, Guardassoni, sometimes young Count Thun, some-

Mozart

times anybody, sweeping the town in a whirl of enthusiasm for themselves and everything they did, and always to the strains of *Figaro*, which pursued them everywhere. The Bohemians adored Mozart, and from the depths of his heart he wrote his greatest opera for them, fired by the unique experience of being wholly appreciated for the only time in his creative life.

So many superlatives have been showered on *Don Giovanni*, so many authorities have agreed that it is the all-round greatest opera, that it is redundant to dwell on it further. It is better to say that *Don Giovanni* does not lack a single element necessary to a perfect opera. It has a subject which is universally acceptable, dealing neither with kings that are unreal to the modern world, nor with fairies that are slightly ridiculous, nor with myths that are dead and therefore boring. Its text, while not classic poetry, is dramatic, polished, and alive. It treats of almost every emotion and sentiment known to the ordinary man. It has humor, from the finest-drawn irony to the broadest burlesque. It encompasses suspense, revenge, lust, anger, remorse, pathos, passion, terror. Love appears in every manifestation from the filial devotion of Donna Anna to the outraged marital fervor of poor Masetto. It includes such elements of human behavior as the flirting *fiancée*, the mocking seducer, the woman scorned. It shows the sinner tempting fate and the wronged thirsting for vengeance. Yet unlike the solemn self-conscious music-dramas of Wagner, imperiously demanding awed deference, it never takes itself seriously. It is theatre, first, last, and all the time. It punishes the wicked villain in terrifying retribution—then (when the performance is authentic) the other characters come forward, reconcile their differences,

Mozart

wink at the audience, and leave every one sure that it is all a play, and a burlesque at that.

The music is Wolfgang's genius flaming and sparkling at its loveliest. It is poised, sure, utterly aware of its dramatic responsibility. It is a masterpiece of characterization, a complete transcription of human behavior from experience into sound. Technically it is a wonder-work of construction, rising and moving with the story and the characters into two amazing climaxes—the ball scene ending the first act and the banquet scene ending the second. And it is delightful. Its extraordinary freshness and its variegated beauty have never palled or lost their quality of delicious surprise. *Don Giovanni* has been continuously alive, permanently in the repertoire of established operahouses for the best part of two hundred years, longer than any opera ever written, with one exception. And that is *Figaro*. Somewhere in the world, every month in the year, *Figaro* and *Don Giovanni* are being sung.

The triple carousal did not last long; Lorenzo had been only a week in Prague, when he received a furious letter from Salieri ordering him back to Vienna to finish the libretto for *Tarar*. Disgustedly he admitted he would have to go; he would miss the première of *Don Giovanni*, and what was much worse, he had the book all ready except for one scene, the confused result of their reluctant cutting when they saw how their original plans would exceed any practicable length. This was Leporello's aria in the second act, after the sextet and recitative, where the rascal has to get himself and his master out of a nasty hole, soothe Masetto, who has been beaten by the disguised Don, attend the perpetually outraged feelings of Donna Elvira, and get off the scene as quickly as possible. Lorenzo had brought things to a pass where radical action was necessary; now he was faced with the possibility of leaving poor little Wolfgang in the lurch. This he could not do. Calling on Mary and the saints, he sat in a wineshop with Casanova and gnashed his teeth. What in the world should he do? He couldn't leave it unfinished, he had no time to write any more poetry. He was stuck, he was worried. Of course, a light broke. Hadn't Casanova been free with good suggestions? Hadn't he added some rich touches to the wonderful seduction scene at Don Giovanni's ball?

'Here,' Lorenzo shouted suddenly, seizing some paper, 'here, what am I thinking of, half-wit that I am! You do it, for God's sake'—sweeping aside protests—'you know what to do, you know the fix Leporello is in. Ah, Giacomo, for the love of Jesus, get him out of it—write this scene for me!'

Casanova was vain of his literary ability, and certainly no man could call himself a great lover who was not something of a poet. All we know is that, not many years ago, in some of Casanova's effects discovered at Schloss Hirschberg in Bohemia, were found two sheets of paper, not titled, but without doubt the ones on which he sketched his plans for extricating Leporello. Later, when Lorenzo had time, he worked those ideas into his book. An alternative version of this theory is that Da Ponte never asked Casanova, of whom he was said to be envious, to help him. But after Lorenzo had returned to Vienna, Casanova went to Bondini and Mozart, criticized Da Ponte's libretto, and tried to have himself commissioned to rewrite it. Failing in that, he did revise the one scene that was causing trouble.

Mozart

However, regardless of who was responsible for it, Wolfgang was inspired by the crafty succession of lies to put the whole thing into a racy burlesque in G major, which, when Leporello—the greatest of nature's rogues—dolefully accuses the Don, *"l'innocenza mi rubo, l'innocenza mi rubo"* (depraved my artless mind!) suddenly drops to a ridiculous, hollow A minor. And, as if to complete the confusion, there are some modern performances from which the whole aria, *Ah, pietà! Signori miei!* is omitted altogether, making no sense out of Leporello's antics. But plenty of chuckles went the rounds of Prague about it, while Lorenzo, back in Vienna, finished a forgotten piece for a forgotten composer, and missed the opening of *Don Giovanni,* the most unprecedented triumph in the annals of the Prague opera.

Poor old Casanova rumbled back to Dux and exile, to quarrel with Faulkircher about the food and affront his patron's guests over trifles. Perhaps, in the brimstone lake where the righteous like to picture him, the thought comes to him that, like certain little bastards with black eyes, Lorenzo's hero proclaims his own lineage.

Franz and Josefa Duschek were unusual in many ways. They gave friendship freely. They were both fine artists —he a pianist, she a soprano—who had the extraordinary good luck to own a charming villa, the Bertramka, at Koschirsch, a suburb just over the Moldau from the city. When every town in Europe had its quota of musicians, not one of whom lived more securely than in some meagre lodging, a couple who had the means to own a delightful country place and keep open house in it were the good angels of the whole profession. The source of the Duschek fortunes, however, was neither a mystery nor a surprise. Josefa Hambacher had started her career as the mistress of Count Christian Clam, a Bohemian noble who treated her kindly and, when the time came, married her off to Duschek with a blessing and a *dot* large enough to purchase the vineyard and farm.

The yellow house is on the side of a high hill overlooking the sharp spires and massive walls of Prague; a typical eighteenth-century villa set in the midst of a green garden and dark old trees, and so built on the side of the slope that a long, smooth grass terrace in the rear is level with the raised drawing-room. The terrace is laid out between the vineyard hills, and surrounded on three sides by thick groves of maple, chestnut, and locust trees. The fourth side is open over the valley, with a stucco balustrade forming an outdoor room where the guests sat waiting their turn at the bowling-games on the grass, or looking down at the comfortable activities of the little farmyard just below.

All day long the house and grounds rang with the exuberant noises of musicians making holiday; somebody playing harpsichord duets in one room; four slightly drunk and very mellow fiddlers practicing quartets in another; Josefa prancing about her household duties with her cap on one ear, singing a new aria at the top of her voice. Franz sat on the terrace with Strobach and Guardassoni, who had run over from the opera house for the afternoon. Each had a long cool pipe and a fine stein of Pilzner. Constanze strolled along the garden paths with Ponziani, the first Leporello, laughing at his sallies; and in a corner by the balustrade, at a little table on the paving, with a glass of punch at his elbow, and the wind

Mozart

ruffling his hair, Wolfgang, scribbling away as hard as he could, tossing off sheet after sheet of even, beautiful manuscript.

Whenever one of the men summed up a lady in a savory phrase, Wolfgang roared with the rest and threw in a word to increase the laughter. Then he grinned and drove his scratchy quill more furiously. When he came to the end of a line, he flapped over the sheet—no more paper.

'Stänerl,' he called, turning around in his chair, 'go in and bring me more paper.'

'You haven't any more like that, it hasn't come from town.'

'Well, then, *Potz sapperment*, bring me anything you can find!'

The paper she brought was another size, the staffs ruled by different measure. What of it, Wolfgang shrugged, plunging his quill in the ink again.

They had come out to stay at the Bertramka about the time Da Ponte had returned to Vienna. Here with the Duscheks were all their friends, gay parties, and no expenses, with two delightful rooms at their disposal at the far end of the house. Each room had a big porcelain stove, of which they were glad when the first frost nipped the hilltop, but Wolfgang spent almost all his time on the terrace. He loved company and particularly the Prague company. Bowls were played all day long and Wolfgang joined every game, leaving his manuscript with a stone on it to keep the pages from blowing away while he took his turn, then dashing back to his little table to write another line or two. Letter-perfect, complete, he set down the marvellous score of *Don Giovanni*. He had hardly a note

Mozart

on paper when they moved to the Bertramka, yet every day, all day, once he had started, he wrote in never-to-be-revised perfection melodies and harmonies that bewildered their first hearers with their loveliness, humor or grandeur. As he finished each part, he sent it off to the singer who was to learn it, and rushed along to the next.

Of course, his whole score stood, "though it be long, complete and finished in my mind," and the time having come to write it down: "I take out of the bag of my memory, if I may use that phrase, what has previously been collected into it in the way I have mentioned. For this reason the committing to paper is done quickly enough, for everything is, as I said before, already finished, and it rarely differs on paper from what it was in my imagination."

Therefore, drawing out of the bag of that God-given memory the complete and perfected score, effacing from the brain what did not please, and dictating all to his busy, scribbling little hands, Wolfgang preferred to sit with his friends in the open air, sharing their pleasure, and shouting at their jokes; for "at this occupation I can therefore suffer myself to be disturbed; whatever may be going on around me, I write, and even talk, but only of fowls and geese, or *Gretel* and *Bärbel*, or some such matters."

Don Giovanni was written in the midst of the things Wolfgang loved best in the world; company, chatter, punch, games, dancing—the weeks at the Bertramka were a festival of happiness.

When the Duscheks did not have a big party on, Wolfgang and Franz, with whatever other men were about, would put on their hats and sway off to town, to spend the evening in a royal bout of music, wit and noise, in

Mozart

some tavern where they were treated like kings. Often they went back to the Three Golden Lions, to riot with their opera friends who lived there, and even these thick walls could not drown the din that poured through and drifted up the street to shock the Martinskirche drowsing in its memories of four hundred years. At three, or four, or dawn, Wolfgang sometimes under Duschek's wing, sometimes alone, would lope off toward the Karlsbrücke —it being too late to hire a hack—and pause on the edge of the bridge-span, at the coffee-house of a burgher named Steinitz, for a hot and much-needed cup. Sometimes he was too late; Steinitz was in bed, and all the shutters up. Wolfgang banged hard on the windows, dancing about in the street and making a fearful uproar. The enraged proprietor finally threw open an upper casement and shouted angrily, 'Who the devil is that? Stop that din or I'll send for the police.' Wolfgang bowed and answered sweetly, "Have no fear, *mein Herr*. It is only a gentleman in a beautiful blue coat with golden buttons, Nanking silk breeches, white stockings, and fine buckled shoes, who ardently desires you to arise at once and make him a cup of coffee. Furthermore, sir"—ignoring the enraged growl from the window—"he prefers it properly strong, *bitte sehr!*"

Pranks like these made Duschek and the opera people a bit nervous, not that they feared for Wolfgang's sanity, but all sorts of difficulties had caused two postponements of the première, and even with the next tentative date two weeks away, there was still a great deal to be done. Wolfgang did not worry. He was used to having malicious obstacles thrown in his way; as for unavoidable accidents—pouf! For the first postponement, a magnificent performance of *Figaro* was substituted, in honor of the visiting Duchess of Tuscany; Wolfgang conducted amid riotous applause.

He had small inclination to stop merrymaking in the interests of serious rehearsal, though the Bertramka was crowded daily with singers, all being coached by the great Mozart himself—who would leave them with their mouths open when his turn came in the bowling-game. However, he was moved to write Jacquin that "there is no such able personnel here as at the theatre in Vienna, so that the opera cannot be learned in a short time"—and the next week, "—a further delay has been occasioned by the illness of one of the singers. As the company is so small, the impresario is obliged to take all possible care of his people, for fear lest some unforeseen indisposition should put him in the most awkward of all awkward situations—that of not being able to stage anything at all!" The company was not only smaller than at Vienna, but not so fine—Teresina Bondini, the manager's wife, either could not or would not grasp the full significance of Zerlina's distress, and more than once Wolfgang gnashed his teeth and swore under his breath, *um Gottes Willen*, if I only had Kelly and Benucci and Storace to sing this opera instead of these bumpkins . . .! "And there are constant delays here because the singers (being lazy) will not rehearse for opera, and the *entrepreneur* (being anxious and fearful) will not force them to do so. . . ."

However, on the 22d of October, the cast was summoned to the theatre for the first stage rehearsal. Only one week was allotted for this work, and Wolfgang labored hard and honorably to whip them into shape. Signora Bondini was his despair—she would not scream behind the locked door as Lorenzo had decreed, and short of hiring some ruffian to double in reality for the Don's fictitious rape, Wolfgang was at his wit's end for a way to teach her. Finally, getting the orchestra started on the scene, he sneaked back to the wings and at the proper moment crept up and pinched her so hard in a vulnerable spot that she screamed like a stuck pig. '*Ah, brava, Signora!*' he cried, 'at least you've learned it. Now continue, gentlemen.'

He found the orchestra far superior to the singers, so superior, indeed, as to be able to appreciate the real meaning of his ideas. They fell in, too, with his peculiar habits of composing, one of which was not to include the brass and drum parts in the original score. One day he finally wrote down the missing parts from memory and brought them in with him, handing them to the players as he said, "Gentlemen, pray be particular at this place"—marking it—"as I believe you will find four bars too many or too few." He was quite right. Another feat of that uncanny memory—to carry the trombone parts, so integrally important in the serious themes, in his head as parts of the whole, and draw them out without the slightest confusion.

But even the serious business of rehearsing could not stop the progress of his holiday, and on the evening of October 28th the Duscheks had a large and very gay party. Wolfgang was, of course, the life of it, dancing to the music of *Figaro*, rushing to the clavier to extemporize a *Deutscher Tanz*, circling the rooms with upraised glass to clink with every well-wisher in the house; and there were many, for the première of *Don Giovanni* was scheduled for to-morrow, the 29th. As it grew late, Duschek, Guardassoni, and Bondini became more and more uneasy, stealing nervous glances at each other, and following Wolfgang's prancing feet with worriedly raised eyebrows. Finally Duschek cornered him and said:

'You know, Wolfgang, this is all very well, but the première is to-morrow and you haven't a note of your overture on paper.' Wolfgang shrugged and waved his hands.

'I'll have it done,' he said.

'Yes,' Bondini put in, '*you* have it done already—in your head—but how is the orchestra going to play it from your head? I know you, Mozart.'

Guardassoni looked his grimmest, and the three finally prevailed on Wolfgang. He sighed and gazed wistfully around the roomful of happy people, shook his white pigtail, and folded his hands meekly.

'Very well,' he said, 'find Stanzi and tell her to make me some punch and bring it to me in my room. And goodnight,' he added sourly. 'Enjoy yourselves.'

When Constanze brought the punch, he was seated at the table, scribbling hard.

'Come here, Stänerl,' he said, reaching for her hand and kissing it, 'and sit right here beside me. I'm terribly sleepy, I don't know how I'll stay awake. Now sit here, little Stanzi-Marini, and for God's sake keep me awake—talk to me, darling, or say verses, or something.'

So she sat down and began to tell him silly stories, chattering as conscientiously as Scheherezade while he dashed off the hollow, portentous chords of the Andante. His whole overture was as perfect in his memory as the rest of the score he had already written out; the problem was only to keep awake, oh, just to keep awake! Constanze's chatter helped, but the punch made him sleepy;

every time she paused his head drooped, his eyelids twitched together, the pen started slipping in his fingers. At three o'clock his chin fell on his breast. Constanze saw he could not go on; she got up, put her arms around him, and propelled him to the couch.

'Only an hour, Stänerl, promise. Only one hour, or I won't get through,' he mumbled. 'You won't let me sleep longer?'

She promised, but had not the heart to wake him in one hour, so she let him sleep until five o'clock. Then he got up and scribbled so furiously that at seven Constanze could send for the copyist. With a great groan of relief, Wolfgang flung himself into bed.

That evening, all streets in Prague led to the yellow opera-house. From the great mansions on the avenues, coaches full of ladies in brocades and jewels, their mountains of white hair glistening with flowers and aigrettes, their escorts gorgeous in velvet and jewelled swords, rolled into the narrow square to the great entrance for boxholders. The good townspeople, brushed and scrubbed, poured into pit and galleries. Even from wretched holes and evil-smelling warrens, hordes of poor but true Bohemians flocked to pay their coppers for a seat somewhere, anywhere, a place under the eaves where they could perch and hear their own new opera. Close to the stage, a box was reserved for the loyal, excited group from the Bertramka. Here were good Franz and Josefa with Constanze between them, and all the other friends who had surrounded Wolfgang and made his working weeks so uniquely happy. The orchestra filed in and took their places shortly before seven. There was a slight hush as the huge audience waited for the conductor; he should appear at once. But he did not. Many a similar occasion would have elicited hisses and catcalls, but they waited patiently for a long twenty minutes. Finally there was a stir at the little door under the stage; that would be he. But no, it was a house attendant, with his hands full of papers. Constanze, white and nervous, could not restrain a faint smile. The boy was bringing in the overture parts, still wet with ink and sticky with sand, and distributing them to the players, who had never seen them before. The copyist had not done as brilliant a rush job as the composer, but when the parts were arranged on the desks, the little door did open for Wolfgang, pale and damp of forehead, but forcefully reassured by a thunder-clap of applause. He bowed, took his place at the clavier and picked up his baton. The first stern, full, unearthly chord flowed out to the tense ears of Prague, then the second. At the resolution into D major, with its enchanting succession of prophetic themes, the house moved as if to break into applause, and the overture subsided in a wave of uncontrolled enthusiasm. With the curtain going up and the violins settling into Leporello's air, Wolfgang winked at the *Konzertmeister* and said out of the side of his mouth, "A good many notes fell under the desks, to be sure, but it went off damn well, just the same."

Posterity has heard finer performances, technically, than Bondini's company gave in Prague that night. But what those singers lacked in voice and training they made up in their magnificent spirit. With the divine inspiration of Mozart himself at the clavier, and with the advantage, not only of having been trained by him, but of being able to watch him as they brought his great work to life in his own hearing, they sang and played like genii. He was deeply moved. He knew the eternal worth of *Don Giovanni,* and the wiser among the players and audience knew it too. At the utterly sublime climax of the first act, where Don Giovanni's ball is the setting for one of the finest scenes in any opera, the house burst into roars, cheers, and bravos.

At the end of the opera, Wolfgang had purposely abandoned in the music all the rough comedy Da Ponte had intended for his *dramma giocoso,* and flung himself passionately into the wild, terrifying punishment meted out to the frightened but always noble reprobate. The solemn, other-worldly notes of the ghostly Commendatore, alternated by stormy, sweeping, chromatic minor scales—the consuming fires of hell and the wails of the damned—gripped and dried every throat in the house, caused eyes to bulge from stinging sockets, breath to come fast and loud. When it was over, there was a moment of tense, pregnant silence; then the graceful white-and-gold interior came suddenly alive. The house was shaken to its cellars by such an overwhelming torrent of applause, shouts, and cheers as it has never sheltered since. In the street outside, the ovation sounded like the reverberation of a battle. Trembling, still bewildered at the violent return to a world of people from his own world of sound, Wolfgang was hoisted onto the stage to take the bows with the deliriously happy singers. Again and again the little man with the plain face and insignificant body was cheered, blessed, and pelted with flowers. Cries of speech, speech, punctuated the salvos of applause and yells of *Viva Maestro!* Someone pushed him, and hesitantly, Wolfgang took a step forward. He stretched out his little white hands in their best lace ruffles, looked for a moment down into the cheering mob. Then, from an overflowing heart, that had known the chill depths of indifference, and would know them more bitterly still, with tears running down his cheeks, he said, *"Meine Prager verstehen mich."*

XVII

1787-1789

WOLFGANG had not realized that the past weeks had been a great strain as well as a memorable fiesta. When the *Don* was finally safe, swashbuckling on Bondini's boards, he turned over the conducting to Strobach with some relief. Then, instead of going straight back to Vienna, he and Constanze lingered on at the Bertramka. The anticipatory excitement was over. They spent lazy days on the terrace watching the last flat baskets of yellow grapes coming down the hill on lovely, balanced heads, and the last golden wine flowing under the brown feet of giggling girls and shouting farmhands. Wolfgang had taken to an occasional pipe now, and he loved to sniff the strong Turkish tobacco floating on the sharp air. The pungent haze of Prague was thickened by smoke from piles of burning leaves, and enriched with gustful smells from the kitchen where onions and herbs and dried mushrooms and great handsome hams went from the black rafters into the blacker pot. Everyone felt intimate and relaxed. Nobody said anything sensible, nobody was expected to. Wolfgang lay back in his chair and wrinkled his nose at the sky and blinked.

'*Aber*, Wolfgang,' he heard Josefa saying through a shrill chorus of birds, 'you are a lazy little lout, you know.'

'You do me wrong,' he said indifferently. 'I'd like to be lazy—but *was ist los?*'

'I'm very cross!' she said.

'*Nun?* And I should do something about it?'

'Certainly. You are talking already about going away and you have not written my aria for me. Lazy! Shameful!' She tweaked his ear.

He remembered he had promised her a new aria. *Ach, Gott!* He ought to do it. Josefa's claim on him was a strong one—hospitality, if not his affection for her and perhaps, if gossip holds any truth, something more. He got up and strolled across to the summer-house. There was a little table inside, and a bench. Well—he shrugged his shoulders and went in. Suddenly the door shut behind him.

'What's that?' he cried. 'Open the door, I don't want it closed.'

'Ha, ha!' Josefa laughed outside. 'Now I've got you. You're locked in!'

'But why?' Wolfgang pleaded. 'I don't like it.'

'Very well. I don't like waiting for my aria.'

He rattled the door.

'*Gott verdammt!*'

'Assuredly. But will you write it now? At once?'

'No! Certainly not. Open the door.'

'Oh, no, *Liebling!* I will open the door when you have written the aria.'

Wolfgang sat down on the bench and laughed.

'You win,' he called. 'Go and bring me my pens and some paper and the poem.' She passed them through the lattice and he started to work. After a time she came back to the door and cried:

'Is it finished?'

'Yes, *dearest* Josefa! It is finished. Unlock the door.'

Mozart

She opened it and he stepped out. Josefa clapped her hands.

'Ah, my aria,' she cried. Wolfgang rolled it up quickly and waved it over her head.

'Oh, no,' he shouted, 'you're wrong! It's my aria!'

Josefa pouted.

'Give it to me, Wolfgang.'

He shook his head, still holding it out of her reach.

'I'll give it to you,' he said, 'on one condition. If you can sing it at sight—perfectly—*aber fehlerfrei*—it's yours.'

By now the others were gathered round them, cheering and taking sides.

'Come on, Josefa! Show what you can do!'

Wolfgang unrolled the paper and held it before her. Josefa took a long look and began. She sang it—the formidably difficult *Bella mia fiamma* (K. 528)—perfectly. Wolfgang put it into her hands and the quarrel ended in a long hug and kiss. Everybody cheered.

The Mozarts stayed on in Prague as long as they dared, but the baby was expected in a few weeks, and it would be dangerous to wait and travel any later. So they reached home in the middle of November. Wolfgang took lodgings in a house near the Hofburg—Unter den Tuchlauben, 281. It has since disappeared, but stood in one of the narrow and poor streets that are so often tucked between a promenade like the Graben and a main square like the Michaelplatz. Here Constanze gave birth, two days after Christmas, to their first daughter. She was christened Theresia for her godmother, Therese von Trattner. From the first she was sickly, and Constanze did not regain her strength as soon as she had after former childbirths. Wolfgang worried; spent more money than he could afford—

or indeed even produce—on nurses, tonics, treatments, and delicacies. He was so preoccupied that he had not time to go about among his friends and hear the reactions to the news of *Don Giovanni's* triumph in Prague. But the Emperor Joseph heard them, and began to ponder.

What if this man should prove to be the greatest composer in the world, as Haydn was reported to have said? Suppose his *Don Giovanni*, when produced in Vienna, should be a wild success as it had been in Prague? Suppose reports of his genius and his difficulties should reach the ears of English or French or Prussian royalty? Mozart would jump at any offer, naturally, and then would Joseph not look a bit sheepish? Or even really be deprived of something worth having? While he was posing these questions to himself, Gluck died. He had still held his position as *Kammerkompositor* to the Emperor, and his salary had been two thousand florins. Pacing in his State corridor, Joseph pursed his lips and pondered. Now that was a good deal of money. All right for Gluck, of course . . . but . . . He sent for one of his confidential lackeys, a rogue named Strak, who, he knew, was an acquaintance of Mozart. As a matter of fact, Strak never missed one of Wolfgang's Sunday morning quartet parties if he could help it, and had always protested his friendship and admiration vehemently, accepting Wolfgang's hospitality as a matter of course. Joseph verified the reports that Strak knew Mozart well. He had been in his house, had he? Many times! And he knew the man's scale of living . . . knew . . . well, what sort of salary he could do with . . . if he were to have a salary . . . that is, if . . . Strak took in the situation and thought quickly. There was no use alarming the stingy king. If Mozart should get a

Mozart

good salary and then not satisfy, who would be blamed, whose judgment damned, but Strak's? The wily liar assured Joseph that if given a court appointment—Gluck's, for instance—he was sure his friend Mozart could do nicely with—well, say eight hundred florins a year. Joseph beamed approval. Fine! Go and send Mozart here at once!

So Wolfgang received his imperial appointment with a reduction of more than half the established salary. He should have been too proud to accept it. But he was not theatrical, and he was also very eager to hold a court position. Humiliation was much more familiar to him than the sweets of realized hope. He had wanted for years to be on Joseph's staff, and now he was. But the one thing happened that Wolfgang expected least in the world. He was practically ignored! Joseph had got him so cheaply that he forgot all about him. He was not, except for balls for the *Redoutensaal*, commissioned for any more music than he had been before. He was puzzled and mortified, and he never found out the real reason for it. His ridiculous salary, which barely covered the rent, was remitted in quarterly payments. After he had received a few of these pittances, having written nothing for them but *Deutsche* and *Menuette*, he took his pen and wrote on a sheet of paper, "Too much for what I do, too little for what I could do." And, sealing it with the receipt, sent it back to court. Every bit of fine music he wrote during his tenure of this court position was commissioned by private individuals for their own parties. He might have been a hanger-on in a crude petty court, instead of Mozart, attached to the staff of the greatest monarch in Europe. Still he did not rebel. He had unshakeable loyalty to his em-

Mozart

peror and his south-German birth, which was the more remarkable since he saw all their disadvantages so clearly.

It was after receiving his salary that Wolfgang began to realize how hopeless was the maze of his debts. Suits and arrests and summonses were nothing new, of course. So far he had managed to keep out of the debtors' jail by robbing Peter to pay Paul, by squeezing this corner or pawning that trinket and hanging onto the edge of security by his fingernails. When a salary actually materialized and he saw how little it did toward solving his future problems, much less toward paying any of his existing debts, he sat down and began to figure. It was plain that he must borrow money. He reviewed all his friends and acquaintances. No musician had any money to spare, and certainly one could not ask it of a nobleman. No, it must be a business man, a merchant, accustomed to dealing with such things. This was not as difficult for Wolfgang as it might have been because there were men of every walk of life in his Masonic lodge. Many of them were in trade, and to them Wolfgang turned now. Michael Puchberg was the first, and if any man in Mozart's life deserves appreciation and gratitude it is this kind burgher and amateur musician who opened his pockets again and again, and helped to stave off, if he could not prevent, disaster.

In June Wolfgang first wrote him.

"Honourable O.B." [*Ordensbruder*, brother Mason]
"Dearest, best of Friends!

The conviction that you are indeed my friend and that you know me for a man of honor emboldens me to disclose all my heart to you, and to make you the following petition. In accordance with the frankness natural to me I will go straight to the point without affectation.

"If you could be so kind, so friendly, as to lend me the sum of one or two thousand gulden for a period of one or two years, at suitable interest, you would be doing me a most radical service! You will no doubt yourself realize and acknowledge that it is inconvenient, nay, impossible, to live from one installment of income to another! . . . If you will do me this friendly service I can *imprimo* (being in funds) more easily meet unavoidable expenses at the proper time, whereas now I have to postpone payment and then, usually at the most inconvenient time, part with my whole income at once, and *secondo*, work with a lighter heart and a carefree mind, and consequently earn more. As to security, I do not suppose you will entertain any doubts! You know, broadly speaking, how I stand, and you know my principles! . . .

"I have now opened my whole heart to you in a situation of great gravity to myself—that is, I have acted as a *true brother*. . . . I do not know, but I think I see in you a man, who, like myself, if it is in any way possible will certainly help his friend, if he be a true friend, his brother if indeed he be a brother. If you should perhaps be unable to spare so large a sum at such short notice, I beg you to lend me a few hundred gulden at least until to-morrow, as my landlord in the Landstrasse"—where he had lived a year before—"was so importunate that I have been obliged to pay him on the spot, and this has put me to great embarrassment! We are to sleep to-day in our new quarters where we shall remain summer and winter. I consider this will do equally well, if not better, for I have little to do in the town, and without the hindrance of numerous visitors, I shall have more time to work. If I have business to transact in the town, which will certainly be seldom, any *fiacre* will take me there for ten kreutzer while these rooms will be cheaper and pleasanter, too, during spring, summer and autumn, as I have a garden. Our rooms are in the Währingergasse, *am Drei Sternen*, No. 135. Now pray accept my letter as a true sign of my entire confidence in you, and remain ever my friend and bro., as I shall remain till the grave,

Your true, most devoted friend and bro.,

W. A. Mozart.

"P.S. When are we to have a little music at your house again?—I have written a new trio!——"

Poor Wolfgang, timidly proffering the only courtesy in his means as acknowledgment! This pathetic gesture was repeated again and again, for he did at first do an enormous amount of work in the new rooms. Puchberg could not spare 2,000 gulden; but he did send 200, and for the rest of Wolfgang's life never refused him money. The Währingergasse where the new lodgings were located is southeast of the central city, and not far from the Jacquins' where Wolfgang loved so much to be. In those days it was a suburb like the Landstrasse. From the time he moved out there, Wolfgang's habits and associations began to change. He was no longer near the Hofburg and the centre of things, no longer accessible to gay and rich and well-born patrons. With a few, like Baron van Swieten and Lichnowsky, who were the most active musically of all the aristocrats, he kept up his connections. But contrary to expectations as a court composer, he hardly ever went to court, and began to find his recreation among plainer and obscurer people, chiefly among musicians of ordinary calibre. He saw more, now, of Constanze's family, from whom he had stayed aloof ever since his marriage. Caecilia had married off all her girls and outlived all her manhunts. Now she saw the Mozarts at other times than when she was needed to help Constanze in child-birth. Sophie, now Sophie Haibl, her youngest

Mozart

daughter, was often with Constanze when Wolfgang had to be away.

As his fortunes waned, though he always thought they would soon and suddenly be made, Wolfgang became a prey for borrowers, cheats and leeches. Borrowed money went even more swiftly through his hands than what he earned. It no more occurred to Wolfgang to refuse a loan to a rag-tag musician than it occurred to him that Puchberg would refuse his appeals. He became known as an easy mark who kept open house and always shared his florins if he had any. The most conspicuous of the leeches was Anton Stadler, a wretched lying thief who took every sort of advantage of Wolfgang and yet made it hard for his poor little friend to believe that such a superb clarinettist could be a rogue. Wolfgang not only shared his house and his pittances with Stadler but immortalized him by writing for him two of the most perfect works in the whole library of the instrument—the clarinet quintet (K. 581) and the concerto (K. 622). And Wolfgang made peace with his mother-in-law so completely that if he went out of an afternoon, Sophie would see him "running up to the house with little packages of sugar and coffee, crying, 'Here, Mama, dear, have a little *Jause!*'"

Just before they moved away from town, as Wolfgang thought, for good, the baby Theresia died. At six months she was too little to have made a place for herself, but Wolfgang could not go repeatedly through these harrowing experiences without suffering. What was the good of these long, dreary spells when Constanze was green and pettish and ungainly, when there was always some doctor to be paid, when a night or day of dreadful agony was followed by the presence in the wooden cradle of a sick,

Mozart

squalling little thing who would soon die—and in dying tear his heart? Four times this had happened, and all that remained was Karl, now a merry four-year-old with charm but not a sign of the promise that his father had shown at the same age.

It was in this depressed frame of mind that Wolfgang began a piece of the most extraordinary work in the history of music—the composition of his three greatest symphonies, completed in eight weeks. First came the E flat (K. 543), finished on June 26. Next, in July, the G minor (K. 550), which has some of the same claims to glory as the quintet in the same key. Last, on August 10, he entered in his little catalogue the Jupiter (K. 551), that noble and imposing work with the *Schlussfuge* (closing fugue) that caused it to be called pure thinking in sound. Wolfgang was a serious symphonic composer. He did not write symphonies in the same off-hand way that he tossed off chamber-music for parties, piano concerti for himself, sonatas for his pupils, and concerti for all the other instruments that his close friends happened to play. He seemed to feel, though he never said, that the symphony had weight and mood and significance, and was the mighty highway on which music was to proceed to its next shining goal. He wrote symphonies at rare intervals; this time for some concerts that would never take place.

Yet his conception of the symphony is perhaps less remarkable than the development he showed from one work to the next. If each symphony had been written a couple of years after the other it would be much more comprehensible. The poetically beautiful E flat has been chosen for the honor of being Wolfgang's farewell to his youth. The dramatic G minor is supposed to be the

Mozart

culmination of all the tragedy and frustration in his life. And the mighty Jupiter is the salute to the future—the promise of the next century. This may or may not be true, depending upon one's taste for reading things into music. Certainly Wolfgang himself had no such ideas. He wrote these symphonies like everything else—in pure creative power and mental delight. "Whence or how they came," he neither knew nor cared. As soon as one was written down he was ready to retire into solitude and start evolving the next. The remarkable feature of his development is not the romantic one, the dividing his life into periods each to be expressed by a type of music, but the plain matter of the instrumentation. In these three symphonies he made successive strides straight into the full-voiced expressions of the nineteenth century, the world of orchestral giants.

Wolfgang had received the symphony form, like the quartet, from Haydn, whom he loved to call his master. But Haydn, who had—and has forever—reached noble heights in his quartets, had failed to realize that the symphony was going to develop from a small ensemble of strings and a few other instruments into a tremendous blending of every voice known to music. Haydn reached for the stars and touched them with his string music, but he never sensed the potentiality of wind instruments. It was Wolfgang who brought the orchestration of the symphony to its fulfillment for that age, sitting in his little garden in the Währingergasse and scoring his masterpieces while he chatted with Jacquin and kept an eye on Karl. He left the field ready for Beethoven, and if he had lived longer he would have changed the whole face of music, giving it a serene, mature quality that it never fully achieved before

Mozart

it was overtaken by the self-conscious emotion of the romantics. Haydn, who lived until 1809, and had the opportunity to study Wolfgang's last symphony scores, was not even able to profit by them; "I have only learnt the proper use of wind instruments in my old age," he said, "and now I must die without turning my knowledge to account."

His three great works of this summer are perhaps the logical indication of Mozart's place in the permanent hierarchy of music. With Bach and Haydn; with Beethoven, Brahms, Wagner, and Verdi, he holds up the main arch; others—and great others—cluster at its sides. Each of the members of the hierarchy made a supreme contribution. Mozart's was unique in the infinite number of its facets. His talent was absolute; his workmanship perfect; his productiveness fabulous; his inspiration divine. He was actually no more prolific and no more of a genius of melody than Schubert; but he had a certain firmness and fullness of conception, combined with great advantages of training, that made his versatility one of the most spectacular things in all art. There was literally no form of music that he did not write supremely well, no instrument whose library he did not enrich; and in that respect he stands alone. Given the necessary stimulus— a definite commission—he was galvanized into unfaltering creation of a sound, masterly, yet incredibly inspired piece of music. And it was immaterial to him whether the commission was an opera, a trio, a symphony, a wind serenade, a set of dances, a concerto, piano sonatas, lyric songs, a mass, or any music else.

Even while one is captivated by the beguiling beauty of his melody and the subtle brilliance of his orchestration,

Mozart

the science of Mozart's music is, in the end, more thrilling than its loveliness. It has irresistible appeal to minds trained in the great schools of art and logic. One word has repeatedly been used about it: architecture. And it is a good word to use, for this music is built with the same instinct for proportion and the same fidelity to elemental laws of structure that built the Parthenon and Chartres Cathedral. Bach's music, in a sturdier and less lyric way, is of the same kind. The surface ornaments of Mozart, like the scrolls and cherubs on a baroque façade, have preoccupied many and have diverted their attention from the underlying structure, but those who see it as a whole know its universal value. The accident that Mozart happened also to be full of spontaneous melody, dramatic fire, tender humor, sophisticated grace, and profound emotion is a bonanza of Providence. Such an accident does not happen twice.

Those who want, in their music, something to fire their brains as well as to touch their hearts and delight their senses are lovers of Mozart. The apparent simplicity of this music, its limpid clarity, are in reality uncompromising forms which exact the maximum from the interpreter. While, with a burst of brilliant, inexact coloratura a singer can create excitement enough to carry off the show, to sing *Dove sono* she has to have a musical conscience, great intelligence, and ten times the vocal craftsmanship. The same is true of the instrumental music. It is sound, ripe, and satisfying. Mozart handles his forms with the sure detachment of the master, dominating yet respecting them. One quality of integrity permeates all his work, whether something so simple as the trio from the third movement of the Haffner symphony, so gay as the *Kleine Nacht-*

musik, so human as *Figaro,* so powerful as the *Schluss-fuge* of the Jupiter, so exciting as the climax of *Don Giovanni,* or so exalted as the *Kyrie* of the Requiem. To come back from these contemplations to a small, homely, nervous man, worrying about his debts in a shabby suburban garden, is to see plainly the workings of the infinite.

Something else contributed to the disturbed and fevered state of Wolfgang's mind at the time he began the symphonies. All the past winter there had been fruitless motions in the direction of a Vienna première for *Don Giovanni,* but it was not until May that Joseph had commanded the new opera to be staged. Wolfgang and Lorenzo had been in a panic of suspense, and had reworked several scenes, cutting, adding, and polishing. But in spite of their work, *Don Giovanni* was a plain failure. There was no applause. Something happened to Wolfgang then and there. The last hopes of a brilliant Vienna success, of final and happy recognition were destroyed in one smashing blow. He knew then that he was not for this Vienna, and perhaps not for this world. Poor Da Ponte was crushed also, but his heart was not bound into the web of *Don Giovanni* like Wolfgang's. Wolfgang became resigned instantly. The hurt was too deep for any action to relieve it. But Lorenzo had fire and fight in him. He swore that *Don Giovanni* should be kept alive, in spite of the giddy indifference of the Viennese to anything that required the least thought and attention. Joseph had said, "That opera is divine; I should even venture that it is more beautiful than *Figaro.* But such music is not meat for the teeth of my Viennese!" Wolfgang's only comment was a quiet remark to Lorenzo: "Give them time to chew on it." So Lorenzo was responsible for the steadily re-

peated performances of the *Don,* persisted in in spite of
public indifference, and "little by little even Vienna of the
dull teeth came to enjoy its savor and appreciate its
beauties."

In Prague Bondini was still coining money with steady
performances of *Figaro* and the *Don.* Wolfgang received
none of the money, but kept his hold on the Prague public.
In spite of this, Bondini allowed his gaze to wander among
other composers and he conjectured that if he increased his
repertoire with more comic operas by a variety of famous
men, he would profit accordingly. So he wrote to Haydn
in December, only a few days after Wolfgang left Prague,
and asked him for an *opera buffa.* Haydn's reply was another of his noble gestures of loyalty to Wolfgang: "If it
is your intention to place the opera on the stage in Prague
I am sorry that I cannot oblige you. My operas are inseparable from the company"—Esterhazy's own, of course
—"for whom I wrote them, and would never produce
their calculated effect apart from their native surroundings. It would be quite another matter if I had the honor
of being commissioned to write a new opera for the theatre
in question. Even then, however, it would be a risk to put
myself in competition with the great Mozart. If I could
only inspire every lover of music, especially among the
great, with feelings as deep, and comprehension as clear as
my own, in listening to the inimitable works of Mozart,
then surely the nations would contend for the possession
of such a jewel within their borders. Prague must strive to
retain the treasure within her grasp—but not without fit-
ting reward. The want of this too often saddens the life of
a great genius, and offers small encouragement for further
efforts in future times. I feel indignant that Mozart has

not yet been engaged at any imperial or royal court. Pardon my wandering from the subject, but Mozart is very dear to me." Haydn wrote, of course, before hearing of Wolfgang's meagre appointment with Joseph.

In anguished haste, Wolfgang was now writing quantities of dances, scrambling to keep ahead of the usurers into whose hands he had fallen. He filled also an order for some piano trios, the G major (K. 564), finished in October, having the wonderfully tranquil Andante with variations that is so much loved. He wrote it for Gottfried Jacquin's sister, Barbara. 1789 opened miserably, the dreariest and saddest year of his life, the least productive, least inspired. From time to time Wolfgang saw Baron von Swieten, who had by now acquired the reputation that was still at its height when Beethoven was living in Vienna. He was the dean of musical patrons, the fiercest and most dreaded of critics. He was director of the court library, and used his influence with all the great nobility to create interest in North German music—naturally too stiff, cold, and intellectual for the flippant public taste. He launched a series of performances of Händel's oratorios in the great hall of the library and in his own house, but had to have them all re-orchestrated for lack of an organ. He engaged Wolfgang to do a number of them,—*Acis und Galatea*, the Messiah, the St. Cecilia's Day Ode, and the *Alexanderfest*. The most direct result of this technical work was its influence on the Requiem.

The countryside that Wolfgang loved was anything but delightful in March. Thaws made the garden a huge gluey puddle. Each time the sun came out he would look up from his table and smile or perhaps get up and move the canary's cage into the open window for the warm spring

Mozart

air. Then a bank of ugly clouds would blot out the light and a cold bitter wind whistle down the garden wall. It chilled Wolfgang through and through. He would sigh— a long, murmuring groan—shut the window, and go back to work. It was fatal to answer knocks at the door these days—more often it was the bailiff than any friend passing by. He had never been able to pay Puchberg the outstanding debts, and now he was mortified at the thought of asking him for more money. He appealed to Franz Hofdemel, judge of the chancery court to ". . . lend me 100 florins till the 20th of next month." While he was torturing himself with worry about repaying that, Constanze told him that she was pregnant once again. Wolfgang could not pretend pleasure or pride. He was terrified. His one thought was the awful burden of debt that would now be enormously increased—how, in the name of God, could he ever hope to get free?

He was none too well himself, and tormented with these apprehensions, when Prince Karl Lichnowsky, who had been his pupil, told him that he was going on a journey to central Germany and to Berlin to pay a visit to Frederick William of Prussia. Would Wolfgang care to go along? Would it help him? It seemed the only thing to do. Wolfgang knew that for all his miserable condition at home, he had by now a great reputation abroad, and his operas had reached most of the important stages in Europe. He thanked Lichnowsky fervently and prepared to set out once more to seek his fortune. It was the first such trip in many years. He had acquired a taste for roving early in life, and like most rovers thought that all he needed for perfect happiness was a permanent home! But he left with misgivings. Constanze was sick and could not manage easily alone; obviously he could not take her; what should he do? Here Michael Puchberg and his wife stepped in and offered to look after Constanze and help her if she needed it. In the first days of April Wolfgang and Lichnowsky left. This was the first time in the seven years of their marriage that he had been away from Constanze. His letters to her from this time on—he had never had occasion to write any before—are a last glimpse of the pure delight and mischief that had always flavored his happiness.

XVIII

1789–1790

8th April, 1789, Budweis.

"Dearest little Wife:

"While the Prince is engaged in bargaining for horses, I joyfully seize the occasion to write you a few lines, little wife of my heart! How goes it with you? Do you think of me as often as I think of you? Every moment I look at your portrait and weep, half for joy, half for sorrow! Look after your precious health which means so much to me, my dear, and farewell!—Do not be anxious on my account, for I am suffering no hardships or inconveniences on this journey save that of thy absence which since it can't be cured must be endured. I write with eyes full of tears. *Adieu.*"

Dresden, 13th April, 1789.

" . . . Dearest little wife, if only I had a letter from you! If I were to tell you all the things I do with your dear portrait you would often laugh, I think! For instance, when I take it out of its case, I say, 'Good-morrow, Stanzerl! Good-day, little rogue!—pussy-wussy! Saucy one! good-for-nothing!—dainty morsel!' And when I put it back I slip it in little by little saying all the time, '*nu—nu-nu—nu!*' with just the peculiar emphasis this very meaningful word demands, and then, just at the last, quickly, 'Good-night, little pet—sleep sound!' Well, I suppose that what I have written is folly (to the world, at least), but to us, loving each other so devotedly as we do, it is *not* folly. To-day is the sixth since I have left you, and by God, it seems a year! *Adieu*, my dear, my only love. The carriage is here—that does not mean, 'Bravo! The carriage is here, but *male!*'—Farewell, and love me forever as I love thee. A million tenderest kisses to thee.

"P. S.—Is our Karl being a good boy? I hope so. Kiss him for me. All kind messages to Herr and Frau Puchberg."

Mozart

In Dresden Wolfgang saw Josefa Duschek, with what joy he wrote Constanze, and both appeared at the Saxon court where Wolfgang was given a gold snuff-box containing 100 ducats. Before he left he wrote, "Dearest little wife, I have a number of requests to make of you:

1mo, I beg you not to be sad.

2do, that you take care of your health and do not trust the spring air.

3tia, that you don't go alone on foot, or better still, don't walk at all.

4ta, that you rest assured of my entire love. I have not written you a letter that I have not had your dear portrait before me.

5to, I beg you to consider not only my honor and yours in your conduct, but also appearances. Don't be angry at this request. You should love me all the more because I make so much of honor.

6to & ultimo, I beg you to be detailed in your letters. I should like very much to know whether our brother-in-law Hofer came the day after I left? whether he comes often, as he told me he would? whether the Langes have come yet? whether he is working on the portrait? what all the details of your life are?"

This harks back to the letters Leopold had written Wolfgang in the old days. Only in details like these can anything of prudent, didactic Leopold be seen in careless, generous Wolfgang. As for his reprimand to Constanze— it was not the first. She meant and did no harm; but her life was dreary and she was always ready to snatch any kind of amusement that came her way. She had not the background or poise to know instinctively what was good taste and what was not. In the most delicate, hesitant way Wolfgang tried to teach her. She reaped the benefit years later, as the wife of a Danish diplomat.

Mozart

Wolfgang went on to Leipzig, which meant one thing in the world to him—the Thomasschule and the music of J. S. Bach. Bach's successor as cantor was Anton Doles, to whom Wolfgang hurried when he arrived. He had concerts to attend to, but spent all the time he could at the organ in the famous Thomaskirche. He played it so magnificently that Doles declared "Sebastian Bach has risen again!" Then the precentor made the choir sing a motet, *Singet dem Herrn ein neues Lied*. With the first notes Wolfgang sat bolt upright, rigid with excitement, following each voice. "There!" he gasped when it was over, "there's music from which a man may learn something." He insisted on seeing all the Bach manuscripts that had lain hidden and unpublished in the Thomasschule since the master's death. He spread the parts on the benches and tables all around him, and on his knees, and studied them in the greatest excitement, turning with quick, passionate little motions from one to the next and exclaiming with intense joy at every page.

He spent every evening in Leipzig at Doles' house and it was there, while playing parts of *Die Entführung* on the piano, that he said, "It is all very well for this sort of thing, but too long on the stage. When I wrote it I was never tired of hearing my own music and didn't know how to bring it to a conclusion."

Two days later he arrived in Berlin and went to put up at an inn. First he asked what opera was being given that evening.

'*Die Entführung aus dem Serail*, by Herr Mozart,' he was told.

'So?' And without waiting for his room or supper he hurried out.

Mozart

He was still in travelling clothes, "short, quick, restless, and weak-eyed—an insignificant figure in a grey overcoat." He bought a ticket and went in. At first he stood near the back of the pit, but as the first act went on, moved unconsciously forward down the aisle. Finally he sat down close to the orchestra and angered all his neighbors by a series of astonishing comments on the performance, which was bad. At last, when Pedrillo was singing *"nur ein feiger Tropf verzaget"* the second violins, for no reason, played D sharp. "Damn you," Wolfgang screamed, jumping out of his seat, "play D, will you?" Pandemonium. He was on the point of being put out when some one in the orchestra recognized him.

'It's Mozart. There's Mozart himself—see?—the funny little man with the light hair—' Word flew about the house.

Wolfgang apologized to the conductor and the performance was ordered to continue. But now there was another uproar. Wolfgang was summoned into the pit. The frantic conductor explained that Henriette Baranius, the soprano singing Blöndchen, had refused to continue.

'Why?' Wolfgang asked in astonishment.

'She says she will not sing another note while you are in the house.'

'Nonsense,' Wolfgang said. 'Where is she?'

He went back to the wings. There, firmly seated with a stubborn glare on her lovely face, in a beautiful costume far too good for the stage, let alone for the character of the maid, was the famous Baranius. Wolfgang bowed low.

'The very greatest pleasure,' he murmured, fixing her with his eye. 'Your singing is heavenly.'

Baranius tossed her head. 'You've been making a good

many remarks for one who thought the singing heavenly,'
she flared.

'Thousand pardons!' Wolfgang begged. 'It was by no
means your singing, Madame. I beg you to believe me. It
was rather the orchestra.'

'Then why didn't you stay outside and coach the orchestra?'

'Because,' Wolfgang said uneasily, looking at her under
a lifted eyebrow, 'because the conductor—implied—that
Madame—' He paused and coughed. Baranius was trying
hard to smother a laugh. In a moment she failed.

'Stupid!' she teased. '*Esel!* Now how are you going to
save the performance?'

'I don't know,' Wolfgang said cheerfully. 'I came back
here to see if I could help. In other words, if I could not
persuade the great prima donna to go on again.'

Baranius shook her head. 'No, you can't. That is, you
can't, except on one condition.'

Wolfgang began to smile. He liked this.

'What is it?'

'That you stop right here and now and coach me in the
rest of my part.'

'But there's no time,' Wolfgang gasped. 'And besides
everyone is waiting.'

'No matter, let them wait. I will not go on until I have
had a lesson from the master—the great *Kapellmeister*
Mozart.' She got off her perch and made a deep curtsey.

'This is your affair,' Wolfgang said with an answering
bow. 'If you break up the performance, be it on your
head.' She gave him her hand and led him away to her
dressing-room. The eye-witness who described this scene
for posterity does not tell us what happened to the audience.

Mozart

Wolfgang's affair with Baranius was a worry to his friends in Berlin, because she was dangerous. She was the kind who cost money. Among other things, she was known to enjoy Frederick William's protection, which made it questionable tactics to fool with her. She wore the most beautiful gowns and jewels in the capital. Certainly Wolfgang could not hope to compete with her rich admirers, and that might result in embarrassment or trouble for him. Baranius had picked him up and stuck him in her cap, her newest feather. Wolfgang was flattered, but while legend likes to say he was extricated with difficulty, there is no reason to believe it. He enjoyed himself and when he was ready to go home, dropped her and turned to Constanze with relief.

Frederick William received him with great cordiality. Wolfgang appeared several times at Potsdam but made himself unpopular with the orchestra by showing plainly his dislike for the king's French musicians, chiefly for Duport the *Kapellmeister*. Duport persisted in speaking French. This was too much for Wolfgang who snorted, "The grinning mounseer has been long enough making German money and eating German bread to be able to speak the language or at least murder it with his French grimaces as best he may." Duport retaliated by starting a nasty cabal and doing Wolfgang every possible injury in the eyes of the king. But Frederick William of Prussia was a just and an intelligent man. He was kind to Wolfgang and offered him a salary of three thousand thalers as head *Kapellmeister*. And did Wolfgang jump at it? Did he grow dizzy with joy as he saw all his debts vanish and lifelong security become sure? He did not. He saw Vienna, heard the warm laughing voices of his friends, thought of his little home in the suburbs with his green garden and his bird and dog. He thought of Constanze, with her love of people and pleasure, exiled with him in this stiff, cold, barrack-like court. He smiled. "Am I to leave my good emperor?" he asked diffidently. Frederick William was touched. "Consider my proposal," he said kindly. "I shall keep my promise, even if it should be a year before you return to claim it." Those (and there are some) who doubt, for lack of a record in the Potsdam archives, that Frederick William ever made this offer to Mozart, base their reasoning on the ground that he could not have afforded to refuse it. The fallacy of their premise is a failure to understand Mozart's salient characteristics—the warm-hearted *laissez-faire*, the casual indifference to money, the same combination of loyalty and inertia that held him to the Webers after he was repulsed by Aloysia. He was capable of rejecting any offer that might take him away from the place where he felt he belonged; but it was no moral issue with him, it was instinct. And he felt his own destiny much more keenly than his childish improvidence ever suggested.

The Prussian king did commission six quartets from Wolfgang, and six easy piano sonatas for his young daughter, and gave him 100 *friedrichsdor*. Of this, Wolfgang loaned 100 florins to "a friend I could not refuse," and started home no better off than he had been. He had broken the stay in Berlin with a return journey to Leipzig, where he gave a concert that made no money because Wolfgang allowed more than half the seats to be given away instead of sold. On his way home he wrote Constanze from Prague not to forget "to bring someone with you"—to meet him at the diligence office—"who can deal with the Customs instead of me. *Adieu*. God, how I rejoice in the thought of seeing you again."

He found her very sick. Her pregnancy was causing more trouble than any previous one, and her legs and feet were affected. They were swollen and painful. This was an omen of the ensuing year—the lowest ebb of his fortunes, his spirits, and his work. "My God," he wrote Puchberg in July, "I could not wish my worst enemy in my present case! And if you, my best friend and brother, forsake me, I unfortunate and blameless, and my poor sick wife and child, are all lost together." Constanze had been ordered by the physician to go to Baden-bei-Wien, a watering-place near Vienna, and take the medicinal baths. This was a nightmare of expense to Wolfgang, meaning as it did that he must keep two establishments running, or pay board for her and Karl, whom she had taken with her. The summer was unremitting hell. Puchberg was his only resort, and though the good man was willing to help, he had not un-limited money. Wolfgang's appeals were continuous and increasingly wild and desperate in tone.

"Oh, God! Here I am with fresh entreaties instead of thanks—with new demands instead of payments! I think I need not tell you over again that I have been prevented from earning anything by this unfortunate illness; but I must mention that despite my miserable condition I de-termined to give a subscription concert at home, so that I could at least meet the great and frequent day by day ex-penses (for which I was sure you would be kind and have patience with me) but—even this failed me! Fate is so unhappily against me (though only in Vienna) that I *cannot* make any money whatever I do. I sent round the list [soliciting subscriptions for the concert] a fortnight ago, and the only name upon it is that of Swieten! Now that my dear little wife seems to be improving from day to day, I should be able to work again if this blow, this hard blow, had not fallen upon me. At least they tell us she is improving—although yesterday, the 14th, I was quite cast down and in despair, she was in such pain again and I—with her! Last night, however, she slept so well and has seemed so cheerful all morning that I am full of hope. . . . Dearest, best friend and brother, you know my present circumstances but you also know my prospects. . . . The point is now, my only friend, whether you will and can lend me another 500 florins? I would suggest that until my affairs are settled I should pay you back ten florins a month. . . . You now know all. . . . Only do not be offended by my trust in you, and remember that without your support the honor, peace of mind, the very life, perhaps, of your friend and brother are forfeit. . . .

"Oh, God! I can scarcely make up my mind to send you this letter! And yet I must! Had this illness not befallen us . . . yet I hope for your forgiveness, for you know both the good and evil of my position. . . . *Adieu!*— Forgive me, for God's sake, only forgive me!—and— *Adieu!*——"

The anguish of these letters is emphasized by the fact that they were all written to one person. It is impossible not to wonder what had become of Wolfgang's loyal friends of two years before, when all his desperate appeals are now sent to this one Masonic brother. Jacquin, who had been so close to Wolfgang, seemed from this time on to disappear from his life. Nobody with whom he had been accustomed to carouse sought him out now; even

Mozart

Lorenzo had more or less dropped him when he moved away from town. Vienna itself had changed as Wolfgang learned when his old subscribers showed they had abandoned him. The greatest pianist—forgotten by a giddy faithless public! Then Joseph himself was not so carefree. He was profoundly frightened by events in France and at home he had plenty of cause for fear. The Turks were pressing his southern provinces hard and at last he had to go to war himself to subdue them. Also, though a comparatively young man, he was tired, disappointed, lonely, and ill. The gaiety of the court collapsed like a pricked bubble. There were not so many dashing young bloods about, nor so many charming singers and dancers at the opera. Life was running downhill.

Toward the end of July Constanze's illness took such a sharp turn for the worse that ". . . she is amazingly resigned to her fate, and waits recovery or death with true philosophic resignation." Wolfgang wore himself to the last shred of energy in taking care of her. She had little physical resistance and not so much intelligence as he, and he had therefore to provide mental strength as well as practical care. It was during this illness, when Sophie Haibl often came in to help with the nursing and housekeeping, that she told a friend how, after Constanze had been ill for fully eight months, ". . . I was sitting by her bed and so was Mozart. He was composing, and I was watching the sleep into which she had at last fallen; we were as quiet as the grave for fear of disturbing her. A rough maid-servant came suddenly into the room. Mozart, fearing that his wife would be awakened, wished to beckon for silence, and pushed his chair backward with an open knife in his hand. The knife struck between his chair and his thigh and went almost up to the handle in his flesh. Mozart was usually very susceptible of pain but beckoned me to follow him out of the room. We went into another room where our good mother was concealed, because we did not wish Mozart to know how ill his wife was, and yet the mother's presence was necessary. She bound the wound and cured it with healing oil. He went lame for some time, but took care that his wife should know nothing of it."

Wolfgang took so much to heart the doctor's orders for complete quiet that he fell into the habit of tiptoeing about the house and hushing everyone who spoke to him, with his finger on his lip and a "Chut!" He became so used to hushing people that if he saw a friend approaching on the street he did the same thing. In August Constanze recovered somewhat—at least enough to draw another rebuke from Wolfgang concerning her behavior in Baden. It is difficult to believe that her illness, brought on by pregnancy, permitted her to undertake anything more than a mild flirtation; yet her indulgence in this, overlooking his recent extraordinary devotion by her sickbed, indicates a certain shallowness of character. Of course she was bored with hardship of all kinds, and glad to smile with anyone who was not associated with illness, discomfort, or worry. While she was in Baden, Wolfgang spent most of his time in Vienna, and went to join her over night or for week-ends. He supervised every detail of her convalescence. "I hope you got my second letter yesterday with the decoction, the electuary, and the ants' eggs. I set off to-morrow morning at five o'clock. Dear little wife! I will be quite frank with you. You have no need to be unhappy. You have a husband who loves you and does all he can for you. As to your foot, you need only have patience. It will certainly get well. I am glad if you are in spirits—of course I am—only I could wish you would not sometimes make yourself so cheap! You are too free, I think, with ——, just as with ——, when he was in Baden. . . . You know the consequences of that. And remember, too, the promise you gave me. Oh, God!—only trust my love—be merry and happy and kind with me—do not torment me with needless jealousy! Have confidence in my love—you have proofs of it, surely—and you shall see how happy we shall be. Do not doubt that it is only by her prudent behavior that a woman can enchain her husband."

This misery could not go on indefinitely. Wolfgang was hounded by innumerable creditors, and so harassed that he wrote nothing of any importance until in September he finished the clarinet quintet for Stadler. This starts in such a lovely, peaceful phrase that it is obviously the expression of the freedom Wolfgang could only long for and dream about. Stadler retaliated by stealing some pawn tickets from a cupboard, selling them, and pocketing the money. Wolfgang remonstrated pitifully, forgave him; that was all. The lodgings in the suburb were more than he could afford now, and the bad late fall weather depressed him extremely. He decided to move back to town, in spite of the bailiffs, who could reach him more easily there. He had received a commission from the Emperor—the first since his appointment—for an opera for winter production. It would be easier to work on it and superintend rehearsals if he were in town, and also he would be accessible to Lorenzo, for of course Lorenzo must write the libretto. So in November, having brought Constanze

Mozart

home from Baden in the last stage of her pregnancy, he chose the best quarters he could find for the miserable rent he could afford, and they moved into them—*am* Judenplatz, 245. Constance, with legs so swollen she could not walk, racked with nausea and pain, was put to bed at once, and on November 16th Wolfgang ran once more for the midwife. This time Constanze's labor was the most supreme agony of all; and after her piercing screams and shrieks had subsided, she was told she had given birth to a girl who died as she was christened—Anna, for Wolfgang's mother.

They reached the nadir of poverty in midwinter. The housekeeping had fallen into utter confusion and half their food was brought in from "The Silver Serpent" in the Kärntnerstrasse, where Wolfgang and his friends had long been habitués. The proprietor, Josef Deiner, could not see Mozart's wretchedness without longing to help. One day he came into the work-room which was deathly cold and clammy. Wolfgang and Constanze, with pale faces and blue lips, were clinging together laughing and dancing crazily around the room. Deiner gaped at them.

'What on earth are you doing? Teaching your wife to dance?'

Wolfgang stopped and began chafing his purple hands. 'No,' he said grimacing, 'we are frozen through, and trying to get warm.'

Deiner looked unhappily at the stove.

'Oh, yes,' Wolfgang said, 'it's cold. We have no wood, you see—and—no money to buy any.'

Deiner made a strange noise in his throat and dashed out. He came back in a few moments with several armfuls of wood.

Mozart

'I can't pay you,' Wolfgang said wearily.

'No, no, don't speak of that.'

'Well—dear, good Josef—put it down in your book, and I'll pay—when I have some money.'

Deiner was not the only one who saw their miserable condition. But nothing was done to relieve them until Wolfgang received his payment for *Così Fan Tutte* (K. 588), the opera he was writing with Lorenzo. For once Da Ponte had not taken some familiar story and reset it in his own bright words. He tried an original tale, a gay and charming trifle, graceful, amusing, and inconsequential even to the point of being preposterous, which does not harm it as a comic operetta. But in comparison with Lorenzo's previous masterpieces it has always been thought trivial. Wolfgang was provided with no such inspiration as in *Figaro* and *Don Giovanni*, and though he produced a witty and a beautiful score, he himself never had much affection for it. It was staged toward the end of January, and was successful, at least in the eyes of a music critic who wrote: "I have again to announce a new and excellent work by Mozart acquired by our theatre. It was performed yesterday for the first time at the Imperial National Theatre. Of the music suffice it to say that it is by Mozart."

The sense of change and depression that had been descending on Vienna was crystallized on the 20th of February, 1790, when the Emperor Joseph died. Aside from the political aspects of his death, the little world of court music was thrown completely into confusion. Joseph's successor was his brother, Leopold II, a stupid, narrow weakling, who neither knew nor cared anything about music. As might be expected of such a small man, his one idea was to assert his new authority in any way that would disrupt the routine of his older and greater brother. He turned on each of the men who had enjoyed Joseph's favor and either dismissed him or made him so uncomfortable that he resigned. Salieri was one of the first to leave, and from the day of his resignation his persecution of Wolfgang ceased. Many of the singers left also; Count Rosenberg was replaced by another director, and, worst of all, Lorenzo was in trouble too.

Wolfgang was bewildered and deeply uneasy. What was he to do now? All this changing about might mean that he would land at the very bottom of the pile. And—on the other hand ". . . I make so bold as very respectfully to beg your Royal Highness [the Archduke Franz] to be so gracious as to speak to His Majesty the King touching my most humble petition to his majesty. Prompted by a desire for fame, by a love of my work, and by a conviction of my own talents, I venture to apply for the post of second *Kapellmeister*." This was before the resignation of Salieri, still head *Kapellmeister* in charge of dramatic music. Wolfgang hoped to be put in charge of the court orchestra and of the cathedral music. He had long ago given up his warm, youthful hopes of triumphing as an opera composer. "Salieri, the very able *Kapellmeister*, has never devoted himself to the ecclesiastical style in music, whereas I have made myself completely familiar with this style from my youth up. Some small renown now accorded me by the world for my performances on the piano-forte encourages me also to beg for the favor of being entrusted with the musical instruction of the Royal Family." Is it necessary to add that Wolfgang never received either appointment? Leopold ignored him.

Mozart

One reason for this may have been the scandals now beginning to seep around Vienna concerning Wolfgang's debts. He could not keep them a secret, indeed did not try. But his miserable debts had been magnified by the public tongue until the formidable sum of 30,000 florins was visited on his head, and the tales reached the new Emperor. He believed them and probably decided with a shrug that any man so unreliable and improvident would be more troublesome than useful, and might get into still worse scandals which would reflect discredit on the court.

There were few alternatives for Wolfgang. Where he had once scorned teaching and reluctantly accepted a few rich pupils just until his permanent appointment should materialize, he now went begging for them. There was no use trying to reënlist his old concert subscribers. Puchberg began to hear from him again. "You will have heard, no doubt, from your household that I called at your house yesterday, intending to dine there uninvited (as you gave me permission to do). You know how things are with me —in short, being unable to find a friend to help me, I have been obliged to resort to the money-lenders; but as it takes some time to seek out the most Christian among this un-Christian class of people, I am at the moment so utterly penniless that I have to beg you, dearest friend, by all that is sacred, to help me with whatever you can spare! If I get the money, as I hope to do, in a week or a fortnight, I will at once repay what you lend me now, though I must, alas! still ask you to have patience touching the sums for which I have been already long indebted to you. If you only knew how all this worries and troubles me! It has kept me all this time from finishing my quartets"—for Frederick William. "P.S. I now have two pupils and would like to make up the number to eight. Pray spread it abroad that I give lessons."

From the moneylenders he had borrowed 800 florins, contracting to repay them 1,000. With this sword hanging over his head, he found it practically impossible to work, swamped in mind as well as in action. He struggled through two quartets, only to write Puchberg, "I have just been obliged to part with them (that difficult work) for a mere song so as to get some ready money. I am now working at some clavier sonatas for the same reason." He was writing from Baden where he had moved, leaving the Judenplatz "for the sake of economy, only going into town when it is absolutely necessary." Constanze had taken to poor health again, never having completely recovered from her phlebitis (which seems to have been her disease) of the previous year. "She will have to take the baths sixty times and go away again in the autumn. God grant it will do her good. Dearest friend, if you can help with the present pressing expenses, oh, do so!"

Wolfgang kept an eye on the musical situation in Vienna and on the Emperor's movements. Leopold was to be crowned head of the Holy Roman Empire at Frankfort in September, which gave Wolfgang the idea of going there for the ceremonies. He took his brother-in-law, Hofer the violinist, with him, and procured the money for their expenses by pawning his silver-plate and some of Constanze's trinkets.

"Dearest, best little wife of my heart! . . . We are at this moment arrived, so we have taken only six days. . . . We had fine weather except for one day; even this caused us no discomfort as my carriage (I should like to give it a kiss) is magnificent. At Ratisbon we dined royally at midday, to the accompaniment of divine music, with angelic cooking, and most excellent Moselle wine. We breakfasted at Nuremberg, a hideous town"—thus eighteenth-century taste. "At Wurzburg we warmed our precious stomachs with coffee. . . . I am firmly resolved to make all the money I can here and return to you rejoicing. What a fine life we shall live then! I will work—work so hard —that no unforeseen accident shall ever reduce us to such desperate straits again." He continued with directions for arranging about the payment of the thousand florins he owed through an advance from Hofmeister, his Leipzig publisher. In the next letter the business began to appear less simple—"I certainly shall not be able to make enough here to be able to pay 800 or 1,000 florins immediately on my return." He expected Constanze to negotiate the advance, which she was not able to do. He had written so sadly and earnestly about it that on reading over his letter he had a twinge of heartache. Poor little Stänzerl! So: "P.S. Tears rained upon the paper as I wrote the foregoing page, but now let us cheer up! Catch!—an astonishing number of kisses are flying about! The devil!—I see a whole crowd of them, too. Ha, ha! I have just grabbed three—they are delicious!"

Wolfgang played one concert with Hofer in Frankfort, and did not make enough to pay his expenses. The Court took no notice of his presence. He played, among others of his works, the piano concerto in D (K. 537) which has accordingly been named the "Coronation Concerto." He and Hofer made their way home by old, familiar ground —first Mannheim, where a performer tried to keep him out of the house where *Figaro* was being rehearsed. "Surely you will let *Kapellmeister* Mozart listen!" the little man (who looked like "a journeyman tailor") remonstrated. This trip had no interludes like the Baranius adventure. Then they passed through Heidelberg, Augsburg, and Munich, Wolfgang looking out at the familiar landscape as it jerked by and harking back to other rides when he had been whisked across Germany in search of fame and fortune. That was all so many years ago. Fame had come, in a measure, but no fortune. Wolfgang was very, very tired. He reached home on the 10th of November, almost hysterically glad to see Constanze again. He clung to her, and relieved his burdened mind and heart in his own passionate way. That was unfortunate; before the month was over she was pregnant again.

Before leaving for Frankfort Wolfgang had moved his family back to town, and on the strength of his hopes of the trip, and a slight improvement in his state of mind, had taken rooms in a house on the Rauhensteingasse, 970. It was called the *Kleiner Kaisersteinchen Haus*, and the building that replaces it to-day bears the name of "*Mozarthof*." They had collected their meagre belongings and Constanze had done what she could to make a home. They had almost no furniture of their own, and all their valuables were in pawn. But such property as they had was disposed in the rooms, and was inventoried after Wolfgang's death, by his creditors. It included, first, his piano-forte of walnut-wood, with white sharps and flats and black naturals, valued at 80 florins. In 1810, when Constanze sent it to Karl who was living in Milan, she wrote: "It is as good as it was, I should say even better than it was; first, because I have taken great care of it, and second, because Walter, who made it, has been kind enough to overhaul it and re-felt it for me. Since then I could have sold it many times;

but I hold it as dear as I do my children, and therefore I shall let no one have it but you, if you promise to take as good care of it as I did, and never to part with it."

The next item of any value was the *Billard* Wolfgang loved, worth 60 florins, and his clothes, in which he had taken such pride, marked at 55 florins altogether. They included his coats of white (his court coat, of course), blue, red (his favorite coat), brown, black, and mouse-gray cloth. His viola, on which he had played the quartets with Haydn, was marked at 4 florins, and three silver spoons, all the plate not pawned or sold, at 7 florins. Among his debts were a bill to one tailor for 282 florins, 13 florins to another, 179 florins to the apothecary, and 208 to the upholsterer. He died in debt to Puchberg 1,000 florins, which Constanze eventually paid, as she did 918 florins in other debts not including loans. Family hardships alone did not force Wolfgang into debt. He bought clothes and trinkets and small luxuries that both he and Constanze could well have gone without. It was his nature to love neatness and a bit of finery; he did not live long enough to learn how to curb his tastes.

By far the most interesting properties he left were his library and his own manuscripts. There were piles of the latter, many of the great scores, some completed manuscripts, some fragmentary; quantities that had remained unpublished. Constanze subsequently sold most of them to André the music publisher of Offenbach, though André had refused to buy any from Wolfgang himself, or to advance him money when he was in Frankfort for the coronation. Wolfgang left forty-six books. Among them were poetry (which he often read in search of lyrics for songs); plays and dramatic texts; technical and theoretical

Mozart

works on music; three volumes of biography; travel books,
periodicals, and almanacs; such miscellanies as Anthoma-
the's *Of the Capacity of Human Understanding* (in the
original English); and some pamphlets protesting certain
evils of the period, such as the Catholic domination, Reac-
tionism, and the practice of castration for the production
of male sopranos. Then he had kept all the textbooks of
his school days, including the *Rechenkunst und Algebra*
he had so loved. Nearly all his books were in German,
but in addition to the English philosophy, there were some
French and Italian works and naturally a Latin Bible. Of
course, he had also owned a quantity of published music
by his friends and those he considered his masters—Bach,
Gluck, and Haydn.

When Wolfgang returned from Frankfort and settled
in his new (and last) home, he sat down and devoted some
careful thought to his condition. He did not blame himself for his financial predicament, but he did realize that it
was months since he had written anything he was proud of,
or anything that had earned any money. The former sort
of works required patrons, the latter required that he concentrate his great power on cheap dance music. Very well.
He set his pale lips firmly. He would do all the work he
could find to do—good or cheap, he did not care. Money
was the vital thing now. If he could get beyond the tormenting creditors, beyond the nausea that swept him
whenever there was a knock on the door, he might pull
himself together and be ready when his big chance came.
The first work done in the new spirit of determination was
a string quintet in D (K. 593) commissioned by some unknown private patron for a salon party. It went easily and
Wolfgang was encouraged to feel that perhaps the fire was
not all gone, nor the well of inspiration entirely dry.

Mozart

Then, at the end of December the finger of necessity points to a new sort of composition for Wolfgang— *"Adagio und Allegro für ein Orgelwerk in einer Uhr."* Later came an Andante and Waltz "for a small barrel-organ," and a Fantasia for a chiming clock. These were all composed for the musical toys that have typified the dainty, tinkling eighteenth-century taste to many minds. Music-boxes with the familiar revolving metal cylinders bristling with little prongs were all the rage in Vienna now —so the best ones must surely have good music, as good as could be had; *Kapellmeister* Mozart's, for instance! But even this was not such a criminal waste of Wolfgang's genius as the work he did in the first two months of 1791 —sets of dances at the rate of one every four or five days. For the carnival balls at the *Redoutensaal,* and for private parties, he produced incredible numbers of *Menuette, Kontretänze, Deutsche,* and *Ländler* (country-dances). He was comparatively well paid for these and for the first time in two years could make a gesture of keeping up with his current expenses. His debts he could not pay. The mass of dances is a telling revelation. There are enough beautiful melodies scattered through the hasty potboilers to provide Wolfgang with material for all the serious music he could have written.

The miraculous recuperation of Wolfgang's creative force in the last year of his life is one of the inscrutable moves of a ruthless fate. His mind and spirits were not reinforced and refreshed. While the flame burned more fiercely and drove him upward to stupendous achievement, his poor body withered, his brain faltered, his tender natural simplicity, as if realizing itself wasted on a crass world, shrivelled and ebbed away. He came to the inarticulate conclusion that his ideals and standards had done little enough for him, his talent even less. The nightmare of the past two years had left welts and scars that he could not look at without a revulsion of horror. Constanze too had suffered. Having grown used to the lengthening separations she made no effort to avoid them, which would somewhat have consoled Wolfgang, but could stay away from him on grounds of lesser necessity. She had no longer to be at death's door to go for a rest-cure to Baden; a slight weakness was sufficient excuse. And there was probably a stronger reason—an officer stationed at Baden who now seems very plausible cause for her protracted visits there. Technically this may be no worse than the slips that Wolfgang made; but weighed in the balance of his necessity and devotion, and the staggering debts incurred for her sake, it is inhumanly cruel. Constanze could not help her nature, could not change the fact that she was an indifferent mother, never caring how little she was with her children. But it is hard to excuse a nature so small, a mind so superficial, that she saw very little more in Mozart than her sister had, who called him "only a little man." Yet perhaps she was as much the wife for him now as in the early days. She had never kept a fierce proprietary grip on him, and she was far from a steadying influence, but her actual presence at home had a significance to him that weakened as she remained away. Wolfgang could never tell when another wave of catastrophe might engulf him. In a plain spirit of abandon—"tomorrow we die"—he threw himself into every prospect that promised diversion; or, better still, oblivion.

XIX

1791

SOME time during the past year Wolfgang had run into an old acquaintance—Emanuel Schikaneder, the wandering theatrical manager he had met ten years before in Salzburg. Since then Schikaneder had had an astonishing career, with numerous scandals, lawsuits, and unsavory vicissitudes. He had tried his hand at trouping and at running repertoire theatres in small cities; once he was banished from Vienna, but had now returned and was settled in a small theatre on the outskirts of the city—*der Theater auf der Wieden*. This building was really a wooden shack, run on a shoestring and patronized by the common populace. Schikaneder had a fairly able company, who made up in versatility and their ability to get themselves talked about what they lacked in dramatic and musical quality. He chose for his shows anything he thought might catch the public pennies—plays or German *Singspiel*. From time to time he had been successful and was known to have made money, which he never used for paying his obligations. But just now he had had a long run of bad luck.

Schikaneder had sprung from the lowest dregs of poverty. He was a big, coarse-faced, black-browed man, with jowls and chin running over onto his greasy linen, a large shapeless nose, and thick lips. He had a loud, crude voice, sang basso parts in his productions, and was a clever comedian. Living by his wits, he had picked up enough reading and writing to be literate, and therefore to steal and garble German plays. But he also had enough taste to stage the dramas of Shakespeare, Lessing, and Schiller, and at a later date grew so respectable as to commission that most proper of operas, *Fidelio*, from Beethoven. If Schikaneder's character was not as low as his repute, it is nevertheless certain that he frequented the Viennese taverns and brothels; and even if his players did not behave as badly as people said, they were not extraordinarily pure in their habits, and their impresario appeared to Vienna like the grand marshal of a troop of profligates. This man came to Wolfgang one spring day (they had only a casual acquaintance) with the surprising proposition that the *Theater auf der Wieden* would have to shut its doors unless Mozart would agree at once to write an opera for it. Wolfgang demurred. He had no idea what sort of production Schikaneder's public would like. And what about a libretto anyway?

But Schikaneder had a story in mind and would write the libretto. As to the music—Wolfgang might 'to a certain point consult the taste of connoisseurs, and your own glory; but have a particular regard to that class of persons who are not judges of good music. I will take care that you have the poem shortly, and that the decorations be handsome."

Wolfgang thought it over. Schikaneder was a Mason, which was the one reason he felt he ought to help him. Aside from that, there might be a bit of profit in it—who could tell? And lastly, it was to be a German opera—something absolutely new to the frivolous Vienna public with its taste for Italian fireworks. In his present state of mind the idea was irresistible to Wolfgang, for it gave him his chance to realize his dearest musical ambition—a true German opera. He agreed to write it. Schikaneder was so close to ruin that he had no money to advance, so Wolfgang arranged with him that he should pay any small sum he pleased for the original score on condition that all copies should belong to Wolfgang. If the opera should be successful he would sell the copies to any theatres who asked for them, and so get his compensation. It seems almost superfluous to add that in the end Schikaneder paid Wolfgang one hundred ducats, kept the score and all the copies and coined money on the success of *Die Zauberflöte* for years while Constanze struggled with creditors.

Then the subject of the piece came up. Schikaneder wanted a fairy opera, a fantasy or an allegory with a magic atmosphere and—wonder of wonders—a good strong moral tone for which he thought the public was ripe. He had got hold of such a piece by the playwright Wieland and was almost through with his transcription when to his horror an opera called *Kaspar der Fagottist, oder die Zauberzither* was produced at the Leopoldstädter Theatre—his bitterest rival. It was of course stolen from exactly the same story as Schikaneder's piece. Schikaneder went to Wolfgang and turned the air blue with his curses. Together they lined up the characters of their own story and with the help of that astonishing poet, Ludwig Giesecke, calmly changed the good ones to evil, the evil to good. The Queen of the Night, originally a benevolent angel, became a priestess of dark magic, and Sarastro, who started as a malevolent sorcerer, was turned into a noble priest of the goddess Isis. This gave the collaborators another idea, and they promptly incorporated it; that the Egyptian mysteries of Isis should represent the rites of their own Freemasonry. Then Schikaneder, who was a

Mozart

much better dramatist than poet, cast about for definitions
for the other characters that would give them strong public appeal. Tamino, the prince who goes seeking for the
imprisoned princess Pamina, was to represent the highest
ideal of the spiritual in conjugal love. As a foil (and
relief) to this, the comic bird-catcher Papageno must em-
body the simple delights of warm physical love. Then
the two mystical characters must each have a retinue of
ministering attendants—a gorgeous opportunity for the
choral music in which Wolfgang excelled. Since it would
not do to have all the evil in the plot concentrated in the
character of one woman, a wicked Moor named Monos-
tatos was delegated to create his share of trouble, and,
with a few additional lesser characters, the cast was
complete.

The plot of *Die Zauberflöte* (K. 620) is absurd. Its combination of morals and magic, Freemasonry and fairy-
tale, allegory and doggerel is laughable. But it is theatre.
When the curtain goes up on the first act all the absurdity
sinks to triviality, and the essential dramatic power rises
up from the stage to engulf the listeners. Wolfgang knew
how silly it was in essence. "If we make a fiasco I cannot
help it, for I never wrote a magic opera in my life." What
he did write was the first true German music-drama. He
forgot Schikaneder's wretched poetry, and the improbable
plot, and the clumsy patching. He forgot everything except
that this was a challenge in ideals, an opportunity to express in dramatic music—the only kind that he felt should
express fact—all his own tremendous loyalties. The German blossoms out in this score with overwhelming conviction. All the purest sentiments of the German mind
appear in brave, noble phrases that do not even trouble to

dismiss the foolish story. Love and faith and friendship and simple trusting devotion were the forces in Wolfgang that guided his tired brain as it evolved this masterpiece.

By instinct he knew that the German voice belongs to clear, pure song. Fireworks for the Italians! In one stroke he laid down the marks that have guided all his German successors, from Constanze's cousin Karl Maria von Weber to Richard Strauss. *Die Zauberflöte* flows along in a serene sweep of lovely melody, broadening into the solemn, mystic choruses that embodied Wolfgang's spiritual ideals. In addition, there are Papageno's delicious German songs and the rollicking Slave Chorus, *"Das klinget so herrlich,"* which suggests nothing so much as a real German holiday, *Männergesangverein* and all. Here, too, Wolfgang was anticipating. The great exception to this rich Teutonic tone was the Queen of the Night's music —the two formidable arias which he wrote for Josefa Hofer, Constanze's oldest sister, whom he had first seen as a girl, doing the housework in Mannheim. There was some argument in Vienna about Josefa's execution and the quality of her voice, but that it was phenomenally high and strong, nobody will deny; nor will anyone question that she was a brave singer. The two arias, climaxed with high F, have remained a nightmare to aspiring coloraturas ever since.

Die Zauberflöte has become an integral, indispensable part of German life. It is moulded into the hearts of the people from the Rhine to the Danube. It is as much a part of every opera-house as the roof and the chairs. And, like all Wolfgang's music, it seems as fresh at the twentieth hearing as at the first. The marvellous beauties of

Mozart

harmony and orchestration increase and enlarge with intimacy, in fascinating contrast with the apparent simplicity of the score. It is not as universal in its appeal as *Figaro* and the *Don*, which have worldwide favor. But it is something they are not. It is the fountainhead of a new German art.

Of course Wolfgang had no idea of this. He wrote the piece in a little pavilion (the *"Zauberflötenhäuschen"* now in Salzburg) close to Schikaneder's theatre, where in the name of conviviality he was virtually imprisoned so that the impresario could keep him at work. Schikaneder had heard of the genius's propensity to procrastinate and was taking no chances. Also—like any other ignoramus—he wanted to be able easily to interfere with the music and argue about everything Wolfgang did. One song for Papageno (the part Schikaneder took) was rewritten five times. "Dear Wolfgang," the manager objected on one note, "herewith I return your '*Pa-Pa-Pa-*' which I like fairly well. It will do at any rate. We shall meet this evening at the usual place. Yours, E. Schikaneder." The usual place was, of course, a tavern where Wolfgang sat and drank with Schikaneder in the same spirit in which he allowed him to interfere with his score—sheer indifference. He simply had not the strength to protest, to say he did not like Schikaneder's loutish pastimes and insolent interference with his music. Wolfgang was in love with his *Zauberflöte*. He loved it as he had loved *Figaro*, with his whole heart. After writing all day in the summer-house and drinking most of the night with Schikaneder, Schack, and Gerl—two of the singers—he would stumble home, pale, dishevelled, and wild of eye, and clinging to the standing-desk, bury his head in his hands and compose. Sometimes a rising dizziness would swirl around him, and the floor begin to tip and sway. Then while he stared it would seem to rise up and hit him. Several times he fainted so.

Once during this summer Wolfgang shut his home for the sake of economy, and stayed in Schikaneder's pavilion, but most of the year his household consisted of himself, his canary, the manservant and valet called Primus, and the housemaid. Primus did not live in the house and Wolfgang was often all alone, which he hated. Constanze had gone to Baden about the 1st of June and had taken Karl with her. Wolfgang joined her for weekends whenever he could manage it. A month before he had applied to the city council of Vienna "to be appointed as deputy to the now aging *Herr Kapellmeister* Hoffmann —for the present without salary—" at the Stefanskirche, which was the city cathedral. This request was easily granted and had the promise of the full position with pay on *Kapellmeister* Hoffmann's death. Wolfgang's mind was a trifle easier, if not his circumstances. He wrote to Constanze nearly every day when they were separated. "I am glad your appetite is good but he who eats a lot must also . . . a lot?—No, *walk* a lot, I mean! But I should not like you to take long walks without me. Only do follow my advice exactly—it is meant for the best, I assure you. *Adieu*, my dear, my only love! Hold your hands up in the air—2999½ kisses are flying from me to you and waiting to be snapped up. Now let me whisper in your ear—now you is mine . . . now we open and shut our mouths—more—and more—at last we say, 'It is all about *Plumpi-strumpi*. . . . Well, you can think what you like. That is the joke."

Mozart

Not so much of a joke was the fact that, after writ[ing] this letter or others like it, Wolfgang would put on h[is] hat and go out to Schikaneder's theatre to find his frien[d] Mme. Gerl in her dressing-room in a frivolous and complaisant frame of mind. She had no particular charm, and did have the conspicuous disadvantage of a husband of whom Wolfgang was now seeing a good deal. But if Wolfgang could not have his solace legitimately, he would have it any way he could get it. There was nothing gay, mischievous, or boyish about this last wretched affair. It was all of a piece with the carousing nights in the pothouses when every one drank without reason, taste, or decency. If he were not to do those things, what should he do? Sit at home and stare at Constanze's empty bed and count up his debts? There were no counteracting influences, either, nothing to remind him of the happy days of Kelly and Storace and the court life that had centred around Joseph, who, in retrospect, seemed the most delightful and generous gentleman he had ever known.

The previous December Vienna had had a visit from Johann Peter Salomon, the London impresario, who had made attractive offers to Wolfgang and Haydn to go to England and write for his concerts. Haydn, whose patron had died, accepted instantly; Wolfgang refused. Again he had rejected the straw held out to him, certainly drowning in his debts and misfortunes Why?—he hardly knew. He was already beginning to believe that his life was over—he sent Constanze "a thousand kisses, and I say with you in thought, 'Death and despair were his reward!'" Could this deep conviction now be removed by a trip to London? Impossible; it was too late. Wolfgang spent the day of departure with Haydn. They

ed sonatas and talked long and intimately. When the
ne came to part, Wolfgang burst into tears and said,
We are taking our last farewell in this world."

Still more upsetting was Lorenzo's departure. Da Ponte
had found the court intolerable under Leopold II, and
after one of the usual blustering scenes, in which he
claimed to be resigning, he was really dismissed, and left
Vienna forever. He had his eye on London too, though he
arrived there later by a circuitous route, stopping on the
way to marry. He begged Wolfgang to go with him.

'No, Lorenzo,' Wolfgang said, 'there is no use now.
It is too late for me to go anywhere.'

'Nonsense, nonsense,' Lorenzo growled. 'Come with me
and we will write some more operas and show the Brit-
ishers what we can do, eh, *pizolo?*'

Wolfgang smiled sadly. 'I love you, Lorenzo. I never
had such a friend. But what can I do? See—I have my
hands full. I have this long opera and I must stay and
finish it.'

'Oh, finish it there,' Lorenzo said. 'Or don't finish it,
we can always write a better one!'

Wolfgang laughed. Then he said quietly, 'No, dear
friend. Now I am thinking only of this German opera,
this *Zauberflöte*—and then—then——'

'Yes?' Lorenzo poked his long face forward.

'Of death,' Wolfgang said in a hushed voice, bowing
his head.

They embraced each other tenderly, both weeping. Lorenzo left. With him went gaiety, delight, the realest
pleasure Wolfgang had ever known.

A young man named Franz Xaver Süssmayr had come
to Wolfgang early in the year and asked to be allowed to

study composition with him. Wolfgang had ne
pupil of this sort, and he took on Süssmayr ver,
because there were too many times now when he fe
and weary and almost incapable of doing his own rou
work. He could teach the youngster by letting him do
He succeeded so well that Süssmayr's own work is like
Mozart's technique without Mozart's genius behind it. The
pupil spent all his spare time running errands and doing
small things to help Constanze in Baden—it was only a
short ride in the diligence. Wolfgang would have gone
much oftener than he did if Schaikaneder had not kept
hounding him about the opera.

"I cannot tell you what I would not give to be with
you in Baden instead of being planted here. I was so bored
that I composed an aria for the opera to-day. I got up at
five o'clock.

"Karl must be a good boy. Kiss him from me.

"(Take an electuary if the bowels do not move—not
otherwise.)

"(Take care of yourself in the morning and evening
when it is chilly.)"

On June 18th Wolfgang got away from town and while
in Baden wrote a short piece for his friend Stoll, choir-
master at the church there. This is an Ave Verum Corpus
for four voices, beautiful of course, but more interesting
in the light of what was to follow. It is easy to see how
Wolfgang's mind was veering. Constanze had heard some
of the rumors about Wolfgang's companions and their
actions, and if she had not heard indirectly he had probably told her himself about Mme. Gerl. He always trusted
her to understand those things. But she was not happy
about it, and worried in her letters. "Where do I sleep?"
he answered her. "At home, of course. I have been sleep-

ell, only the mice bearing me honest company.
d regular discussions with them. . . .

all answer Süssmayr by word of mouth. I would
r not waste paper on him. . . .

P.S. It might after all be a good thing if you gave
arl a little rhubarb."

A few days later Wolfgang was ready to orchestrate his first act and could not find it. *Basta!* Süssmayr had it with him in Baden. He is to "put it together and dispatch it by the first coach to-morrow morning, so I shall have it by midday. A couple of Englishmen have just called, not wishing to leave Vienna without making my acquaintance. But of course the *real* truth is that they wished to know Süssmayr, and came to see me to ask where he lived, having heard that I had the good fortune to be intimate with him! I told them to go to the *Ungarische Krone* and wait till he returns from the baths. *Snai!* They wish to engage him as a lamp-polisher."

Constanze's time was very near, and Wolfgang worried miserably. She wanted some extra money—indeed, had not enough to pay her regular expenses. He was forced to write, for the first time in months, to ask Puchberg for some. But this time he tells his creditor—"It won't be many days before you receive 2,000 florins in my name." What hopes he had! Puchberg sent the new loan and Wolfgang forwarded it to Constanze. "Do not be melancholy, I beg you! . . . I hope to hold you in my arms Saturday, perhaps sooner. As soon as my business here is over I shall be with you, for I mean to take a long rest in your arms. I shall need it, too, with all the mental worry and distress. . . .

"And what is my second fool [Süssmayr] doing? When

Mozart

I reached the 'Crown' yesterday, I found the En⟨g⟩
lying there quite exhausted still waiting! *Snai!*"

Constanze, who by now had little enough right
so, was growing more unhappy about Wolfgang's do⟨⟩
in Vienna, and protested ironically—in her letters. ⟨H⟩
pretended not to know what she meant. He had no
real interest in carousing and revelling, and what he
said to her was more truth than expediency: "You would
never believe how long the time seems to me since
I left you! I cannot describe my feelings to you—there
is a kind of emptiness which hurts me sharply—a kind of
longing, never ceasing, because never satisfied, but per-
sisting, nay, increasing, from day to day. When I think
how merry we were together in Baden— Like children!
And what sad, weary hours I live through here! Even my
work gives me no joy, because I am accustomed from time
to time to break off and exchange a few words with you,
and that pleasure is alas! now impossible. If I go to the
clavier and sing something from the opera I have to stop
at once—my emotions are too strong.—*Basta!* the very
hour I finish my business I shall be away from here. . . .
I will inquire at the Court apothecary's where perhaps
they can procure me the electuary after all. If so, I shall
send it at once. Meanwhile if it should be necessary, I
would advise you to take tartar rather than cordial."

Wolfgang suspended his "business" in time to get to
Baden by July 26th, when his last son was born. This boy
was christened Franz Xaver Wolfgang, suggesting that
he was either named for Süssmayr or that Süssmayr's
name was taken because no other could be thought up as
readily. Constanze's foot was still slightly affected, but

Mozart

no way as ill as she had been the previous time. overed quickly. But Wolfgang, back in Vienna and at work in his lonely rooms, was bearing a mental en that seemed to clamp down around his temples and y a heavy, hard hand on his throat. It was very hot, the narrow street was filthy and stifling; often he felt faint and dizzy. On such a day he was startled by a slow knock at the door.

'*Herein!*' he cried.

A tall man stepped across the threshold and closed the door. He was a total stranger, thin, solemn, and dressed from head to foot in sombre gray. Wolfgang looked up at him and shivered at his strange appearance before he remembered his manners and rose from his chair. The man bowed coldly and with a few conventional remarks handed Wolfgang a letter, a folded heavy white sheet with a plain seal. Then, murmuring a direction as to where an answer would reach him, he opened the door and vanished. Wolfgang stood looking after him, trembling with surprise and with a vague sense of terror—a strange sort of fright, almost premonitory . . . he was staring into space. Presently he remembered the letter, and opened it. There was no signature. Wolfgang turned it over and looked carefully. Nothing to identify it. He rubbed his forehead and began to read. Suddenly he sat up, taut . . . rigid.

The letter began with several flattering but commonplace allusions to the accomplishments of the great *Kapellmeister*, and assured him of the writer's profoundest regard. Then it went on to ask him to name his price for composing a Requiem Mass— Suddenly there seemed no breath in Wolfgang's body. A cold wind, on this hot

afternoon, seemed to stab him, coming from.
Wolfgang shook his head quickly and finished
If willing to compose the mass, he was to state th
est time in which he could have it finished. There w.
further condition. Wolfgang was to make no attemp
any kind ever to discover who had commissioned the wor
Any attempt would prove in vain. And that was all.

Wolfgang tried hard to think of it all as a piece of
business. He got up and walked around the room, flapped
over some music, took a drink. He looked out of the window, whistled at the canary, settled his hair before the
mirror. But the thing was there. It wasn't a thing really.
Nonsense. It wasn't a man either. Damn it . . . it was
something. You couldn't shrug off a thing like this. It
was in the room. Finally he gave up. He might as well
stop trying to control his poor tired mind. *The thing was
a message from the other world. A call from Death.*

Wolfgang went out to Baden to see Constanze. He did
not tell her what he really thought. No, by now death
had become beautiful. Death was a friend, a far-away,
wonderful friend to whom he was forging his way. He
wouldn't tell anybody! This was his secret affair, his secret love and desire. Like madmen who grow cunning,
Wolfgang at first kept his secret friend sealed up in a
vault. He was not going to reveal him—to run the chance
of argument with stupid blind fools who would stare at
him incredulously. He merely told Constanze that he was
going to accept the commission and that there was nothing he could think of that he would rather write. He even
said (despite his promise of anonymity) it was a good
chance to impress the new Emperor Leopold with his ability as a church composer. Ha, ha! Emperor Leopold!

...ed to town and communicated with the tall
...ger. He named his price as 50 ducats. With *Die*
...öte still unfinished Wolfgang could not name a
...or delivery. Besides . . . besides . . . he knew
...this thing was no ordinary commission. He could not
...omise something—when—there was so much he could
...ot yet tell— The stranger appeared promptly, paid 50
ducat...assured Wolfgang that the terms were satisfactory
and that he would receive an additional payment on com-
pletion of the score. There would be no restrictions on the
style and detail of the music. Then he looked down at
Wolfgang with his cold gray stare and repeated his in-
junction not to try to discover the patron. Then he disappeared.

Wolfgang could not know, of course, that the whole
incident had a simple explanation. There was in Vienna a
certain Count Walsegg who had a fantastic desire to be
known as a composer. He could play the cello but had
never written anything. So he made a practice of keeping an eye on all the poorer and finer composers and sending them anonymous commissions for work. He paid them
well and then had the works performed in his house as
his own compositions. This Requiem was to be his composition in memory of his recently deceased wife. The
tall gray man was his steward, Leitgeb. But if Wolfgang
had been told the whole story then and there he would
hardly have believed it. For him the experience was unearthly and other-worldly. Nothing could so have shaped
and tinctured his brain, nothing could so have inspired the
Requiem.

But he was prevented from beginning the work by an
unseen and annoying interruption. The Emperor Leopold

Mozart

II was to be crowned king of Bohemia in early S[...]ber and the national States assembly at Prague ha[...]Wolfgang a commission to write the festival opera. A[...]Prague showed a loyalty that Vienna had never once [...]dicated. Wolfgang would not refuse. He wished he ha[...]done so, however, when he learned that he was expected to write a new score to Metastasio's *La Clemenza di Tito* (K. 621), a stiff, tiresome tragedy of the Italian vintage of Wolfgang's boyhood in Naples. But for this there was no remedy. Taking Constanze along—the children were boarded out with a family in Perchtoldsdorf—he left for Prague in the middle of August.

As he was stepping into the coach Wolfgang stopped and shuddered. A hand had touched his arm. He whirled round, to meet the gray stranger.

'You are going on a journey?' the man said. 'And the Requiem Mass?'

Wolfgang went weak with fear and surprise.

'I have to go,' he gasped. 'It is an opera—for the Emperor. But I will be back soon.'

'Very soon?' the stranger asked.

'Very soon,' Wolfgang repeated. 'I will work on it immediately when I arrive at home. Tell—the—the——'

The stranger bowed. 'I will tell him,' he said. 'I think he will be satisfied.' He walked away.

White-faced, Wolfgang climbed into the coach and sank against the cushions. Constanze looked at him, alarmed, and not fully understanding.

Wolfgang had also taken Süssmayr along to help with the orchestration and recitatives of the new opera. The whole piece had to be finished and produced in eighteen days of tense, nerve-racking work without any relief.

[361]

..ng was irritated by the contrast with *Die Zauber-*
..which was still active in his mind. It was terribly
..cult to go back to another age and style from which
.. thought he had graduated, and apply himself to it with
..ch intense concentration.

Even Prague, for the first time, was not a joy. He saw
his friends, but there was no time for the old parties at
the Bertramka, nothing to divert him. He was pale, very
nervous, always weak, sometimes ill, and continually taking medicines. Prague called up a host of memories that
were now actually painful to contemplate. He could not
look at the great palaces without remembering his first
introduction to them, nor at the taverns and inns without
hearing the joyful roars of Lorenzo and Casanova, good
friends whom he would never see again.

Tito was a failure. Some of Wolfgang's loyal old
friends insisted it was a fine opera, a splendid opera. The
noise and excitement of the coronation had temporarily
overshadowed it, that was all. Wait and see! But Wolfgang knew better. He knew that *Tito* was dull and cold
and perfunctory, and that he had only written it because
he could not afford not to. He cried at the première. The
beautiful white and gold opera house had too many dear
and glorious associations.

When he returned to Vienna in the middle of September he was immediately set upon by Schikaneder, who was
getting ready for the première of *Die Zauberflöte*. Was
Wolfgang all ready? Wolfgang was not. He had some
chorus and orchestra parts still to write, and the overture. Schikaneder dragged him out to the theatre, made
him give suggestions for the settings, filled him full of
wine and punch and drove him hard. He finished his

beautiful overture—one of his most thrilling and also most popular fugues—on the 28th; the première was set for the 30th. The bill read:

DIE ZAUBERFLÖTE

Grand Opera in Two Acts

By Emanuel Schikaneder.

Then followed the cast, by now all cronies of Wolfgang, including Mme. Gerl and her husband; Schack; Nannina Gottlieb, who had created Barberina in *Figaro* (it seemed so many years ago!); all the members of Schikaneder's family, and of course Josefa.

The music is by Herr Wolfgang Amade Mozart, *Kapellmeister* and Imperial Chamber Composer. Esteem for an appreciative public and friendship for the author of the work have induced Herr Mozart to consent on this occasion to conduct the orchestra in person.

Books of the opera, with two copper-plate engravings representing Herr Schikaneder in his actual costume as Papageno, may be had at the box-office, price *30 Kreutzer.*

The scenery and stage accessories have been intrusted to Herr Gayl and Herr Nessthaler, who flatter themselves that they have performed their task with all due regard to the artistic requirements of the piece.

These were circus-showman tactics indeed. It was quite traditional for the composer to conduct at the first performance, and as for the opera "by Emanuel Schikaneder" —both *Figaro* and *Don Giovanni* had been billed for their premières with no mention at all of poor Lorenzo, a librettist deserving of fame if ever one lived. The cynic, however, may be dimly reminded of certain of Leopold Mozart's advertisements when he was dragging his two children around the continent of Europe in quest of royal patronage; though Papa had more taste, and was appealing to different audiences entirely.

And here it is simple justice to point out the wonderful logic of Leopold's mind. Leopold had known his world. All his emphasis on the importance of obtaining a permanent court position, all the crabbed letters he had written to that end, were thrown into sharp and clear perspective by Wolfgang's miserable contact with Schikaneder. Wolfgang had thrown aside Papa's worldliness in the gaiety of his heart; now, inevitably, Nemesis was upon him. To write *Die Zauberflöte*, he had sunk to the very bottom of the musical world and could never extricate himself again from the mire.

Yet the significance of his fall was almost incredibly profound. He was down among the people. The glitter of fashionable applause was foregone, the tinselled sword of the Elector was put away. His life had been reduced to its elements—German loyalties, and music. These, with Constanze, were all he had left of meaning or desire. Not that he dramatized this, like his romantic successors, nor that he was even aware that he had undertaken the burden of democratic art: he knew only that he was unhappy, that the golden days were gone. Yet his fanatical obsession with the tall stranger who had commanded the Requiem, and his persistent refusals to accept favorable offers outside of Vienna, indicate that he felt the new significance of his life with a kind of deep instinct. Had he gone to Frederick William in Berlin, had he followed Lorenzo to London, or worse still, had he obtained any of the fine positions for which Papa had clamored, he might never have taken this final, deathless step into the night of the future.

Mozart

Die Zauberflöte might very well not have opened ⸝
operatic world; the Requiem, with its supernatura⸝
spiration, might very well not have been written. Yet
his miserable circumstances the strain of the new insigl⸝
brought death with it inevitably. He had attained that
strange combination of death in life which is possible only
for the truly great. This, to be sure, was the last person
that Papa had intended to make of his baby at the clavier.

Wolfgang had his fears about the reception of *Die
Zauberflöte*. He himself knew it to be great, but he had
learned well to distrust the trivial Viennese public. The
first act was received in silence. He was thrown into a panic
and rushed behind the scenes to Schikaneder.

'Wait,' the manager said. 'Calm yourself. I know this
game. Give them time.'

He was right. The public had been too surprised at the
novelty to do anything but gape. The applause began during the second act, and while not a triumph, the première
was satisfying. Schikaneder knew that it was the sort of
piece that must be pushed hard, and therefore presented it
steadily for the next ten days. Presently the reaction began; within a few weeks it had caught on and smart society
was staring through its lorgnon. It became the amusing
thing to do, to take one's guests out to the queer little
theatre and hear the new, amazing music. All the musicians in town heard it. But nothing pleased and touched
Wolfgang like the praise of Salieri, who spoke his first
kind words to Mozart in connection with this German
opera.

Wolfgang was now in very bad condition. He still had
fainting-spells, sometimes he had violent headaches; he
grew paler and more nervous, and his eyes took on a

Mozart

..e lustreless stare. The gray stranger of the Requiem .. not appeared again, but Wolfgang was tensely aware ..is promise. He began to work just as soon as *Die Zau-öte* was off his hands. Lorenzo Da Ponte was on his travels, heading for London, and wrote to Wolfgang, again urging him to go along. Wolfgang read the letter in a daze. England might have been another world, even Lorenzo seemed a vague, half-strange character. "I wish I could follow your advice, but how can I do so? I feel stunned, I compose with difficulty, and cannot get rid of the vision of this unknown man. I see him perpetually; he entreats me, presses me, and impatiently demands the work. I go on writing because composition tires me less than resting. Otherwise I have nothing more to fear. I know from what I suffer that the hour has come; I am at the point of death; I have come to an end before having had the enjoyment of my talent. Life was indeed so beautiful, my career began under such fortunate auspices; but one cannot change one's own destiny. No one can measure his own days, one must resign oneself, it will be as providence wills. I must close. Here is my death-song; I must not leave it incomplete."

Wolfgang made no greater revelation than this. Obviously he thought he must have told Lorenzo about the stranger at some earlier time. Everything had now narrowed down for him to these fine and fearful points: the stranger; suffering; the death-song; death.

Constanze had every reason to know all this, yet she had gone back to Baden after the *Zauberflöte* première, leaving the children boarded out, and there she was now. She was not sick any more—just a bit ailing. It seems not to have occurred to her that Wolfgang might need now,

as he had never needed, a little care, some good nourish[ng?]
food, loving companionship, and peace. Instead he spe[nt]
his days pouring his last drops of lifeblood into his Requiem, eating anyhow, snatching scraps of tiring pleasure,
writing letters to her. Wolfgang—who loved and longed
for friendship, and craved simple tenderness, spent his last
weeks alone in a deserted house, tended by an innkeeper
and a clumsy servant.

"Just after your departure I played two games of billiards with Herr *von* Mozart (the man who wrote the
opera being played at Schikaneder's theatre). I then sold
my old nag for fourteen ducats." (He was too ill and grew
dizzy too easily to ride any more.) "Next I got Josef
[Deiner] to get Primus to fetch me a cup of black coffee,
smoking a splendid pipe of tobacco the while. I then orchestrated almost the whole of Stadler's rondo. . . . At
half-past five I went out through the Stübenthor and took
my favorite stroll by way of the Glacis to the theatre.
What do I see? What do I smell? Why, here is Don
Primus with the cutlets! *Che gusto!* Now I am eating to
your health! It is just striking eleven o'clock. Perhaps you
are asleep already! Sh! I won't wake you!

"Saturday, 8th. You should have seen me at supper yesterday! I could not find the old tablecloth so I got out one
as white as driven snow—and the double candlesticks with
wax candles!" Just because he was alone Wolfgang saw no
reason for eating off a bare table. He had always loved
elegance, and always would. "The time drags for me without you—I foresaw that it would. If I had had nothing to
do I would have spent the week with you out there, but I
have no suitable place in which to work and I am anxious,
as far as possible, to avoid all chance of money difficulties.

Mozart

...ere is nothing more desirable than to be able to live in ...ome peace of mind, which means that one must work diligently, and glad I am to do so."

Next day he went, as usual, to the theatre to hear the *Zauberflöte* he loved. "To-day I went behind the scenes for Papageno's aria with the glockenspiel, for I felt a great desire to play it myself. For a joke I played an arpeggio when Schikaneder had to speak a few words. He started, looked into the wings, and saw me. He stopped then and would go no further. I guessed his thoughts and played a chord again. He then struck the glockenspiel muttering, 'Stop it!' Everyone laughed. I think my joke disclosed to many for the first time that he does not really play the instrument himself! You cannot imagine how enchanting the music sounds from a box close to the orchestra—far better than from the gallery. As soon as you come back you must try it.

"Sunday morning, 7 o'clock. I have slept very well and hope you have too. I have greatly relished a half-capon Friend Primus brought me. At ten o'clock I am going to divine service at the Piarists' chapel, as I can then get word with the director. . . . Next Sunday I shall certainly come out to you. Then we can go to the Casino together and travel home on Monday.

"P. S. Kiss Sophie for me. A few good nose-pulls to Siesmay and a thousand compliments to Stoll. *Adieu*—the hour strikes! farewell!—we shall meet again!

"N. B. I think you must have sent the two pairs of yellow winter riding-breeches to the laundry, as Josef and I have hunted for them in vain. *Adieu!*"

If Wolfgang gave Constanze no idea of his real condition, others did. Hofer saw him from time to time and re-

Mozart

ported to Constanze that Wolfgang was ill, miser[...]
lonely. So she came home at the end of October.
gang's pleasure was pathetic. She was horrified to see
his little white face had shrunken so that all the bones
his large skull stood out clearly—particularly his prom[...]
nent eye-sockets and the long nose. But she was still more
troubled at his talk. What on earth was he thinking about,
with his constant allusions to death and dying, his unre-
strained spells of despair and tears? The weather was still
beautiful, and Constanze hired a carriage and took him to
drive in the Prater, where the clear autumn air was sweet
and fresh blowing up from the Danube. They got out and
sat on the grass. Wolfgang remembered another day in
the Prater, long ago. That had been springtime, and he
had made knots of primroses to tuck into her breast, and
had kissed her and they had lain with their arms around
each other and whispered their dear, tiny secrets. He had
never forgotten that day—how sweet she had been, and
tender! It was just before their first baby was born . . .
one who had died.

Suddenly Wolfgang began to sob. He doubled over and
buried his head in his folded arms. Constanze turned to
him in alarm.

'Wolfi, *Liebchen*, what is the matter?'

'Nothing, nothing,' he muttered. 'I am just so very
tired and sad.' He raised his wet face and looked at her.
There was something in those eyes that Constanze did not
want to see. She wanted to turn her head away. But Wolfgang was looking at her. She could not move.

'Wolfgang,' she said slowly, 'what are you thinking
about?'

His eyes softened and he took her hand.

ittle Stanzi-Marini,' he said gently, 'I am think-
eath.' Constanze shuddered. 'I am always thinking
ath now, you see. That is why I must finish my Re-
m.' He put his cheek down on her hand and looked up
her. 'I am writing it for myself, dear. Don't you understand?'

Constanze was terribly frightened. Wolfgang was so
calm. He spoke as if this had already happened, long ago.
She put her arms around him and clasped him fiercely.
'No, no, Wolfi,' she choked. 'Don't say those dreadful
things . . . please. . . .'

'Those are not dreadful things, Stanzi, darling. Those
are beautiful things. Death is very beautiful. Have I not
said I think it the true goal of life?' She shook her head
again.

'Please, Wolfi, please. . . .'

'Don't be sad, darling,' he said. 'It *is* beautiful, truly,
nearly all of it. But there are other things—things . . .'
His tone changed. Constanze looked at him quickly. His
drawn face had suddenly set in cold, hard lines. He was
staring into space. She touched his arm timidly. He turned
back to her. His eyes had changed. They seemed larger,
and as he gazed at her Constanze shrank back. She had
seen something terrible.

'Constanze,' he said, in a low tense tone, 'there is something on my mind. I have known this for a long time.'
Her chin shook but she still stared at him. He leaned forward. 'Constanze, I have been poisoned.'

'No, no, no,' she whimpered.

'Yes,' Wolfgang said firmly. Again his eyes filled with
tears. 'I have certainly been poisoned,' he said. 'I cannot
rid myself of this idea.'

Mozart

Constanze tried to say something. She opene[d her] mouth, moved it. She could not say "Who?"

Wolfgang understood. 'Never mind,' he said, shak[ing] his head. 'I shall not say.' The strange gleam had com[e] back into his dim eyes.

Of course it was a pitiful delusion. No human hand had poisoned Wolfgang, but in his desperate hours he wove the idea out of his harried brain. And secretly he thought Salieri had done it. The poor Italian was horrified when the ghoulish tale reached him. It haunted him the rest of his days, and on his death-bed, a played-out old man, he looked at a friend and said piteously, "I did not poison Mozart." And while Wolfgang still lived Salieri went to every length to show his real and honest if belated admiration. He needed to—there were some with whom the rumors might have taken root.

Constanze realized at last that Wolfgang was suffering something more than an indisposition. She sent for Doctor Klosset of the general hospital who examined him and agreed with her—whose idea it was—that the score of the Requiem (K. 626) must be taken away from him. Wolfgang assented. He was tired and feeble; he had faint strength left for composing; none for anything else. His Masonic brothers were having a festival and with Schikaneder he wrote a cantata for them, which was sung in the middle of November and rapturously greeted. He came home in the first good spirits Constanze had seen for weeks. He was happy, even mischievous. He teased to have his Requiem back. Constanze never looked beyond the surface appearance of anything. She thought Wolfgang so much better! She gave him his unfinished score.

It was destined to remain unfinished, of course. But

ing could not bear to admit the possibility. Ready
ath, and sure it was not far away, he wrote his death-
g in a passionate race for the greatest of all stakes—a
y measure of life after the span is up. He lost, but his
little pupil Süssmayr made a faithful effort to fill the gap.
Wolfgang worked slowly on the Requiem, putting all the
force of his wonderful brain into each note that he left. Of
the twelve parts, he completed the first two entirely. The
next six he left unfinished, but in such condition that
Süssmayr's work was technical and merely automatic. For
parts eight and nine—*Domine Jesu* and *Hostias*—he left
sketches from which Süssmayr carried out his rough ideas.
The next two parts, *Sanctus* and *Benedictus,* were written
entirely by Süssmayr. The *Agnus dei* has put scholars to a
deal of trouble but no one doubts that the fierce pleading
of the opening phrase is Wolfgang's idea, just as the moving but conventional prayer, *dona eis requiem,* is Süssmayr's. The pupil was thoroughly imbued with his master's
unearthly passion for the work, and had the good sense to
allow himself to be swayed by that and not by any desire
to create or interpolate something of his own. What has
seemed like a stroke of genius on Süssmayr's part—the
use of the fugue from the first movement as recapitulation
and climax and ending—was what Wolfgang was direct-
ing him to do on the evening of his death.

The Requiem has been discussed, written about,
analyzed, pulled apart, put together, criticized, rational-
ized. For what? The Requiem is one of the eternal epics
of man. It is so much a mass for the dead that it transcends
life, for there can be no death that has not cooled the fever
called living. Like life and its inseparable death, the Requiem is universal. It is one of those things that comes

out of space and stays with us. It has no tem~~~
ning or end, unless it can be said to have begun ~~~
feeble child first wailed in Salzburg and ended w~~~
weary man last sighed in Vienna. Even then it do~~~
stay within the bounds of thirty-five little years. It ~~~
back to the source of experience and it comes down ~~~
strike to the heart of reality.

The idiom of the Catholic ritual is an accident. It might
have taken any form, but it took that of a mass. Mozart
could not have died without fulfilling his mind, soul, heart
and cosmic force, in some such way. If he had died without it, he would not be so completely what he is—a fundamental factor in a fundamental art. Yet he had no such imposing idea. Of all the motives that provided fuel to
create this burning thing, his feeling for death was the clear-
est. He was about to die, and he was writing a requiem for
himself. That is simple. The rest is a matter of hearing
the terrific beat of life marching by, when the men shout
"Quam olim Abrahae" and the women answer in a shrill
cry that is all the cries ever wrung from women—and
Wolfgang knew them well. It is a matter of knowing the
meaning of the strings snarling upward against the middle
phrases of *Dies irae*—a day of wrath that comes in every
life, when fear is known even by the coldest mind. It is
realizing, through the two slow, simple minor scales of
Lacrimosa, rising, then falling against the sobbing violins,
that those who do not know tears do not know anything.
It is acknowledging humility in the *Recordare,* and devotion in the serene balance of *Hostias.* Lastly, in the mighty
triumphant fugue of the *Kyrie* and *Cum Sanctis* there is
the fierce and burning beauty of the mind, whose passion
belittles every other passion, and whose fruit lives forever,

Mozart

...ther fruit has gone. The Requiem is a matter
...g that Mozart, whose personal creed was not to
...se among his fellows, ended his tortured bit of
...th joy—in a clear, blissful open chord in D.

...n the 21st of November, a cold, gray afternoon,
...olfgang wandered into the Silver Serpent. He looked
...stlessly around the large main room, shrugged with distaste as he saw all the tables filled, mostly with strangers.
He made his way on into the rear room, where he selected
a corner and threw himself wearily into a chair. He
stretched his right arm along the table and dropped his
aching head on it. The marble table-top was cool—thank
God. What matter now that admirers in Hungary and
Holland had just sent him promises of generous commissions? For a long time he sat there, eyes half closed and
slight shoulders moving almost imperceptibly as he
breathed. Presently he raised his head and beckoned a
waiter.

'Bring me some white wine,' he said indifferently.

The waiter knew him and was surprised at the order.
Kapellmeister Mozart usually had beer in the afternoons.
The boy set the wine down, polished the glass, rattled
some spoons, moved away. Wolfgang sat staring at the
flagon as if it were painted on the table. He did not touch
it. Josef Deiner appeared at his elbow, the kind proprietor
who had all but kept house for him in this past hectic year.
He pursed his lips and slowly shook his head as he looked
at Wolfgang. The little face was even thinner than a week
ago, and in addition to its usual dull pallor had a heavy,
waxy texture. Then there was a bright rosy spot on each
cheekbone—or was that only the afternoon light? The fine
blond hair of which Deiner knew Wolfgang was so proud

was rumpled and gnarled, carelessly powdere
tied queue-ribbon falling off. The queue was full
—plainly it had not been dressed for several days
gang raised the neglected head and looked at Dein

"Well, how are you to-day?" he asked.

"I think it more my place to ask you that," Deiner sai
"You look like a very sick man, *Herr Kapellmeister!* That
trip to Prague you took in September—now you know, I
don't think that was good for you. That air didn't agree
with you."

Wolfgang stirred uneasily. The good faithful soul was
getting on his nerves; but then, what would not?

Deiner went on. "I see you're drinking wine now.
That's a good thing. Doubtless you drank beer in Prague,
and that upsets the stomach, you know . . . very upsetting."

Wolfgang turned in his chair and smiled gently.

"My stomach is better than you think, Josef. I taught it
at a very early age to digest anything." He sighed.

"Well, that's a very good thing," Deiner said, "since all
diseases start in the stomach, as Marshal Laudon said
at——"

Wolfgang suddenly felt very ill. He pressed his lips
together and gripped the edge of the table, and staggered
to his feet.

"Josef," he said, "I—I've got a chill . . . that's queer.
I'm going home. You drink my wine. Take this *siebzehner*,
and come to my house to-morrow morning to help us.
Here it is winter already and we need wood. My wife
will order it. . . . I'm going to have a fire made right
now."

He gave the waiter a coin and went out. He stumbled

....tnerstrasse and across the Stefansplatz. When
...a the Rauhensteingasse he could hardly manage
...flight of stairs. Oh, God. Oh, *God!*——

...nie Haibl was there with Constanze and they put
... quickly to bed. He vomited and shuddered violently
...d his cheeks began to blaze with fever. He lay on his
back and clutched the sides of the mattress and the room
rocked this way and that. During the night Constanze,
helping him to turn over, noticed that his little hands had
changed queerly. She asked him if they hurt. No, but—
she looked at his feet—swollen just like his hands. Constanze waked Lisl the housemaid and told her to run for
Doctor Klosset.

Next morning when Deiner called to see what Wolfgang wanted, Constanze took him into the bedroom where
Wolfgang was stretched flat under the white counterpane.
He opened his eyes weakly and winced as the light struck
them. But he summoned a smile for Josef.

"Not to-day, Josef," he said gently. "To-day we have to
do with doctors and apothecaries." . . . ('And death,' he
murmured to himself peacefully. He knew quite well.)

In the afternoon his friends began to come in. Word
soon went the rounds that Wolfgang was too sick to go out
and the men at Schikaneder's theatre arranged among
themselves that some of them should always be with
Wolfgang in the afternoons to keep him company. He was
only interested in music and did not want to talk about
anything else. Süssmayr planted a chair by the bedside and
could hardly be induced to leave it. Wolfgang was grateful; he was much too ill to write but he could give "Siesmay" directions for scoring and orchestration. The sheets
of the Requiem were scattered all over the bed, and every

afternoon when the men came in, four of them, usua
Schack and Gerl, Hofer, and Wolfgang himself wou.
sing the parts that were nearly finished, Süssmayr accompanying on the clavier which had been moved into the
bedroom.

Wolfgang's kidneys had been weakened by an illness
some years before, and now gave him agonizing pain. The
swelling in his hands and feet rapidly grew worse. On
November 28th Klosset called Doctor Sallaba in consulta-
tion, but they were baffled by the symptoms and nothing
definite was done. It was so painful for Wolfgang to move
or to turn himself in bed that Sophie and her mother "made
him night-shirts that could be put on without turning him
around, and arranged a cloth which was slipped under him
so that he could be drawn forward without making any
effort. Not realizing how ill he was, we made him a
wadded dressing-gown against the time that he should be
able to sit up. His good wife, my dear sister, gave us all
the material for it; it very much amused him to follow our
work as it proceeded."

Every day when the men came from the theatre, Wolfgang had to be told all about last night's performance, and
when evening came he liked to lay his watch on the pillow
beside him and follow *Die Zauberflöte*. "Now the first act
is over." "Now comes the great Queen of the Night."
When he was very weak he still tried to sing *"Der Vogel-
fänger bin ich ja,"* and Roser, one of his visitors, went to
the clavier and played it for him. Wolfgang tried to
stretch out his hand.

'Oh, thank you,' he said, 'thank you very much, Herr
Roser!'

Constanze began to go to pieces and was treated by the

ctor; she would have been helpless but for her sister Sophie who came every day and really superintended the nursing. She kept an eye on the housekeeping too. Surrounded by the plain friends of his later years, Wolfgang would lie and watch them contentedly and listen to their talk. He did not call often for Constanze. After a week in bed he began to be very helpless, actually partially paralyzed. At night, however, he was apt to be violently ill. All day he was quiet, peaceful, and spoke little except about music or to reassure someone who showed concern for him. The wildness in his eye, the strain in his tired brain were past now. He was going to meet his friend, in great contentment.

On Sunday afternoon, the 4th of December, he asked to be propped up with pillows, and motioning his friends to take their places around the bed, he gave them the *Lacrimosa* to sing. He took the alto, as usual, Schack the soprano, Hofer the tenor, and Gerl the bass. Süssmayr was at the clavier. They began; quietly, for Wolfgang was very weak now and could just make his voice heard. As the minor scale rose slowly to its height, his placid expression and drooping eyes gave way to a flash of visible anguish. Ah! he was young, after all. It was not so easy to die! So much unfinished! So much still to do! The white face twisted in a painful grimace. The swollen, flabby little hands dropped their sheet of manuscript— and Wolfgang burst into a flood of tears.

Later his excitement subsided. Toward evening Sophie came for her usual visit. In a panic, Constanze met her at the door.

"Thank God you are here!" she said. "He was so ill last night I thought he could not live through the day; if it comes on again he must die in the night." Sophie conquered her fright and went quietly to Wolfgang. She touched his hand. He smiled faintly and whispered, "I am glad you are here. Stay with me to-night and see me die." Sophie began to tremble and might have wept, but she controlled herself and reassured him. Dearest Wolfgang; he would be all right.

Calmly he answered, in a tiny voice, "I have the taste of death on my tongue—I *taste* death; and who will support my dearest Constanze if you do not stay with her?"

Sophie left him lying quietly, and hurried home to tell Caecilia Weber. As she left the house Constanze, quite hysterical, ran after her and asked her "for God's sake to stop at St. Peter's and ask one of the priests to come." Wolfgang had been careless about his religious duties of late years and had no regular confessor. It was only with the greatest difficulty that Sophie made one of them promise to go to him. When she reached Wolfgang once more he was whispering to Süssmayr who again had the parts of the Requiem spread on the bed. Wolfgang gazed at them with blurred eyes. "Did I not say I was writing the Requiem for myself?" he asked gently.

He had no requests and no messages to leave, except to ask Constanze to keep the news of his death secret until Albrechtsberger—the musician next in line to him for the post at the Stefanskirche—should have been notified. Constanze had sent out in despair for Doctor Klosset, but he was at the theatre and did not come until very late. He looked at Wolfgang, and calling Süssmayr into a corner, told him there was no hope. Nevertheless he ordered cold compresses to be applied to Wolfgang's head. This was done; he began at once to shudder violently. In a little

Mozart

while he sank into unconsciousness which was occasionally broken by a delirious cry. Once they saw him raise his hands as if holding something, and puff out his cheeks—trying to blow the trombone of the *Tuba Mirum*.

Constanze, Sophie, and Süssmayr. They knelt by the bed, each repeating the prayers for the dying. At midnight Wolfgang tried to raise himself. From the black swoon the clouded gray eyes opened wide for the last time. Then he laid his rachitic little body down. He turned his face to the wall.

At one o'clock in the morning Wolfgang died.

XX

WHAT of the pitiful funeral in the Stefanskirche? What of the important Baron van
Swieten who came back into their poor world
from his great one to arrange for the third-class (pauper's)
funeral, for eleven florins, twenty-six kreutzer, that Constanze paid? What of the straggling little group—Süssmayr, Swieten, Salieri—that gathered in the chapel to hear
the corpse blessed, and then, huddling under their um-
brellas, to leave it halfway to the burial-ground because
the weather was too bad to endure? What of the wild rain
and sleet that beat down on the cheap board box? And the
solitary old ghoul who lowered it into the poor-pit in the
Marxer Friedhof? He knew that its contents were no different from the other lumps of dead unwanted clay.

But the music is alive!

APPENDICES

I

CONSTANZE AND THE SONS, KARL AND F. X. WOLFGANG MOZART

Mozart's body was prepared for burial by the two servants and Josef Deiner. Constanze was in a state of hysterical prostration. After the corpse was carried out to the Stefanskirche, she paused to write a few words in Mozart's notebook, commemorating their years of "tenderest, most inseparable wedlock," and praying that she might soon go to join him forever. She then threw herself (according to her own subsequent account) onto the deathbed, in the hope of contracting her husband's mortal illness—most probably nephritis aggravated by nervous exhaustion and under-nourishment. She did not go to the church or to the grave. She pulled herself together soon enough to face the mass of debts that was her only inheritance, and to be a party to a petition written in her name to the Emperor Leopold, dated December 11th, six days after the death. The Emperor authorized a benefit concert under his own patronage, and subsequently allowed her a life pension of 22 gulden (about $10.00) a month. With this, the proceeds from sales of Mozart's manuscripts to publishers, and the income from occasional benefits, she rented lodgings and took in boarders as her mother had done in the same circumstances.

In 1799, Constanze received as a lodger Georg Nikolaus von Nissen, a counsellor of the Danish Embassy in Vienna. Shortly afterward, she became his mistress. He treated her well and helped her to provide for her sons, who were boarded out in Prague, where both were receiving a fair musical education. Karl was taught by his father's friend Franz Duschek. In 1809, when Nissen was preparing to return to Copenhagen, he married Con-

…at she might accompany him without scandal. She had
…ren by this marriage. In 1808, evidently in expectation
…ving Vienna, Constanze went for the first time to the
…xer Friedhof and asked to see Mozart's grave. The sexton who
…d put the body into a mass-grave seventeen years before had
…ied, and there was no other way (as the mass-graves were dug
up every ten years) of identifying the spot where Mozart was
buried. No one had thought to order a cross or a marker for his
funeral.

Constanze von Nissen lived with her husband in Copenhagen
for ten years, after which he resigned from the diplomatic service and they returned to Austria to work on the first biography
of Mozart. Nissen died in 1826, and Constanze superintended
the publication of the book by Breitkopf & Härtel after she was
left a widow for the second time—"Constanze, Wittwe von Nissen, früher Wittwe Mozart" was her signature. The Nissen biography is unreliable in everything pertaining to the personal life
of Mozart and his family, as it was thoroughly tinctured with
Constanze's prejudices and with her care for sundry reputations.
The letters used are also doctored. After Nissen's death Constanze settled permanently in Salzburg (where Nannerl died,
blind, in 1829) and remained there the rest of her life, receiving
visits from her sons and from distinguished musicians on pilgrimage to the birthplace of Mozart. On March 6, 1842, at the age
of seventy-nine, she died, and was buried in St. Sebastian's church-
yard in the same grave with her implacable enemy, her father-in-
law, Leopold.

Her elder son Karl never showed marked ability in any field,
and was successively a merchant, a musician, and a petty job-
holder in some official capacity in Milan. Unmarried, he died
there in 1859. Franz Xaver Wolfgang had more musical ability
and was known as a conductor and a pianist. He was attached to
a noble house in Lemberg as musical instructor, and later he settled
in Vienna. He made some attempts at composition which were insignificant not only of themselves, but by inevitable comparison
with his father's music. He also never married, with the result

Appendices

that there are to-day no descendants of Mozart ˅
Wolfgang died at Karlsbad in 1844.

Constanze made rather a favorite of Karl, and dem
in her letters to him a firmness and shrewdness totally α
from the character of the giddy wife she had been to Mc
This change was due entirely to Nissen's influence; he taught .
to keep her affairs in order and to know the value of every penny
She did so to a mercenary degree. She lost her easy-going ways
and her casual attitude toward virtue, and at the same time
showed, in retrospect, the sentiment for Mozart and his music
that she had never manifested in his lifetime. That was natural;
Constanze had no idea of his significance while she was his wife,
and in that, as in other matters, she took her cue from the world.

II

MOZART AND MONEY

His financial difficulties are so much a part of Mozart's story that it is of major interest to understand his income and his expenses. The currency he used means little to modern Europeans and almost nothing to Americans. And, though many economists have made elaborate attempts to correlate the values of different national moneys in different ages, there is still no practical table to which one may refer for such information. The innumerable changes in the basic value of commodities such as gold, wool, and wheat; the varying gold and silver contents of different coins, differently weighed in each country; the fluctuating and unrecorded rates of exchange; the loose demarcations of national authority, and thus of the right to coin and issue money—all these factors make the problem a difficult one.

But while it is therefore impossible to show, in absolute terms, how much Mozart earned and how much he paid for what he purchased, it is at least desirable to grasp these values *in relation to one another*. Such can be accomplished within reasonable limits of accuracy by simply reducing florins to their silver content, and equating this to American silver dollars of approximately that time. This is an informal and inexact procedure, disregarding entirely the fluctuations in the purchasing power of money (and particularly of the silver dollars referred to), and it is intended solely as a guide for general information, not for any practical use. I have made a rough table of these values:

Austrian Currency (*circa 1760–1800*)	*U. S. Currency* (*1792*)
1 ducat (gold)	about $2.25
1 florin 1 gulden } (silver)	about 45 cents
1 kreutzer (copper)	45/100 of a cent, or just less than half a cent.

[386]

Appendices

On the same basis, the French louis d'or mentioned
and his mother in Paris was worth about $5.80. The th.
lar) of Prussia was equal to about $1.00.

The purchasing power of Mozart's money may be g.
from the debts he left. He died owing a tailor about $127.00,
apothecary about $80.00, and an upholsterer about $94.00. H
viola was valued at less than $2.00. The cost of his living may be
estimated from the fact that his apartment in the Schulerstrasse,
the best house he ever lived in, was rented for about $207.00 a
year; and that beef cost him about two cents a kilogram. Mozart's
salary as *Kammerkompositor* to Joseph II was about $360.00 a
year, and he paid his housemaid (and other servants, each) about
$5.50 a year. In his boyhood, on the staff of Archbishop Sigis-
mund of Salzburg, his pay was about $67.00 a year; and as
Kapellmeister to Hieronymus, after returning from Paris, about
$225.00. He borrowed almost a thousand dollars, in amounts
ranging from $4.50 to $90.00 (and once even $360.00), and
died owing Puchberg about $450.00. The inadequacy of his in-
come may be judged from the fact that about $200.00 was all he
ever received for *Figaro*; about $225.00 for *Don Giovanni*; the
same for *Die Zauberflöte*; and about $112.00 for the Requiem.
His funeral cost about five dollars.

III

THE PIANO

The instrument of which Mozart was a virtuoso, and for which he wrote so many great compositions, was the predecessor of the modern piano. I have called it indiscriminately by all or any of the terms by which it was then known, partly for convenience, and partly to imply how little distinction was then made among them. Whether German clavier, Italian forte-piano, French clavecin, all were the same type of instrument, sounded by means of hammers striking on single strings. Their forerunners among keyed instruments were the harpsichord and its variants, cembalo, clavichord, and spinet, the strings of which were plucked to produce sound. Mozart's own piano, made by Walter, and now in the Mozart Museum at Salzburg, had two octaves less than a modern piano, and its "forte-piano pedal," mentioned by Leopold Mozart, was a crude forerunner of the present pedal which raises the dampers and so sustains the tone. While the tone of Mozart's piano was somewhat more sustained than that of the harpsichord, his instrument had not the resonance and breadth of tone of the later pianoforte, and did have the tinkling quality that was eventually eliminated by triple stringing, cast-iron construction, and many other technical improvements. Not until early in the third quarter of the nineteenth century did the piano reach its general development as the instrument we now know.

BIBLIOGRAPHY

I

Keller, Otto, *Wolfgang Amadeus Mozart, Bibliographie und Ikon-graphie.* Berlin-Leipzig: Gebrüder Paetel, 1927.

Köchel, Ludwig Ritter von, *Chronologisch-thematisches Verzeichnis sämtlicher Tonwerke Wolfgang Amade Mozarts.* Leipzig: Breit-kopf & Härtel, 1905.

Wyzewa, T. de, et Saint-Foix, G. de, *W.-A. Mozart, Sa Vie Musicale et Son Oeuvre de l'Enfance à la Pleine Maturité.* Paris: Perrin et Cie., 1912.

II

Abert, Hermann, *W. A. Mozart, Neuarbeitete und Erweiterte Ausgabe von Otto Jahns Mozart.* Leipzig: Breitkopf & Härtel, 1923.

Cohen, Hermann, *Die Dramatische Idee in Mozarts Operntexten.* Berlin: Bruno Cassirer, 1915.

Groag-Belmonte, Carola, *Die Frauen im Leben Mozarts.* Wien-Leip-zig: Am Althea-Verlag, 1923.

Jahn, Otto, *Mozart-Paralipomenon (Gesammelte Aufsätze über Musik).* Leipzig: Breitkopf & Härtel, 1867.

Lach, Robert, *W. A. Mozart als Theoretiker.* Wien: A. Hölder, 1918.

Leitzmann, Albert, *Mozarts Persönlichkeit.* Leipzig: Insel-Verlag, 1914.

Lert, Ernst Josef Maria, *Mozart auf dem Theater.* Berlin: Schuster & Loeffler, 1918.

Mörike, Eduard, *Mozart auf der Reise nach Prag.* Boston: D. C. Heath & Co., 1904.

Mozart, Konstanze, *Briefe — Aufzeichnungen — Dokumente, 1782–1842; Herausgegeben von Arthur Schurig.* Dresden: Opal-Ver-lag, 1922.

Mozart, W. A., und Seine Familie, *Die Briefe; Mozart-Ikonographie; Herausgegeben und eingeleitet von Ludwig Schiedermair.* Mün-chen und Leipzig: Georg Müller, 1914.

Mozarteums-Mitteilungen, Herausgegeben vom Zentralausschuss der Mozartgemeinde in Salzburg. Salzburg: Im Verlage des Mo-zarteums, 1918–21.

Nagel, Willibald, *Gluck und Mozart.* Langensalza: Hermann Beyer & Söhne, 1908.

—— *Goethe und Mozart.* Id., 1904.

Bibliography

.....ozart und Casanova, Eine Erzählung. Prag: Verlag
   ....herstube," 1929.

   .....te, Casanova, und Böhmen. Alt-Prager Almanach, 1927;
   ....9–148. Id., 1927.

   .....nek, Franz, W. A. Mozarts Leben. Prag: I. Taussig, 1905.
   ....eprinted from original edition of Herrlischen Buchhandlung,
   ....rag, 1798.)

.....sen, Georg Nikolaus von, Biographie W. A. Mozart's. Leipzig:
   Breitkopf & Härtel, 1828.

Nohl, Ludwig, Mozarts Leben, Neu Bearbeitet von Dr. Paul Sakolow-
   ski. Berlin: Schlesische Verlagsanstalt (Schottlaender). G. M. B. H.

Nottebohm, Gustav, Mozartiana. Leipzig: Breitkopf & Härtel, 1880.

Paumgartner, Bernhard, Mozart. Berlin: Volksverband der Bücher-
   freunde, Wegweiser-Verlag, 1927.

Pohl, C. F., Mozart in London. Wien: Carl Gerold's Sohn, 1867.

Prochàzka, Rudolf Freiherrn, Mozart in Prag. Prag: H. Dominicus
   (Th. Gruss), 1892.

Schiedermair, Ludwig, Mozart, Sein Leben und Seine Werke. Mün-
   chen: C. H. Beck'sche Verlagsbuchhandlung, Oskar Beck, 1922.

Schlichtegroll, Friedrich, Mozart. Supplementband des Nekrologs,
   Abtheilung II. Gotha: 1798.

Schurig, Arthur, Wolfgang Amade Mozart. Leipzig: Insel-Verlag,
   1923.

Tenschert, Roland, Mozart. Leipzig: Philipp Reclam, Jun., 1930.

Tottmann, Albert, Mozarts Zauberflöte. Langensalza: Hermann Beyer
   & Söhne, 1908.

Waltershausen, Hermann W. von, Die Zauberflöte, Eine operndrama-
   turgische Studie. München: Drei Masken Verlag, 1920.

Wurzbach, Constantin von, Mozart-Buch. Wien: Verlag der Wal-
   lishausser'schen Buchhandlung, 1869.

Blazek, Vlastimil, Mozart A Bertramka. Hudba a Škola, Ročnik I, Čislo
   I, p. 8. Praha: Rijen, 1928.

Barraud, M. le Docteur J., À Quelle Maladie a Succombé Mozart?
   La Chronique Medicale, 12me Annee, No. 22. Paris, le 15
   Novembre, 1905.

Bellaigue, Camille, Mozart. Paris: Henri Laurens, 1927.

Boschot, Adolphe, La Lumière de Mozart. Paris: Librairie Plon,
   1928.

Kufferath, Maurice, La Flute Enchantée de Mozart. Paris: Librairie
   Fischbacher, 1914–19.

Photiades, Constantin, Mozart à Paris. La Revue de Paris, Tome IV,
   p. 208. Paris, 1928.

Bibliography

Prod'homme, J.-G., *Mozart, Raconté par Ceux Qui L'Ont Vu.* Paris: Librairie Stock, Delamain & Boutelleau, 1928.
—— *Mozart en France. Le Mercure de France*, No. 662, Tome CLXXXV. Paris, le 15 Janvier, 1926.

Barrington, Daines, *Account of a Very Remarkable Young Musician. Philosophical Transactions of the Royal Society*, Vol. LX, pp. 54–64. London, February 15, 1770.

Engel, Carl, *The Mozart Couple.* Essay in volume entitled *Discords Mingled.* New York: Alfred A. Knopf, 1931.

Gounod, Charles, *Mozart's Don Giovanni.* Translated from the third French edition by Windeyer Clark and J. T. Hutchinson. London: Robert Cocks & Co., 1895.

Hitchcock, Thomas, *Unhappy Loves of Men of Genius (Mozart).* New York: Harper & Bros., 1891.

Holmes, Edward, *The Life of Mozart.* London: Chapman & Hall, 1845.

Hussey, Dyneley, *Wolfgang Amade Mozart.* New York and London: Harper & Bros., 1928.

Jahn, Otto, *The Life of Mozart.* Translated from the German by Pauline D. Townsend. London: Novello, Ewer & Co., 1891.

Kerst, Friedrich, *Mozart, the Man and the Artist, as Revealed in His Own Words.* Translated into English and edited by H. E. Krehbiel. New York: B. W. Huebsch, 1905.

Mozart, Wolfgang Amadeus, *Letters.* Selected and edited by Hans Mersmann. Translated from the German by M. M. Bozman. London and Toronto: J. M. Dent & Sons, Ltd., 1928.

Pole, William, *The Story of Mozart's Requiem.* London: Novello, Ewer & Co., 1879.

III

Angerville, Mouffle d', *The Private Life of Louis XV.* Annotated by Albert Meyrac. Translated from the French by H. S. Mingard. London: John Lane The Bodley Head, Ltd., 1924.

Bradby, G. F., *The Great Days of Versailles.* London. Ernest Benn, Ltd., 1927.

Bryce, James, *The Holy Roman Empire.* New York: Macmillan & Co., 1880.

Buck, Mitchell S., *The Life of Casanova from 1774 to 1789.* New York: Nicholas L. Brown, 1924.

Coxe, William, *The History of the House of Austria* London: Henry G. Bohn, 1847.

Ellis, S. M., *The Life of Michael Kelly, Musician, Actor, and Bon Viveur.* London: Victor Gollancz, 1930.

Bibliography

Endore, S. Guy, *Casanova, His Known and Unknown Life.* New York: The John Day Company, 1929.

Kelly, Michael, *Reminiscences.* London: H. Colburn, 1826.

Le Gras, Joseph, *Casanova, Adventurer and Lover.* Translated from the French by A. Francis Steuart. London: John Lane The Bodley Head, Ltd., 1923.

Ponte, Lorenzo Da, *Memoirs.* Translated by Elisabeth Abbott from the Italian. Edited and annotated by Arthur Livingston. Philadelphia and London: J. B. Lippincott Co., 1929.

Russo, Louis Joseph, *Lorenzo Da Ponte, Poet and Adventurer.* New York: Columbia University Press, 1922.

Walpole, Horace, *Memoirs of the Reign of King George the Third.* London: Richard Bentley, 1845.

Beaumarchais, Pierre Augustin Caron de, *La Folle Journée, ou Le Mariage de Figaro.* Paris: Furne, 1826.

Deffand, Madame du, *Corréspondence Inédite.* Paris: Chez Leopold Collin, 1809.

Épinay, Madame d', *Memoirs, Avec des Additions, des Notes, et des Eclaircissements inédits, par Paul Boiteau.* Paris: Charpentier, 1863.

Genlis, Madame la Comtesse de, *Memoirs Inédits.* Paris: Chez Ladvocat, 1825.

Grimm, Frédéric Melchior, *Corréspondence Littèraire, Philosophe, et Critique.* Paris: Garnier Frères, 1878.

Sainte-Beuve, C.-A., *Causeries du Lundi,* Sixième Édition. Paris: Garnier Frères.

Seingalt, Jacques Casanova de, *Memoirs,* Édition Originale. Paris: Ernest Flammarion.

Komorzynski, Egon von, *Emanuel Schikaneder.* Berlin: B. Behr's Verlag (E. Bock), 1901.

Meissner, Alfred, *Charaktermasken.* Leipzig: 1861.

—— *Rococobilder.* Lindau: 1876.

Noorden, Carl von, *Europäische Geschichte im Achtzehnten Jahrhundert.* Leipzig: Dunker & Humblot, 1870–82.

Reference has also been made to Grove's *Dictionary of Music and Musicians,* to the *Encyclopædia Britannica,* and to Brockhaus' *Konversations-Lexicon.*

ADDENDA
TO THE BIBLIOGRAPHY

Blom, Eric, *Mozart*. London: J. M. Dent & Sons, 1935.

Einstein, Alfred, *Mozart, His Character, His Work*. Translated by Arthur Mandel and Nathan Broder. London: Cassell & Co., 1945.

Hutchings, Arthur, *A Companion to Mozart's Piano Concertos*. London: Oxford University Press, 1950.

King, A. Hyatt, *Mozart in Retrospect*. London: Oxford University Press, 1955.

Köchel, Ludwig Ritter von, *Chronologisch-thematisches Verzeichnis sämtlicher Tonwerke Wolfgang Amade Mozarts*. Dritte Auflage bearbeitet von Alfred Einstein. Leipzig: Breitkopf & Härtel, 1937.

Mozart. *The Letters of Mozart and His Family*. Chronologically Arranged, Translated and Edited with an Introduction, Notes, and Indices by Emily Anderson. With extracts from the letters of Constanze Mozart to Johann Anton André translated and edited by C. B. Oldman. Three vols. London: Macmillan & Co., 1938.

Nettl, Paul, *The Other Casanova*. New York: Philosophical Library, 1950.

Novello, Vincent and Mary, *A Mozart Pilgrimage*. Transcribed and compiled by Nerina Medici di Marignano, edited by Rosemary Hughes. London: Novello & Co., 1955.

Sitwell, Sacheverell, *Mozart*. London: Peter Davies, 1932.

Turner, W. J., *Mozart, The Man and His Works*. New York: Alfred A. Knopf, 1938.

INDEX

Index

Index

Index

Index

Index

Index

Index

The Best in Biographies from Avon Books

IT'S ALWAYS SOMETHING
by Gilda Radner   71072-2/$5.95 US/$6.95 C

JACK NICHOLSON: THE UNAUTHORIZED
BIOGRAPHY *by Barbara and Scott Siegel*
76341-9/$4.50 US/$5.50 Can

ICE BY ICE
by Vanilla Ice   76594-2/$3.95 US/$4.95 Can

CARY GRANT: THE LONELY HEART
by Charles Higham and Roy Moseley
71099-9/$4.95 US/$5.95 Can

I, TINA
by Tina Turner with Kurt Loder
70097-2/$4.95 US/$5.95 Can

ONE MORE TIME
by Carol Burnett   70449-8/$4.95 US/$5.95 Can

PATTY HEARST: HER OWN STORY
by Patricia Campbell Hearst with Alvin Moscow
70651-2/$4.50 US/$5.95 Can

PICASSO: CREATOR AND DESTROYER
by Arianna Stassinopoulos Huffington
70755-1/$4.95 US/$5.95 Can